René & Me tells the story of George and Donella East's attempt to live off little more than their wits in an isolated corner of Normandy.

Arriving at Le Moulin de la Puce with no experience in country living (especially in a foreign country) the Easts struggle to survive with a selection of hare-brained schemes, while coming to terms with a vastly different culture where time is of little value, and reluctant tractors are brought to life with a tot of homebrew *Calvados*.

As René Ribet - the wily Fox of Cotentin - moves on to their land and in to their lives, plans for crayfish farming, natural spring water bottling plants and metal-detecting weekends to uncover the miller's secret hoard crash about the couple's ears, and disaster looms.

Following a series of hilarious encounters with bizarre situations and unforgettable characters, tragedy comes to the tiny community, and the newcomers finally discover where the real treasure of their new home is to be found…

René & Me

BY

GEORGE EAST

ILLUSTRATIONS BY ROBIN EVANS

LA PUCE PUBLICATIONS

My wife and I first met René Ribet when he moved on to our land and in to our lives at Le Moulin de la Puce. During an eventful year, he taught us much about the countryside and people of the Cotentin, and in the process, much about ourselves.

For that, we will always be grateful to our friend The Fox.

Merci, mon pote.

French Letters and Home Truths

As usual, and for those who may wish to know what I *think* I mean when using French words or phrases throughout *René & Me*, there is a glossary of sorts at the end of the book. To avoid hindering the action for those readers whose command of the language is as shaky as mine, I have also hopefully managed to make most of the words in italics self-explanatory by context, or the simple device of using an English equivalent in the direct vicinity.

On the subject of action and content, all the following events were either experienced directly by my wife and I, or related by the people named.

Finally, however this homage to the people of a small corner of a great country is ultimately perceived, I would like to make it very clear that we shall remember our year with the Fox of Cotentin and everyone else mentioned with no other emotions than sincere gratitude and affection.

NB: All the recipes in this book are as genuine as the characters described. Due to my condition when sampling and recording most of them, I may have got the proportions wrong, or left out or mistakenly included any number of ingredients. But, as all enthusiastic cooks will know, half of the fun is in the experimentation. The only items which may not be left out in any circumstances are, naturally, the home-made cider and calva. To get your hands on the genuine article, you may have to visit its source, but that, I promise you, will be a journey well worth the making.

René & Me

Published by
La Puce Publications
87 Laburnum Grove
North End
Portsmouth PO2 0HG

Telephone: 023 92 678148
Facsimile: 023 92 665070
e-mail: info@la-puce.co.uk
Website: www.la-puce.co.uk

© George East 1997

First impression 1997
Second printing 1998
Third printing 1999
Fourth printing 2000
Fifth printing 2001
This edition 2002

ISBN 0 9523635 1 8

The author asserts the moral right to
be identified as the author of this work

Designed and typeset by Nigel at Christianson Hoper Norman
Reprographics by SP Digital Limited
Printed in Great Britain by Borcombe Printers PLC, Hampshire

The reason that all of us naturally began to live in France is because France has scientific methods, machines and electricity, but really does not believe that these things have anything to do with the real business of living.

Life is tradition and human nature.

French people really do not believe that anything is important except daily living and the ground that gives it to them...

Gertrude Stein (from *'Paris France'*)

When people learn we live in the Cotentin, their first question is invariably 'Where's that?'

When we tell them it's the top bit of the Cherbourg peninsula, they often look disappointed on our behalf, and are quite likely to say 'Oh, you're not in *real* France, then.'

Contrary to popular British belief, real France does not start south of the Loire valley, and the Cotentin is as French as it is unique.

When they have spent a little time in our particular neck of the *bocage*, another comment visitors frequently make is: 'It's just like rural England must have been a hundred years ago.'

Of course, it isn't.

The most isolated or rustic cottages may not have inside toilets or a bathroom, but there's usually a television aerial on the original 18th-century roof, and a car parked outside, even if its primary function is as a chicken coop. What is so evocative of a long-gone time about the small and isolated rural communes of the Cotentin is the people and the way they look at life.

They are every bit as sophisticated as other modern Europeans, and (as they will waste no time in telling you) much more so than the most *avant-garde* Parisian.

It's just that they have thoughtfully watched the world around them change, and much prefer to keep to the old ways when it comes to family, friends, daily life in the countryside, and other matters which, in their opinion, really matter.

And that suits people like us right down to the ground.

WINTER

December 20th:

Midnight, and the Néhou Christmas party is in full swing. I am outside counting stars from the vantage point of the village *pissoir*. My wife is dancing to the Birdie Song with Christian the Goat, and Mr Maurice is telling an audience of schoolchildren about the night the Yanks invaded his wardrobe. René has not begun his whirling dervish routine, but the night is yet young. Jean-Pierre has done us proud with the catering arrangements, and is twirling his moustaches in a most lascivious manner at his understandably nervous wife. Given his track record for these occasions, it would not take a local Nostradamus to predict a welcome addition to the commune head count by next summer.

All is as it should be at this trial run for the seasonal celebrations, but I am worried about the bar bill. Our evening started at the Bar Ghislaine with a round or so of *Ricard* merely frightened with the water jug, followed by a brace of *calvados* to see us through the hundred metre walk to the hall. Since we arrived, however, our Jolly Boys Club has been drinking its way around France, and I have not bought a single bottle. So far on our journey of exploration, detailed analysis and criticism, we have visited the Loire, Bordeaux, Burgundy and Gascony.

Along the way, we've paid tribute to food of the relevant region, with JayPay unveiling and presenting each complementary course like a magician pulling a ready-cooked rabbit from the ether. Every time our table reaches the bottom of a bottle, another takes its place courtesy of Big Freddo, official vintner for the evening.

As he leaves to visit the open-air facilities, I follow to tackle him about the likely size of the drinks bill and, most importantly, who will be settling it. Now, we stand shoulder to shoulder beside the *épicerie* window and solemnly observe local custom by aiming at the epicentre of the enamelled *Gauloises* poster. As usual, Freddo is spot on. Across the road, the church clock chimes the witching hour and a nearby stallion snorts with derision at my feeble efforts to match my companion's head of pressure, trajectory and pinpoint accuracy.

Eventually and as relief comes, I ask how we are to sort out the finances. I appreciate his generosity, but surely it must be my turn to buy a round?

Sighing with contentment, Big Freddo turns towards me and I see that his nickname is not entirely attributable to the size of his moustache. Shaking vigorously and casting a sympathetic glance downwards in my direction, he explains. As it is Christmas and a good time for party pieces, we will be playing the sausage game. Pressed for further details of this ancient Cotentinese ritual, he summates the basic rules. At the end of the evening, all the men at our table will line up at this very spot. As one, we will unzip, display and compare our assets. The member of the cartel with the furthest to reach to the *Gauloises* poster will be (like the poor chap's wife) the loser, and must stump up for all bottles consumed that evening.

Now I see why, in the midst of such informality, the table plan was drawn up and enforced so rigidly by Freddo. And also why it occasioned so many sly comments and asides by the women of the village.

"If you like," says Freddo politely as we zip up and make our way back to the celebrations, "...we can ask your wife to be the judge?"

" No need to bother," I reply limply, "...will you take a cheque?"

At our table, Freddo explains in an unnecessarily loud voice that I have offered to pay for all the drinks this evening, and suggests another round. He, I note, orders a giant two litre bottle of farmhouse cider.

I, in final and complete capitulation, call for a miniature of scotch.

*   *   *   *   *

Some hours later, and we are nearing the end of our vigil by the big pond. At this time of year, we do not expect any sightings of the local wildlife, but are determined to savour every minute of this, our first night as proper residents at La Puce.

For the past three years we had made the monthly pilgrimage from our terraced house in Portsmouth to the heart of the Cherbourg peninsula, and driven off the ferryboat knowing we must desert our Normandy home in a few days time. Each visit had been a frenzy of activity, battling to restore the ruined farmhouse and make some impression on the even more ruined mill cottage at La Puce before time and funds ran out. We had slept with the cement mixer, learned the patois for 'actually, we wanted the toilet bowl in the bathroom, not the kitchen', and experienced the full horror of employing French and British craftsmen at the same time and in the same place. We had a property in each country, and felt truly at home in neither. Like a gallic *Brigadoon*, La Puce would vanish in the legendary Cotentin mists as we left, existing only in our imagination till the moment we drove again down the old cart track to walk the fields, touch the trees and pretend to live there for another heartbeat of its long history.

Back in England and in between those brief encounters, I would find myself drifting away to the water meadow and leaking septic tank while discussing the practicalities of a topless darts match with a Nottinghamshire licensee or inventing a fairly credible PR story for a London publican with no sense of publicity. Worse, I would find myself driving on the right hand side of any road without a white line down its middle, and seeing our friends dive for cover each time some innocent asked how the place in France was coming on.

Each night in Normandy we would sit beside the grotto at La Puce, listing a dozen good reasons why we should take the final step across the Channel. The following week in the UK we would invent thirteen good excuses why we could or should not.

For nearly thirty years we had lived in Portsmouth, moving regularly towards the city boundary like a convict edging towards the prison wall. Finally, we had arrived within a mile of the ferryport, and both realised that it was time to make a final bid for freedom, or give up our dreams and settle for a lifetime stretch on home turf.

Then, as if an impatient deity had grown weary of our timid gestures and mewling excuses and decided to take a hand, three of our best brewery customers called in the same week to give us the sack. Re-organisation, re-shuffling and reducing costs meant that they would not be renewing our retainer fees in the autumn. They would, of course, still be interested in any ideas for public house publications, PR and publicity packages we might wish to offer, but could not guarantee us an income.

In shock, we sat and considered our immediate reactions and alternatives. We could start again and trawl the country seeking new clients for my specialist talents of writing about pubs and spending a lot of time in them. We could also conduct our own cost-cutting exercise, which would require somehow living off a quarter of last year's income. This would involve selling La Puce to the highest bidder, but any sort of bidder would be hard to find in the current market, and two years is a speedy property transfer time in France.

Something had to be done, and as usual when big problems surfaced, we went down the pub.

At the end of a long session in our Portsmouth local, we took stock of our situation and our options. On the debit side, we had a terminally failing business, a minus equity figure in our Portsmouth home, an overdraft at the bank and no pension fund or any source of regular income.

On the plus side, we had La Puce, which was in hock to the *Crédit Agricole* bank for a relatively small sum, and the farmhouse building was virtually ready for habitation.

Then, as we have often found, inspiration arrived with the last round. Starting on her fifth *pastis*, my wife observed that we could just cover our UK and foreign mortgages by renting the two properties out. With unassailable logic, I pointed out that this would leave us with nowhere to live on either side of the Channel. She responded swiftly that I had forgotten the tiny mill cottage at La Puce. It had been good enough for cows to live in for the last half-century; with a little imagination and a lot more work, it could make a comfortable if basic home while we sorted ourselves out. We could simply reverse our situation and base ourselves in Normandy, a move we had endlessly discussed and rejected. Then, we could return each month like latter-day Vikings to raid and pillage any pub publicity business in England, and virtually live off the land at La Puce in between times. There was more than enough room to grow vegetables and graze sheep, pigs, ducks and every other creature below us in the food chain. Also, how often had we considered and devised foolproof schemes for making money out of our property in France and its proximity to England? Were we not a nation of explorers, entrepreneurs and traders? It was time to put our heritage to the test. And just think of the book I could write about our year in Normandy with René Ribet and all our other friends at Néhou.

It would be an adventure beyond compare, and we would still be hedging our bets. If, after a year, we had not waxed fat on the fruits of the land and my fertile imagination, we would be on the spot and in a better position to sell La Puce and return to reclaim our home in England. At least, she concluded, we would have given it our best shot. To surrender now and meekly await certain financial disaster would be unworthy of us. It would also be an insult to all our ancestors, who had set forth from Portsmouth harbour to make a new home in far remoter corners of the earth than the Cherbourg peninsula with hardly a sovereign in their breeches. Were we going to talk about it for another thirty years, or were we going to make the break and follow our hearts desire?

As a young couple at a nearby table broke into spontaneous applause at my wife's moving address, I sat and considered the arguments for the defence.

I could and probably should have pointed out that her

experience of living off the land was limited to a yearly harvest of grow-bag tomatoes in the back yard of number 87 Laburnum Grove, North End. Or that the closest she had come to animal husbandry was taking the dog for a walk. Or that we had seen dozens of other people's schemes for survival in France go tragically wrong. Or, indeed, that most of our immediate ancestors had limited their adventuring abroad to the odd trip on the Isle of Wight ferry. Finally, and thanks to Peter Mayle, statistics proved that there were now more British people trying to write and sell books about their adventures in France than actually live there.

But the way things were, it seemed to me that someone somewhere was trying to tell us something. The fates had rolled the dice and mischievously pushed us into a corner, and it was time to put up or shut up. I ordered another pint of Dutch courage and agreed that it would be so.

We would have our year with René, and take each day as it came.

*   *   *   *   *

Above us, the big Normandy sky goes on for ever, and the night is as still as death. I start to tell my wife that she was right, and that I love her for it. A terrible fear for the future still grips my heart, but I would rather be here with her at this moment than anywhere else in the world. I reach towards her but she stays my hand and silently bids me listen.

Somewhere, from out in the velvet blackness, a visitor has arrived. A crackle of breaking undergrowth is followed by a regular series of low, breathless grunts. Donella turns to me, her face alight with joy.

"There," she says, in a voice trembling with emotion, "I told you we had a badger. *Now* will you believe me?"

I smile and nod and take her hand.

I have heard that sound before, and know it is René trying to re-start his moped after falling into the roadside hedge. Unlike him, sound travels best at night, and the Christmas party at Néhou must finally have ended.

I shiver and suggest we return to the mill, lest we scare the badgers away and spoil a perfect day.

December 21st:

Having settled the monumental bottle bill, we decide to take a break before our first Christmas in Cotentin and visit friends in the South. Colin and Anne Scott had taken the plunge, sold their two very successful pubs in Sussex and moved permanently to the Dordogne a year ago. Perhaps they will have some sage words of advice on how to adapt, survive and prosper in France.

We travel through the night, and twelve hours later sit in their tiny restaurant on the outskirts of the village of Catus as they get us up to date with their situation.

Learning the ropes of running an Anglo-Irish restaurant in a rural area of France has been, they tell us, an interesting, frustrating and sometimes expensive business, not helped by their initial communication problems. Both had picked up the basics of the *lingua franca* during visits to their holiday home in the village, but Anne's soft Irish brogue does not convert well to Dordognese.

In the first week, she had made what she thought was a modest order of coal, and taken delivery of two lorryloads. This had not been a total disaster, however, as the black mountain had become a local landmark and site of pilgrimage for the villagers, and a playground for their children. Determined that they should get to grips with the language before any more expensive mistakes were made, Colin had heard two travelling salesmen from Nantes discussing their surefire language system and plumped for the complete course of books, video and audio cassettes. Taking delivery a week later, the couple had eagerly opened the packing case and found a comprehensive guide to mastering every aspect of the English language.

Despite these early setbacks, Colin told us, they seemed to be winning the battle to capture the hearts, minds and stomachs of the local people, which would keep the business afloat during the long and lonely winter months. The summer season was no problem, with more English visitors in search of familiar food and accents than could be packed at any one time into Scott's

Restaurant. The premises had also become the HQ for the local expatriate community, where members would regularly gather to curse the French and their funny ways and recall the golden days of their lives and times at home in Luton and Leeds. We had arrived on market day, and already the bar was filling with natives come to gaze in undisguised fascination at the shrine in the corner where Anne had set up a trading post stocked with vital commodities for the English residents. Packets of suet, bottles of brown sauce, tins of real baked beans, custard powder and rental videos of ancient episodes of *Coronation Street* were obviously at a premium.

But, as our friends explained, the brisk turnover of Marmite and Sugar Puffs would not pay their way. They would know they had made it when the locals came to eat, and returned for more.

The big breakthrough had come recently, when Scott's restaurant had been elected the official lunchtime venue for council workmen resurfacing the road outside. A long, impeccable and paid-for midday meal was a mainstay of their working conditions, and the men chose where it would take place. With a catch in his throat, Colin explained that the workers had voted to break with tradition, loyalty to the French-owned bar down the road and a lifetime's schooling in the horrors of English cooking. The foreman had arrived a month ago, and after much inspecting of the kitchen, the proposed menus and a lengthy interrogation as to the patron's attitude and commitment to the pleasures of the table, the deal had been struck. They would give Scott's a chance.

Starting conservatively with well-rehearsed regional favourites, Colin had then taken their reputation and financial future literally in his hands, and started to introduce his own specialities to the set menu. On the first Best of British day he had unveiled and presented a giant steak and kidney pudding to the silent and suspicious crew. With bated breath, he and Anne had watched through the porthole in the kitchen window as their guests sniffed, poked, prodded and finally tried the offerings. One muscular navvy had even taken the dish outside to analyse the contents in

10

the full light of day. After an agonising interlude of delicate yet stringent sampling, debate and consideration, the men had declared the pudding not only fit for human consumption, but even acceptable. Aflame with enthusiasm and missionary zeal, Colin had moved on to Lancashire hotpot, Bedfordshire clangers, and ultimately, Anne's particular *pièce de resistance*, boiled bacon and cabbage *à la* Donegal.

Unfortunately, there was a downside to the bold experiment. The culinary conversion of the road gang had been such a success that the men had started to demand similar foreign adventures at table from their wives.

Where, they would ask irritably at weekends, were the spotted dicks and apple crumble they had grown to know and love at the *Café Ecosse?*

Why could Madame not create a gravy *solide* which would cling to the plate like ivy and turn a morsel of bread into a thing of sodden beauty?

Worst of all, there were now tangible signs of their infidelity as the men were getting noticeably fatter. Mutterings were heard in the market that the classic cuisine of the region was being undermined. The very French way of life might even be under threat. If things continued as they were, a petition would be drawn up and sent to the *Académie Française* demanding action and retribution.

Fortunately for international relations and local harmony, the road outside was now repaired, and the men had moved on to another village. The British special would be officially dropped from the menu during the winter months, though still be available under a coded heading for English residents - and those locals bold enough to put their longing for *saucisse paysanne* (bangers and mash) above the risk of marital discord. With a final and inspired touch of English duplicity, Colin had invited a committee of local women to advise on and oversee the preparation of classic regional specialities for Scott's. In a moment of wild enthusiasm, Anne had even suggested that she respond in kind by hosting evening classes in British and Irish cuisine. Perhaps wisely, the couple had decided that, cosmopolitan as it was becoming, Catus and particularly its womenfolk were not yet ready for this ultimate example of *entente cordiale.*

December 23rd:

Having driven straight back from the south much enthused and heartened by our friends' success, we arrive to find a new member for our ditch of the month club.

It rains frequently in Cotentin, and the sensibly deep channels on each side of every road and lane lie in wait for unwary drivers like still and patient lions at a waterhole.

Curiously, it is invariably the locals who play the part of doomed gazelles. Visitors soon learn to keep clear of the treacherously soft verges, while the Cotentinese seem almost proud of the way their clinging embrace claims so many victims. There is still talk in the village of an encounter with *les accotements non stabilisés* by a rather proper English lady some years ago. A new member of the Bricquebec twinning committee, she arrived very late for a reception and meal and apologised during her after-dinner speech, made in her best Franglais. She had, she haltingly explained, pulled off the road to get her bearings on the way to the venue, and become bogged down. 'Everything about your countryside is so charming,' she gushed in schoolgirl French, '…but you do have such soft… *verges.*' Understandably, she had not known the correct term for the dangerous grassy bits on the side of the road, so in the way of Britons abroad had used our 'verge', saying it confidently and loudly in English with a French pronunciation, assuming that the audience would get her drift. She had also obviously not known that *verge* is the French word for penis, and that she had consequently offered the male members present the most deadly insult imaginable. After convening a hasty meeting, the bemused leader of the all-men hosting committee had responded by welcoming her to the region but passionately rebutting her claim that it was famed for its impotence. Necessary steps should surely be taken to disprove this regrettable

12

misunderstanding, and the entire committee was happy to volunteer with a demonstration at the time and place of her choosing. History and local legend do not, sadly, record whether the offer was taken up.

La Puce sits alongside the main route from St Sauveur to Bricquebec, so we have seen much evidence of the Cotentinese affinity for ditches and their magnetic properties. Hardly a visit goes by without our finding an injured car on its side and off the road, and any offer of help will inevitably be met with a frosty look and curt rejection as if acceptance would be an admission that the position of their vehicle is anything other than deliberate. Of all the many examples of cultural idiosyncrasy, the French approach to driving seems the most bizarre and potentially lethal. On our earliest visits to their country, we found many preconceptions about the French and their strange habits to be patently untrue, but in the matter of road safety, they are even worse than we give them credit for.

I have never seen a copy of a French Highway Code for British visitors, but have already begun a manual which will be based upon some basic lores and laws. Sub headings will include:

1. Close Encounters

The favoured position for any driver (male or female) is about six inches behind your rear bumper. So much do they like this position that they only leave it regretfully, and then preferably on a particularly dangerous and sharp blind corner, or just before a hump back bridge. In particularly bad weather and visibility, the distance between bumpers will decrease pro rata.

On one occasion my wife actually thought she was towing a car in a thunderstorm, so closely was it following her every move. Looking into the rear-view mirror after navigating a particularly tight bend, she saw that it had disappeared, and stopped to investigate.

Rounding the bend on foot, she found the ancient Citroën

lying wounded in a waterlogged ditch, with two elderly ladies sitting calmly inside. Both refused all offers of help and may, for all we know, be there still. On another occasion, I grew tired of counting the liver spots on the face of an aged pursuer through miles of winding country lanes, and after taking a dozen random turns to try to shake him off, finally careered into a convenient driveway to escape.

As he arrived alongside and skidded to a halt in a shower of gravel, I got out to apologise for parking outside his house. He looked at me as if I were mad, and said that he lived elsewhere in the region, and was merely following me to see where *I* lived...

2. After You

The right of way on any roundabout may belong to the driver already on it or arriving on it, depending on local tradition and established usage. All drivers with foreign - ie not local* - number plates have no legal right to be on any rond point, and are therefore fair game for every other vehicle in any situation. Local drivers may and probably will gang up together to box in, intimidate or even force intruders off the road.

* In Britain, number plates follow a sequence obviously designed by a former and very demented MI5 codemaker. In France, the last number in the sequence sensibly indicates where the registered owner lives. All plates on vehicles belonging to the inhabitants of Manche end with a 50, while numbers on cars from neighbouring Calvados conclude with a 14. Officially, this at least enables the police to know immediately where a gang of escaping bank robbers stole the getaway car. Unofficially, it allows local drivers to use their superior knowledge of the highways to tempt outsiders into mortal danger.

3. Taking Sides

Depending on the area, season of the year or time of month and day, traffic entering a main route from a side road or lane may or may not have priority. Tractors towing long and badly loaded trailers obviously win extra points for stalling halfway out on to the highway.

4. Jump or Die

Pedestrian crossings are not there to guarantee safe passage, but to channel potential targets for bored or irritable motorists, and will always be located in a particularly ill-lit or obscure location. Some villages have as many as five crossings in a row, giving local pedestrians a whole range of choices as to where they would most prefer to be run down.

On an early visit to Bricquebec, I drew up at a pedestrian crossing as an elderly lady hobbled off the kerb without looking in my or any direction. Not only did the queue of drivers behind sound their horns in a frenzy of outrage at being cheated of their quarry, but the old woman glared ferociously and shook her fist at me before continuing on her painful way. My wife believes there were two possible reasons for her anger. Either my actions implied she was now too elderly and infirm to play the traditional dicing-with-death crossing game, or she felt I had cheated her of the opportunity to ensure future security for her family, courtesy of a foreign and therefore soft insurance company.

NB. *All or any of the above rules, regulations and conventions will not apply between the hours of 2 and 5pm, when drivers are returning from their luncheon venue. During this time, any vehicle from a tractor to a seventeen tonne juggernaut is likely to come and go to and from wherever fancy dictates, and on either side of the road.*

*   *   *   *   *

Investigation of the van occupying the ditch outside La Puce reveals that our new club member is Mr Janne. A local farmer, he follows the Cotentinese tradition of being close to the earth, and is somewhat wider than tall. His hands are about the same size as the blade of my wife's trenching spade, his moustache almost as luxuriant as Big Freddo's, and on a good day he looks like his favourite breakfast dish is live rats. He is, however, a gentle and considerate man who raises thoroughbred horses at his farm a mile away from La Puce, which makes him one of our closest neighbours. The latest victim of the ravine outside our farmhouse, he presently lies slumped motionless behind the wheel of his Renault, and we fear he is injured. Closer examination of the empty lemonade bottle in his lap reveals, however, that he is merely paralytic.

With no little effort, we ease his giant bulk from behind the wheel and help him into the kitchen. Here, his story unfolds over several mugs of coffee, brewed to local taste. As they say, the perfect composition is as black as night, as sweet as a young nun, and as thick as a bull's most important appendage.

The present condition and position of Mr Janne's van is, he explains with a shrug of his massive shoulders, entirely the responsibility of the ridiculous laws appertaining to the transport of the region's favourite beverage. It is simply because he is such a law-abiding citizen that things have come to this pretty pass.

At this point, it is perhaps useful to attempt an explanation of the complex relationship between Norman countryfolk, the apple, what they do with it and the importance it plays in their everyday lives.

As with Somerset, the soil and climatic conditions found in the north-western region of France particularly favour the growth of small, sweet and often exceptionally ugly apples. I have never seen a Norman actually eat one fresh from a tree, but they know more ways to preserve, cook or distil its essence for consumption than there are days in a leap year. The women are naturally the experts in all matters concerning apple tarts, puddings and cakes, while every Norman countryman absorbs with his mother's milk the family recipes for the specialist drinks the fruit will provide with little effort and less cost.

By tradition, every country dweller will have at least one apple tree in his garden, or access to someone else's. The harvest will be taken in October, either during the day or night depending upon who it officially belongs to, and the apples left in a pile in the open air to mature, or as we might say, rot.

Over the long winter months, the ancient rituals will then begin in conditions of almost obsessive secrecy and security. The basic ingredients for cider are apples and more apples, but most households in our region will make some small addition at a vital stage to ensure unique flavour and taste. Pieces of dead animal are much favoured for the creation of further zest and body, and one elderly brewer of our acquaintance is alleged to add a pinch of gunpowder to every litre to increase its purgative qualities. As with English prize vegetable growers, competition is fierce to produce best in class each year. Unlike vegetable growers, however, Cotentinese cider buffs will rarely allow anyone else to taste their produce without money changing hands, so most judging and subsequent status relies on the claims of the maker and the forensic evidence of the odd tasting or burglary. This leads to much debate and argument in the local bars as to who produces the superior vintage each year, but that's how they like it. Occasionally, a villager will bring a bottle of his best cider into the bar and leave it casually on a table for observation and comment, and a purely visual process of judging will begin. Points will be awarded for degree of murkiness and the number of small pieces of apple and other grisly remains suspended in the liquid, and even the age, design and general grubbiness of the bottle may win grudging approval.

A by-product of the apple fermenting and distilling process is a viscous liquid called *pommeau,* usually made and drunk solely by the women of the household. Defying the laws of nature and science, any bottle will contain more dissolved sugar than its own volume and weight. A favourite trick to demonstrate its sweetness and medicinal properties is to leave an ancient and discoloured 20 centime piece in a glassful overnight. By morning, the coin will be in mint condition, unlike the teeth of the persistent drinker.

In extreme cases, the coin may have disappeared, though whether as a result of total disintegration or the legendary Norman reluctance to leave hard cash laying around will depend upon the circumstances and situation.

Unquestionably the acme of the regional home brewer's art is *calvados*, named for another county, but (according to our village) hijacked after its invention by the Cotentinese. This fierce distillation of cider is loosely described by those who have never tried it as a sort of apple brandy. All patriotic Normans, however, place *calva* somewhere higher up the league table of great French beverages, and local conviction claims it to be the prototype for the mythical elixir of life which foreign alchemists have been trying to create since the dawn of time. As every Norman knows, a tot of classic *calva* will cure a host of maladies, preserve life when all other practices of modern medical science have failed, and start the most reluctant of tractors on a frosty morning.

Also known colloquially as *trou Normand* because of its traditional use to fill the hole between courses at table, locals may refer to farm or home made *calvados* simply as *goutte*, elsewhere meaning any small amount of strong drink. Though they will take a glass at any time and with the slightest excuse, most Cotentinese are also firm believers in its employment to cleanse the palate during meals. Actually, the smallest glass will briefly paralyse all nerve endings in the upper body while perversely liberating the vocal chords, stimulating the libido and burning out all sensations of taste. Having attended a number of Norman dinner parties, I believe this may provide a strong clue to the real reason for which it was first conceived and created.

According to local tradition, regular consumption also negates the need for dental hygiene, and the purchase ratio of toothpaste and brushes in Cotentin is, it is proudly claimed, the lowest in France.

Because of the special and enduring relationship between the Cotentinese and their *calva*, a whole set of rules and regulations governing its production have been in place for centuries. To the outsider, some may seem archaic, illogical and even bizarre; virtually all are completely ignored by the locals.

In our region, for example, it is still an offence for the orchard owner to allow foreign growths to infest his trees. Mistletoe flourishes on apple wood, and the *gendarmerie* has the power to call at an appropriate time to solemnly check that the parasite is not strangling its host and threatening the next harvest. In practice, every leaf and berry of *gui* will have been carefully collected for seasonal export by the bemused farmer, amazed at his good fortune that the English will actually pay to display the weed in their homes as an excuse (as if one were needed) to kiss a pretty girl.

An attempt to control the production and circulation of farm *calva* and placate the region's licensed vendors is enshrined in a law permitting each amateur grower to employ the services of a travelling still once a year. Then, the golden essence of the season's harvest will be created and reverently transferred to oaken barrels, where it will hibernate contentedly away from the light of day for up to a decade. A considerable amount will never reach the barrel stage, however as a sample must be bottled for immediate assessment, possible trading, and to start the tractor when all else fails.

Officially, the amount produced by each orchard owner is regulated by the number of trees and their yield, and be strictly for home consumption. Given the going rate for illicit *calva*, it is hardly surprising that there is a permanent shortage of empty bottles in our neck of the woods, and that manufacture takes place on a considerable scale in the most unlikely places. Many properties in our area have security systems worth more than the outhouses they protect, and we know of a local man who somehow produces 3,000 litre bottles of *goutte* a year while living in a bed sitter.

To stem the annual torrent of bootlegging activity, there is also a law which could only abide in France. A sealed and full bottle of *calva* in a car could be in transit for illegal sale, reasoned the authorities, so a suitable statute would have to be framed and enforced to prohibit the practice. With supreme gallic logic, the legislators decreed that only the transport of unsealed and part-filled bottles of home-made *calva* should be permissible. Consequently, anyone found driving a car with an unopened bottle in the boot risks investigation and prosecution. If the bottle is loosely corked, half empty and rolling about on the front seat, the driver is obviously complying with state requirements and using it for personal consumption only, so is in the clear.

*   *   *   *   *

After a reviving *goutte* from our emergency supply, Mr Janne recovers enough to tell us his story. Hearing from René of our imminent arrival from the ungodly south, he had selected a bottle of his best *calva* to welcome us back in traditional fashion. Before departure, he had broken the seal and poured a little of the golden liquid safely away into a jug to conform with the law. Obviously, it would have been unthinkable to have done so without ensuring that all had gone well since the contents of the bottle had last breathed the evening air. In all modesty, he assured us, it was close to perfection. To be doubly sure, he had tried another glass before setting out, and even stopped off at a convenient point on the mile-long journey to check that his precious cargo was travelling well. Somehow and most probably due to a fault in the steering, he had eventually found himself in the ditch outside La Puce, and kept his spirits up while awaiting our arrival with the remains of the gift bottle. Now we must help him out of the ditch, but much more importantly, out of trouble with Madame Janne.

Would it be possible, he pleads, for us to go to his farm and find Henri the labourer, explain the situation and return with the necessary equipment to rescue the car? If he were to return on foot, Madame would ask all sorts of awkward questions, and the implications with regard to both his capacity for strong drink and driving skills would surely diminish his standing throughout the region. A confrontation with a ditch is, as we realise, of no consequence to the average Norman, but, as we also know, Madame Janne is not as understanding about his occasional tippling as most wives of hard working farmers…

A little later, and Henri, the tractor and a tow rope have been summoned, and the road is completely blocked with motorists anxious to observe and advise if not actually help. They are mostly dispersed by a passing policeman, who arrives on his *mobylette* to sympathise with Mr Janne's predicament, make copious notes about the incident and officially take over arm-waving, traffic directing and shouting responsibilities.

At last the van is parked in our yard while Mr Janne, Henri, the bobby and two complete strangers settle down in the kitchen to celebrate a successful conclusion to the evening's drama. Donella visits the medicine cabinet for another bottle of emergency *calva* and suggests she run Mr Janne home to ensure that he arrives safely. All the men look at her as if she has just suggested they have soft *verges*. A better idea, proposes Mr Janne, would be for him to drive us all to the Bar Ghislaine, where he may properly thank us all for our assistance and relate the story of our adventures to the Jolly Boys Club. In spite of much nodding and general agreement, we politely refuse his invitation.

There are at least two miles of ditches *en route*, and besides, we know of Ghislaine's general opinion of men, men drinking, and especially men drinking off the premises.

December 24th:

Christmas Eve, and we decide to visit all the bars in the area for a traditional British pub crawl. Donella suggests inviting Mr Janne to be our chauffeur, but we settle for playing snap to select the driver. I win with a grand slam of Mr Bun The Baker and we set

21

off in high hopes of a convivial evening. Unfortunately, the doors to virtually every bar in the area are firmly shut. From inside come the sounds of much jollity, and we conclude that Christmas is still a strictly family affair in Cotentin. Eventually, we find a warm welcome from Madame Nellie, who unbolts the doors to her bar at St Sauveur le Vicomte and invites us to join the small gathering of lonely people without families or friends to be with at this special time. A large, lovely and extremely maternal young woman, Nellie seems to attract a certain type of clientele who are not always at ease in other company. Soon after arrival, Donella is in deep conversation with Mike The Bike, a Néhou resident and new friend who often cycles down our track with his briefcase containing lengthy magazine articles about himself, colourful pictures of his many operations, and detailed notes of his complete medical history. Michel is a local celebrity by virtue of contracting a mystery illness which kept the most distinguished Parisian doctors perplexed for almost a decade, and speaks a little English as a result of being regularly exhibited to visiting Harley Street specialists. He is a complete innocent, kind and trusting with a childlike enthusiasm for the little gifts which Donella regularly brings him from England. I, meanwhile, have been backed into a corner between the juke box and football table by a tall man with staring eyes and a marked facial twitch who is interrogating me about our plans for La Puce. His patois is even stronger than René's, but from what I can make out he is threatening to visit us at dead of night and kill every living animal if we decide to go into livestock farming. I make my excuses and go to the toilet, only to find he has followed me and is brandishing a huge and deadly looking knife. I promise that we will stick to purely arable pursuits, and apparently disappointed, he sheaths his weapon and leaves.

After settling my nerves with a swift glass of *calva*, I relate my experience to Madame Nellie, who explains that I have misconstrued the situation. Mr Guy is a harmless individual who happens to work at the local slaughterhouse. Unofficially, which means totally illegally, he earns a little extra income by making late night visits to smallholders who wish to have their animals butchered, and was merely offering me this service should we have need of it. It is understandable that the misunderstanding has taken place, Nellie remarks as she notes my shaking hand and pours another measure in the glass with some difficulty. Mr Guy is a lonely, withdrawn and sometimes intense personality even by local standards, and people say he carries the smell of death with him wherever he goes. As I now know, he also carries the main tool of his trade.

December 25th:

Christmas Day. We rise late and exchange presents. Opening mine, I solve a month-long mystery regarding the contents of the large and strangely shaped parcel beside the gaily decorated fir tree in our orchard. Donella has thoughtfully bought me a new wheelbarrow, complete with a list of pressing outdoor tasks attached by a pretty bow to the handle. She seems equally pleased with her second-hand chainsaw, which I bought from René after his assurances that it is as good as when his father bought it twenty years before, and far superior to modern rubbish with all the unnecessary safety devices.

Like children impatient to play with our new toys, we decide to spend the day outside. Loading my new wheelbarrow with a picnic, bottle of wine and the chainsaw, we make our way down to the water meadow so that my wife may give her presents to the livestock.

Unable to keep our own animals in the past as mostly absentee landlords, we have sublet the land to a variety of tenants in an attempt to keep the land in trim, and Donella has adopted them all. Two goats belonging to our distant neighbour Christian do good work on the scrub in the one acre garden behind the farmhouse, and my wife has bought them a gift-wrapped packet of extra strength Capstan cigarettes, which are their favourite brand.

We learned of this enthusiasm for tobacco from an eccentric Englishman in a neighbouring village who shares his house with an alpine goat. Whilst most amiable, the creature also likes pot plants and is not house trained, so even my wife has not invited the happy couple to dinner as yet.

Apart from the occasional arrival of friends' sheep or pigs in need of rough grazing, the two sloping and well-drained roadside fields at La Puce are reserved for the beef cattle owned by Jean Chevalier, the mayor of Néhou. We inherited the arrangement from the previous owner, and are very glad to have done so. Typical of the farmers in the region, John and his wife Solange have their own fields around their farmhouse in a nearby hamlet, but rent extra grazing land at a very nominal fee. Apart from keeping the land, hedges and gates in impeccable condition and their tireless efforts in helping us become accepted by the community, having such a close relationship with the local mayor has been of great practical assistance during the restoration of La Puce. Every commune in France has its own elected mayor, and each wields considerable power, particularly in matters of planning consent for building works and improvements. Even before buying our first house in Cotentin we had learned that the French love of bureaucracy is matched only by their total disregard of due procedure when it suits them or the situation. One of our first requirements at La Puce was to seek the best way to let some light into the former hay loft which would become our bedroom, and this at first seemed to present no problem. Skylight windows being as common as crows in this region of traditional single storey Norman longhouses, we made some rough sketches of where we thought they should be fitted, and wishing to go by the book from the start of operations, asked John to help with any necessary paperwork.

The next day, he arrived with a sheaf of forms and wearing a tie with his usual bib and brace overalls and gumboots to signify the official nature of his visit. We then spent an hour going through the details of how to proceed with bureaucratic communications. Firstly, we must take photographs from all angles of how the roof looked at the moment, and commission professional drawings of how it would look after the alterations. Also, we must fill in three duplicate forms asking such relevant questions as how long we had been married and where our children went to school. These would be despatched to the local *mairie*, to the main administration centre for the department, and to Paris, presumably to ensure that the President had no objection to our changing the aesthetic outlines of a roof which was about to collapse before we bought it. Over the coming days, we diligently complied, confidently ordered the windows, and awaited a favourable outcome of our application. Three weeks later, a most apologetic John told us that for some unexplained reason, our request was *irréconciliable*. For whatever reason, the authorities appeared to have decided that it must remain forever midnight in our bedroom, and the farmhouse at La Puce be the only property in the region without even one roof window.

Fired with indignation and having taken advice from a local English expatriot who had developed a small outhouse into a sprawling five bedroomed home without bothering to ask anyone's permission, we decided to take the law into our own hands and risk fines, imprisonment and expulsion. Following the necessary adjustments to the upper part of the gable end wall with a five pound sledgehammer, we fitted an economy size pair of french windows which would let in more light to the bedroom than a dozen skylight windows. While the mood was on us, we also designed and erected a massive wooden balcony, giving incomparable views across the whole of our terrain. As we slapped a final coat of wood preservative on the huge timber legs, the mayor arrived to move his cattle from the field alongside. While we held our breath, he took off his hat, scratched his head and spent a long moment surveying the totally unapproved structure with a quizzical frown. Then he shook our hands vigorously, complimented us on the standard of workmanship and speed of erection, and graciously accepted our invitation to officially open the new *balcon* with a drinks and ribbon-cutting ceremony later that day.

It was some time before we discovered that skylight windows are the one alteration to any existing building that do not require planning permission in France.

*   *   *   *   *

Down at the big pond, we find the crayfish gang have extended their territory and reign of terror.

Reggie and Ronnie Cray and their heavy mob appeared in the east end of the pond shortly after we had it dug, and immediately set about ruling their new manor with almost inhuman ferocity. We had first spotted their aggressive swagger through the shallows as they visited the frog colony and put the frighteners on, and even the largest trout would turn tail at their approach. Burrow holes had regularly appeared around the bank as new generations of the gang set up home, and now it seems they hold total sway. They are, according to our enquiries, a particularly large and succulent species of native freshwater crayfish, who have reappeared since we began clearing out the stream and generally attempting to restore life to the polluted waters of La Puce. Hearing of our new tenants during a visit to the *Café de Paris*, Freddo the patron had told us of his happy childhood days at our grotto fishing for cray and trout, and advised that we keep their return a deadly secret. The first action we should take would be the removal of the No Fishing signs Donella has put up all around the terrain. Their very presence would let everyone in the area know there were now fish to be caught at La Puce, and the temptation would be too strong for the most law-abiding Norman angler. Even more importantly, we must make sure that René does not find out there is anything remotely eatable or sellable in our waters.

We know this to be sound advice, having become aware of our friend's appetite for unusual delicacies when we dug a tiny pond in the garden at La Puce and filled it with goldfish cunningly smuggled across the Channel in a couple of large thermos flasks. The day after they had taken up residence, Donella had found him looking thoughtfully at the innocent creatures, and asked if

26

goldfish are as popular in France as they are with English people. He had nodded enthusiastically, and told her of his special recipe for *poissons rouges* in batter.

Given the rapid expansion of the Cray gang as evidenced by their territorial gains, René has hopefully not yet noted their presence, in spite of their tendency to wreak havoc when in drink.

We had first become aware of the Crays' liking for alcohol when preparing a special dinner for a visiting Burgundian friend. Wishing to impress him with our mastery of his regional classic dish, we had visited JayPay with a bottle of scotch and a request for a crash course in creating *boeuf bourguignon*.

Following the lengthy verbal and written instructions to the letter, we marinated the beef for the requisite time, and then fished out the carrots which had been sitting in a bottle's worth of best Burgundy for a day and a night. This, JayPay had stressed, was a vital step, as they would become discoloured in the process and totally ruin the overall visual effect if left in place. Having read that crayfish are not averse to vegetables, we had taken the thoroughly soused carrots down to the big pond and dropped them by Reggie and Ronnie's front door. In moments, the duo had emerged and snapped up the unexpected treat. Inevitably the alcohol had taken effect and trouble broke out. With nobody else to pick on, they had started a drunken brawl with each other and we were unable to separate them. Eventually, a lost claw declared Big Reg the winner, and all was still again as they retired to sleep it off.

Knowing their susceptibility to strong liquor, Donella has prepared them some pork crackling in low alcohol lager, and respectfully leaving their special Christmas lunch at the entrance to their manor, we continue our rounds.

*   *   *   *   *

At his caravan, all is quiet, which means René has found an open bar, is visiting The Widow of Negreville, or sleeping off the effects of the night before. We leave his present of real ale-flavoured

Christmas puddings and a bottle of malt whisky, and an invitation to join us for dinner.

René Ribet and his mobile home arrived in the big field last year, shortly after he told us that he was being evicted from his tiny cottage on the outskirts of Néhou and needed somewhere else to stay till times became better. The arrangement, he said, would be to our great benefit, as his presence would deter poachers, burglars and other miscreants who would otherwise take advantage of our absence. Under his stewardship, our estate would be in safe hands, and he would not only manage the land, but carry out all restoration work on the buildings at La Puce at half the price of any other specialist tradesman in the area. As anyone would tell us, there was little he did not know about nature, farming and building work.

In fact, most people in the area seem keen to tell us that René is known locally as Ribet The Fox and is not to be trusted, but, for all his failings he has a big heart and has become my friend. From him, I have already learned much about the culture and character of the Cotentinese people, and am prepared to pay the price for that knowledge. My wife seems to think that the price is often too high, but I am sure she will warm to him now that we are here to stay.

*   *   *   *   *

The roast is almost ready when René arrives. As Donella prepares the drinks, he explains he has been out on the traditional Christmas Day hunt, in full hue and cry for what must be one of the few surviving mammals bigger than a water vole in Cotentin. As in other regions of France, the country people seem to like to pursue and kill any wild creature that can be broadly classified as either eatable or a pest, and take a very liberal view of the results of the occasional mistake. Last year, two ramblers in the St Sauveur forest were quite badly injured by a salvo from a hunting party, but the trial judge said it was their fault for being there at the start of the wild boar season.

Before we sit down at table, René passes me a carrier bag

containing our Christmas present, and I see that it is a dead squirrel. Hoping that it is not the same undernourished animal that my wife has been encouraging to take up residence in our copse, I thank him and slip the still warm corpse in the rubbish bin whilst Donella hands him a glass of mulled wine spiced with nutmeg and ginger. Our guest takes a sip, makes a grim face but eventually pronounces it as perfectly acceptable for English tastes as he puts the glass to one side. It is the first time in our acquaintance that he has not finished a drink.

After dinner, which seemed to go quite well except for the vegetables, René accepts a tumbler of whisky and asks if our burglars had taken anything. Pressed for details, he describes a dramatic incident at La Puce during our visit to the south. Just after dusk, the mayor had arrived at René's caravan in a state of high excitement. Knowing of our absence, he had stopped off at the farmhouse to check all was well and that all doors and windows were secured. As he had walked around the building, however, an outside light had been turned on and off, indicating that intruders must be inside. Armed with René's ancient shotgun and a billhook, they had surrounded the farmhouse, when once again a light had signalled the presence of careless trespassers. As the official keyholder, René had then led an assault through the front door, only to find the building empty.

An investigation of the premises proving fruitless, they had concluded that the would-be thieves had made good their escape during the search upstairs, that the flashing lights had been operated by a power surge, or even more likely and satisfactory that it was the manifestation of some supernatural force. After disconnecting the electricity supply we had stupidly left on, the intrepid pair had returned to René's caravan for a steadying glass of *calva* and a full debate on the mystery.

I express our thanks for their brave action in protecting our property, and think it best not to point out that, before leaving to visit our friends, I had installed a set of newfangled British security floodlights with special sensors which react to any movement in the yard.

And so, the legend of the *fantôme* of La Puce was born.

December 30th:

We are invited to dinner with the mayor, a signal honour. It should be an interesting evening. Other guests will include my mother, who has joined us to see the New Year in, and Helen Patton, grand daughter of the famous American general. Patton was based at an orchard just down the road from La Puce during the D-Day operations, and Helen is restoring a grand house in Néhou in memory of the great man. Twenty miles from Cherbourg, our area has always played an important part in the history of the peninsula, and many illustrious figures have visited, stayed or died here, especially in times of war. Like the extravagant claims of patronage by Queen Elizabeth I made by so many English innkeepers, Rommel seems to have spent at least one night in every farm house and *chambre d'hôte* in the region, despite having his permanent defence headquarters at the Old Chateau hotel in Bricquebec. We also know that Richard The Lionheart was a frequent traveller through the nearby port of Barfleur on his way to the Crusades, but the local tourist board does not seem to consider the passage of an English king worthy of plaque or record, despite the fact that he spoke better French than English. A considerable celebrity in the area, Helen Patton is much respected in the village, and has just asked John Chevalier to take on the responsibility and honour of aiding progress with restoration work on the orchard and house. A grim coincidence, she confides over a pommeau *apéritif*, is that like her grandfather, John's predecessor was killed in a car accident. She asks us not to make this fact public, as we know how superstitious the locals can be.

Over a simple but excellent dinner of pressed bull's tongue followed by roast chicken in a sauce made from its entrails, John tells us how his farm was a billet for German troops during the occupation. He was just fourteen at the time, and some of the soldiers were even younger. Others were too old to do much more than wear a uniform, and none were brutal or even unfriendly. In stark contrast to our long memories and dislike of those who have as much as threatened our shores, we have found that none of the residents seem to bear any malice towards their former occupiers. Donella believes this to be another example of Norman pragmatism, as German visitors contribute greatly to the economy of the area by revisiting the scene of their crimes. Indeed, our informal survey of local restaurateurs indicates that they are the most popular visitors as they tip so generously. Next favourite are the British, who are not as open handed, but never complain. Universally despised are all Parisians, who want everything for nothing, refuse to tip, love to criticise the food and have the audacity to believe that they are not only equal but even superior to the Cotentinese.

As the evening progresses, we learn that La Puce saw some honourable action during the D-Day landings. According to John, a German machine gun nest was set up in the roadside attic, frustrating the efforts of a platoon of American infantrymen to advance on St Sauveur le Vicomte. After a lively exchange of fire, the platoon leader called on the services of a passing fighter plane, which strafed the farmhouse until the inhabitants surrendered. According to elderly locals, they were then marched away to our copse by resistance fighters and never seen again. The holes in the kitchen ceiling and great chunks missing from the attic rafters are evidence of the aerial attack, as I will have noticed. It would be fitting, the mayor ventures, to leave the wounds intact during our restoration as a permanent reminder of the incident and the ultimate pointlessness of war. I agree and wish I hadn't spent so much on getting the rafters repaired and timbers treated by René, who assured me the culprit was a particularly savage termite which would eat the whole building if not exorcised.

After dinner, we are introduced to yet another variety on the *calva* theme. The regional economy version of Grand Marnier, *quarante quatre* is made by every rural housewife to serve at special occasions and the method of marinating an orange and some coffee beans in *calva* for the required 44 days could not be simpler.

The resulting sweet and fragrant liqueur is just as lethal as *calva* but has an innocence of taste which invites overindulgence, as my wife and mother proceed to confirm.

It is now time for us to present our party pieces, and Helen breaks the ice by performing a tuneful American folk song. Rather thoughtlessly, I take mother's advice and respond with my speciality of standing on a chair and declaiming some of the loud and very francophobe extracts from the St Crispin's Day address in Henry V. Happily, the text appears to lose much in the translation, and Solange calms us all with a patois lullaby, serenely delivered in her pure, sweet voice.

Emboldened by the *quarante quatre*, my wife stops the show with Land of My Fathers in the original Welsh, and mother gives a stirring rendition of Hearts of Oak. John then tells a polite anecdote about a gendarme and a lady motorist, which mother, who is obviously feeling homesick and therefore at her most patriotic, follows with Rule Britannia before inviting the assembly to join in with a grand finale of Land of Hope and Glory. To even the score a little, I suggest we all sing the *Marseillaise* before going our separate ways.

Fuelled with another glass of the *calva* liqueur, mother is now beginning to make tart comments about the overall performance of the French and the late entry of the Americans into the war, and unfortunately Helen is translating. I thank our hosts and escort her to the car as she recalls how her great-great-great-grandfather played a leading part in the Battle of Trafalgar, and how he would oft recall that the Lords of the Admiralty quite rightly considered one English tar to be worth at least eight French matelots when planning engagement tactics.

Around midnight, I have a strange dream, in which I am visited by a lady in 18th-century clothing. She summons me, and I follow her down the stairs and out to the orchard. There, she points at the base of an old apple tree. I wake Donella and tell her of my experience. It is well known, I point out, that all millers were renowned for fiddling their customers and burying a spare pot of gold somewhere on the premises. Perhaps this is a supernatural visitation to tell me where a fortune in *Louis d'or* is buried. She yawns and reminds me that I ate nearly a whole round of goats cheese after dinner. Knowing the Norman reputation for closeness to a shilling, any treasure would have been discovered long ago. Perhaps, she grudgingly concedes, I might find our German stormtroopers there.

I return to bed, nevertheless determined to buy a metal detector on our next visit to the UK...

Recipe for *Quarante Quatre*

1. Take one orange
2. Pierce with 44 coffee beans
3. Place in a jar and cover with rough farm calva
4. Leave for 44 days
5. Taste in sitting position and on a day off
6. Drink some more
7. Go and lie down...

January 11th:

An uneventful crossing home - yes *home* - on the overnight from Portsmouth.

Now that Christmas and the worst excesses of the booze cruises are over, it is at least possible to use the toilet and avoid certain confrontation with a pool of vomit or its previous owner.

The last time we ventured into a Cherbourg supermarket in the run-up to Christmas, a British youth wearing a monstrously inflated condom on his head was being sick over a table in the cafeteria as his mates made encouraging comments on style, volume and content. Thankfully, the table was not occupied at the time.

As we hurried away trying to look like locals, I commented admiringly on the reaction of the French diners. Rather than looking angry or disgusted, they were watching the display with the bemused air of foreign spectators at a village cricket match.

I put their attitude down to classic gallic tolerance and respect for individual liberties. My wife thought it was probably because the French are so used to being invaded, the odd barbarian at a neighbouring table is no big deal.

Besides, she reminded me, I of all people should refrain from complaining about pillaging raids by duty free hunters, as I was responsible for helping stage the biggest organised booze cruise in history.

I began my long relationship with the Cotentin peninsula when a friend asked for my assistance in staging the first ever floating trade show, with a thousand publicans and their wives to be taken on a day trip from Portsmouth to Cherbourg. In theory, the idea was to hire a ferry for 24 hours and convert the car deck to an exhibition featuring prominent drinks and pub products. The captive audience would inspect, sample and hopefully place orders for the goods on the way over, take a leisurely lunch at the quay side, then return at the end of a long but entertaining day.

In practice, it didn't quite work out to plan. Apart from the captain asking if we could call a halt to the simultaneous microwave, electric oven and juke box demonstrations so that he could have his radar back on line, the outward journey was as calm and benign as the mill-pond seas.

When we arrived however, the entire complement of landlords and landladies ignored the bars and cafes and made straight for the nearest hypermarket.

Three hours later, I stood at the top of the gangplank with the managing director of the brewery which had sponsored the event, and watched as a raggle taggle army staggered back to the ship laden down with tons of duty free beers, wines and spirits. Taxis, supermarket trolleys and even the odd pram had been commandeered to help them take maximum advantage of the opportunity to buy their next month's stock-in-hand at remarkable prices. The fact that re-selling the goods would be illegal, and that anyway they were all supposed to buy their products direct from the brewery was not lost on our host, who consequently decided not to repeat one of his company's most successful PR promotions the next year. Or ever again.

*   *   *   *   *

We have been over the water to raid the dwindling supplies in our Portsmouth bank account. We could have had the money transferred direct, but our manager doesn't yet know we have moved, so it seemed a good idea to show our faces in the Southsea branch and forestall any awkward questions about why we prefer banking in a foreign country.

At Bricquebec, we stop off at *Crédit Agricole* to inject some life into the separate restoration and survival funds, which are both dangerously close to extinction. Though so liberal in other areas, the French attitude to spending money you haven't got by signing dud cheques is far from understanding. If we don't keep the payments on our Cotentin home up to date, we could soon be asking René for a share of his mobile home.

When we bought La Puce, we thought it best to take out a

mortgage with our French bank, and it has proved to be a serious mistake. At that time, the exchange rate was more than ten francs to the pound, and the interest level comparatively low. Besides, not too many British financial organisations expressed interest in lending money on a pair of architecturally interesting ruins in a field in France. Now the rate is little more than seven francs, and we appear to owe more on La Puce than this time last year.

In a black moment last month, Donella calculated that if things go on as they are, we will end up with a bigger debt than the place cost to start with. This bizarre equation is reflected in the bank, where the longer we wait, the further we get from the counter. If there is a French word for queue, the Cotentinese have obviously yet to learn it.

Eventually, there is only one customer in front of us, a very small monk with a very large sack of cash to deposit. We have seen him before, and know him to be the bagman for the Trappist monastery overlooking the square, where it is said the finest *charcuterie* in all France is made. The impressive gothic building is next door to a grocery store where it is said the finest cheeses in all France are to be found. Naturally, stocks are limited to the 27 varieties made in Normandy.

As the monk is fortunately from a silent order, the usual ten minute dialogue on intimate health details and exchanges of x-ray plates from recent operations does not take place, and we are soon at the counter. Even better, we are to be served by our regular cashier, which should cut down on the usual formalities like fingerprinting and gene matching before we are allowed to pay any money in. After the usual greetings and polite enquiries, I pass large wads of English banknotes across the counter, pocket the receipt and ask for five hundred francs to do the shopping. With a perfectly straight face, the girl asks if I have any identification to show that I am, indeed, entitled to draw upon the account I have just filled to overflowing. Checking my passport for the hundredth time in two years, she presses some buttons and regretfully informs me that our account does not hold sufficient funds to cover the withdrawal, and we have, as we should know, no overdraft facility. The manager is more sympathetic, and explains that there will be a slight delay of no more than a few days before our three thousand pounds is electronically converted to real (i.e. French) money and credited to Mr and Mrs East at the Agon-Coutainville branch where we have chosen to keep our main account. Till then, his all-purpose shrug confirms, he can in no circumstances let us have a single centime. Had we honoured this branch with our account, of course, it would be a different matter.

We get as far as the foyer before he joins us to point out that, as we will know, due to the vagaries of the sophisticated system, our cash card will perhaps not be aware of the situation, and were we so inclined we could quite illegally draw up to a thousand francs from our temporarily empty account. Not, of course, that we would consider committing such an offence.

We do and do so as he discreetly averts his eyes and wishes us success with our shopping, recommending as he does the superb facilities and range at the nearby *Huit à Huit* grocery franchise owned by his cousin.

After all this excitement, it is time for a coffee break at the *Café de Paris*. Besides, as my wife reminds me, the Eight to Eight doesn't open until nine a.m.

* * * * *

Of the half dozen bars in Bricquebec, the *Café de Paris* is our favourite local. Like every other bar in the region it falls considerably short of the traditional attractions of a good British pub such as carpets and a choice of beers beyond lager, lager or lager. Except on market days, a busy session for the average small town or village bar is when the customers outnumber the proprietor, but big Freddo's place is a regular and popular haunt for most of the town's serious drinkers and socialites. As the owner of the most monumental moustache in Bricquebec, Freddo is naturally an important figure in the community, and we come to him for regular advice on all matters of local etiquette and best practices.

As it is a Tuesday, our host will be at his day job as a master at the local secondary school. Donella is sure he teaches English, but as a smattering of German appears to be his only foreign language, I think this is unlikely, even in Cotentin.

Madame Collette and her mother are at their usual posts, and we are each awarded the four kisses normally reserved for close friends. There is a special bond between us, as the kind and gentle Collette was born in Néhou. In the reverse of the usual situation in an English village, we have been almost instantly accepted as members of the community, unlike the foreigners at nearby St Jacques de Néhou. We have yet to discover the reason for the fierce rivalry between the two villages which stand in permanent antipathy on either side of the D900, but believe there was a serious falling out a hundred years or so ago. This is no more than a whisker on Freddo's moustache in the scale of time locally, so the two neighbouring communes with their similar names and history keep strictly to their own territory, shops, bars and affairs. Scandals concerning each other's residents are of course very much in the public domain.

In the way of things locally, La Puce is actually closer to St Jacques, and we are official reinforcements to the dwindling commune of Néhou simply because the mayor nipped round and signed us up first.

As ever, it is difficult to see more than a metre inside the *Café de Paris* due to the comfortable fog of tobacco smoke. Last year, we were severely traumatised to learn that a universal ban on smoking in public places, including all bars, had been decreed from Paris in our absence, and was shortly to come in to force.

From the dawning of what for some unfathomable reason was dubbed Blue Elephant day, every bar in France would be strictly smoke-free, with just one table in a clearly defined separate area set aside for hopeless addicts. An orgy of posters, leaflets and advertisements bearing the blue elephant logo having prepared us for the day, we visited the *Café de Paris* determined to show our intransigent British dissent by sitting outside and sullenly fuming in the rain. As it transpired, Freddo and every other bar owner in the region had taken a very French approach to the new legislation. There were now two overflowing ashtrays on each table instead of the usual one, and the few non-smoking regulars had lit up to express their contempt for this unacceptable threat to fraternity and liberty. Bets were also being placed on whose glass the ever-growing column of ash on Freddo's *disque bleu* would contaminate as he puffed with his usual determination over the pumps. Elsewhere, some wag had sketched a large cigarette protruding from an unusual orifice in the blue elephant which was watching with watery eyes from the poster behind the bar. The law being the law, however, Freddo had taken all due precautions. A single table marked *non-fumeur* had been placed in the dingy passageway at the rear of the bar, wedged in between the fridge-freezer and toilet door.

Nobody, he told us, had chosen to use it so far, but you never knew when a spy from the relevant ministry might drop in to check that the new law was being scrupulously observed and administered.

*   *   *   *   *

After catching the *Huit à Huit* just before the standard two hour lunchtime closure - which allegedly also applies to some restaurants in our area - we depart for La Puce.

*   *   *   *   *

Making our way straight down the ancient cart track to where the remains of the tiny mill stand beside *le Lude*, we are greeted by a host of snowdrops and a newly delivered mountain of sand.

Now that René has finished restoration work on the farmhouse and has promised to find us an impeccable tenant *tout d' suite*, he is obviously preparing to turn his attentions to the mill. As all interior and exterior stone walls are to be left unplastered and the heap of sand is almost as big as the building itself, it appears he has over-ordered. Probably, I reassure my wife, René has gained considerable savings on our behalf by buying in bulk, and sand

39

always comes in handy. She sniffs and reminds me that her researches and our latest bill from Mr Ribet prove it would be cheaper to have a lorry load delivered by the local builders' merchant than a wheelbarrow's worth via The Fox of Cotentin.

I promise to do something about the situation, and pointedly suggest she might like to spend the afternoon re-stocking her feeding stations with the expensive selection of quality victuals she has brought all the way from the Portsmouth branch of Pets Are Us.

January 12th:

Having risen early to give her dependants a full English breakfast, my wife returns to the farmhouse and announces that it is raining.

This comes as no surprise as it is neither July nor August. One of the older residents of Néhou claims to recall a dry week in the winter of 1924, but he is a notorious liar. It is said that the weather on the peninsula is so changeable that four seasons can take place in just one day. This we have found to be true but not particularly remarkable, as all seasons in Cotentin are rainy. This is why the countryside is so green and so often empty of people, who sensibly prefer to stay indoors during inclement weather. It is also said locally that a walking stick pushed into the ground will eventually blossom in the rich and fertile soil. Providing, of course, that nobody cuts it down for firewood before it has a chance to root. Wood, and preferably someone else's wood to be used for free fuel is a prized commodity in Cotentin, either in spite of or perversely because of its abundance in this heavily wooded region.

No visitor to Cotentin could fail to notice that, as with the size and shape of the Manche moustache, the dimensions and design of the woodpile outside each home is a most important status symbol for its creator. Virtually all cottages will have a monstrous woodpile, either freestanding or stacked against the gable end, and style is almost as important as size. There is constant competition to build the most complex and impressive erection

40

of the hardest and therefore most expensive woods, much in the way that neighbours in England might compete to achieve and display the most immaculate and flattest lawn. A curious phenomenon is that the woodpiles do not seem to diminish as winter progresses, and often seem to grow as the cold weather intensifies. I know of some upwardly mobile villagers who have oil central heating, yet still work feverishly all summer to build the biggest and best woodpile in the neighbourhood.

January 16th:

Sunday morning. It is so quiet we can hear the church bells at Néhou calling the faithful to prayer. Though this is a strongly Catholic region with roadside shrines in abundance, the men of the region are far more likely to be found in the PMU betting shops and bars at this time.

On our first Sunday in La Puce, we decided the lunchtime session at our local bar would provide an ideal opportunity to make ourselves known to the locals. Accordingly and to the best British traditions, we rose late, put a lamb roast in the oven, and arrived at the Bar Ghislaine on the dot of noon.

The place had obviously been under siege, but was now deserted. As we learned, peak hour for the Sunday morning session here is around eight am, with lunch on the table at midday sharp. But, as we also discovered, it all starts again at two pm, when most of the customers return to settle their stomachs with a selection of interesting *digestifs*.

It was during our apprenticeship at one of these lazy afternoons that I was to commit a serious social gaffe.

As usual, JayPay was the centre of reverent attention as he described a recent adventure with a cuttlefish and some fine herbs, and I made the mistake of saying I would stand next to him at the bar so he would feel slim by comparison. This pub ploy usually goes down well when breaking the ice with someone who is about my build, but at the Bar Ghislaine it resulted in a sudden, cold and complete silence. Feeling like a gunslinger from out of town who has unwittingly confronted the local quick-draw specialist, I tried to make things well again by asking his opinion on the best way to cook English lamb, but the damage was obviously done.

Re-settling his massive stomach on the bar and with his moustache quivering with suppressed fury, the local hero took on my challenge by calling for Madame Ghislaine's bathroom scales. As the entire congregation held its collective breath, we took it in turns to weigh in.

Unfortunately, I won by a clear five kilos.

Since then we have become good friends, and I have made sincere attempts to lose weight and restore the heavyweight championship to JayPay.

I have also learned that, in a culture with such different values and standards my nickname of Mr Beerbelly is anything but a disrespectful jibe.

January 22nd:

René arrives after lunch to find me tooled up with my new metal detector, carefully hoovering the spot next to the apple tree where the Grey Lady indicated the location of the miller's gold. I consider telling him the device is a revolutionary silent British grass cutter and the headphones are tuned in to Radio Jersey, but he is no fool. Thinking quickly, I say that I am ensuring there are no water pipes below the earth, as I have decided to plant a new cherry tree. He sucks his teeth, looks at me for a long moment, then explains patiently that it would be stupid even for an Englishman from a city to dig so close to an ancient apple tree. The ground will not bear two trees so close together, and besides, cherries are a waste of time, except as flavouring for Mr Maurice's *calva* collection. And anyway, the birds will eat all the fruit before it ripens. René has a keen interest in the welfare of the orchard trees because, as he explained when we made our original arrangements, honourable tradition and long standing custom dictate that the estate manager has the rights to the entire harvest. In exchange, we are awarded one bottle of *calva* per tree. As, thanks to his year-round ministrations, our trees produce the finest *goutte* in Cotentin, I would be most ill-advised to risk the health of this one. I nod in agreement, and determine to start digging at night when he is safely tucked up in his bed.

January 25th:

René has called a caravan conference to begin discussions on the creation of another *étang* in the water meadow. Now that the crayfish gang have taken over at the big pond, Donella is anxious to create a safe haven for the victims of their protection racket. René says he and his tractor-owning pond specialist can start next week, so I calculate that the first sod will be turned over around June.

Over the past year we have learned that, in the local work vocabulary, 'tomorrow' means at least a month or so, and 'next year' more than likely never. While it is true that tradesmen in rural areas elsewhere in France are not known for their commitment to a schedule, the Cotentinese are recognised as past masters at avoiding future start dates, and have their own version of *mañana*. When asked if he will be sure to arrive at the agreed time and place, the local craftsman will invariably shrug, look at the sky for a while, remove his hat and cigarette, scratch his jaw, fiddle with his moustache, then grunt '*p'tet bankwee... p'tet bankno*'. Technically, this means 'perhaps yes... perhaps no'. In practice, the acceptance of the negative option is usually a very safe bet.

This is one of the reasons why my relationship with René is so important. In my dealings with our estate manager, I am daily learning how to adapt to the ways and wiles of the Cotentinese, said quite unjustly in other regions to be as crafty as two barrels of particularly cunning monkeys.

From the beginning, my understanding of The Fox of Cotentin has been developing through a series of encounters, with each of us striving to establish and maintain the advantage. He has knowledge of the land, the people and the ways of the region. I like to believe I have the worldly-wise sophistication of the modern city dweller, and am experienced in striking a shrewd business deal in the urban jungle. Since we arrived and the game began, my wife has been keeping score and says there is no contest. René has been playing with me like a farm cat with a particularly stupid mouse. What she does not know is that I have been biding my time, learning the local rules of engagement, and while appearing to appease him at any cost, am actually conducting a complex strategy which will result in a sound working relationship for the future.

Now, the sand mountain outside the mill has become a symbol of our struggle, with the advantage to him growing with its size, and to me as it diminishes.

I am resolved not to become obsessive about the sand pile, but have my plans.

Our original deal to start a suitable working arrangement was struck over a bottle of my best malt whisky at his former home, and concluded with the general agreement that all restoration and development projects should be carried out by him or his representatives, and in exactly the way he proposed. This, he argued, would work completely to my benefit, as he could secure the sort of labour charges and material costs that I, a foreigner, could not hope to achieve. In return, he would merely ask for the odd specialist commission for himself, and that our refrigerator be kept stocked with an adequate supply of beer. After a year of being a mostly absentee landlord, I had not been able to ensure that the first part of our bargain was working to my advantage, but had achieved considerable success with the beer rationing. Depending upon the season, temperature and nature of the work, my wife and I had long established the best and most productive rate for the job.

In mid-summer and when an acre or so of garden grass needs

cutting, René will operate his scythe to optimum efficiency and safety standards on one bottle of *Kronenbourg 1664* every twenty minutes. Any less and he will begin to dehydrate and sulk, and his lunchbreak lengthen to three hours; any more, and he will work faster, but endanger his own limbs and those of any creature within range of the flashing blade.

Sorting out the price for each project has proved a much more complex and demanding operation. Traditionally, negotiations take place in a bar, and begin with a presentation of a bottle of scotch. This is never opened, but left on the table as a sign to the locals that business is going on, and also the high level of esteem in which we hold our man. Scotch whisky, as frequent visitors to France will know, is one of the few British products held in universal favour.

After an initial beer or two, negotiations open with the presentation of a detailed drawing of our vision of the project, complete with precise details of location and dimension. This will be fleetingly acknowledged, then put to one side. We will then hear all the reasons for doing the job differently, on a different scale, and usually in another place. Having agreed on these provisos, it is time to settle the price.

It is most important at this stage to establish whether we are working in new or old francs, as this will affect the price considerably.

Initially, and not knowing that René was the River Authority for the region, we had asked for an estimate from a professional pond maker. He had arrived with all sorts of machinery and complex equipment, surveyed the water meadow for an hour or two and finally declared the terrain suitable to hold an *étang*.

This came as no surprise to us, as the meadow floods to gumboot level every winter, is marked on old plans of La Puce as *le réservoir*, and was used as a storage lake by the miller for around two centuries.

What did come as a surprise was the price quoted for a fairly large pond, complete with feed and drainage pipes from and to the river just fifty feet away. A suitably large and impressive *étang* would cost us only slightly less than we had paid for the ten acres, farmhouse and cottage. It was time to consult with René for an alternative estimate.

Having changed the location, size and shape of the pond and dismissing the professional pond builder as a rank amateur in a few minutes, it took him three hours and eight beers to come up with a price. Finally, the calculations were completed, scribbled on the back of a beer mat and slid conspiratorially across the wet table top beneath his horny hand.

Getting into the spirit of things, I picked the piece of card up like a particularly secretive poker player, looked suspiciously round the empty bar, then tried to decipher his computations beneath the table. The special price for our pond would appear to be *trois millions*. At ten francs to the pound, this would be approximately £300,000, which would appear to be a little optimistic of our presumed wealth and gullibility, even for René. I sighed, expressed my disappointment with an English expletive and rose to go to the outside toilet. There, I would mull over how we would raise the cash for the professional pond maker's services. I had promised Donella her *étang*, and it was a vital step on the road to creating our trout farm. We would have to find the money somehow.

As I set off in obviously high dudgeon, René frowned, caught my arm and waved me back to my seat. I must understand, he hastily explained, that the price was, according to the countryside tradition, couched in ancient francs. In modern terms, it would, *naturellement*, be 3,000. And the *grand étang* would be built before our next visit. I clasped his hand and sealed the deal.

A year later, and our pond was ready. It was at the wrong end of the water meadow and much smaller than we had hoped, and, without any piping to or from the river, the water level drops alarmingly in summer. It's also difficult to reach as René and his *spécialiste* disposed of the excavated earth by simply dumping it around the edge and creating a massive rampart which is almost impossible to scale in the rainy season. However, they did lose the use of the tractor for a week when it got stuck in the mud, and at £300 the price was exactly right.

This was my first experience in negotiating with and getting the better of The Fox. My wife still feels that had we been as incredibly wealthy and stupid as René had hoped, he would have taken the £300,000 without a blink, and disappeared to a pleasant retirement in the south. She also believes it was the last time I got the better of him, that the low price was just a loss leader, and that Ribet The Fox has been making up for it ever since.

But at least, as I constantly remind her, we have the cheapest artificial *étang* in Cotentin.

February 5th:

A Saturday evening in by the fire, and we are missing the Lottery. They have the same sort of thing here, but for some reason it's less fun not winning vast sums of money in a foreign currency. As in England, nearly everyone here believes they will hit the jackpot before the numbers begin to appear on screen, then spend the rest of the evening sulking when they don't.

My brother phones from Hampshire to say he hasn't won again, and tells us a story which he swears is true.

Last Saturday, he and his wife went with another couple for dinner at a local pub. The husband is apparently a fervid Lottery player. As soon as they arrived and found a table, their friend placed his ticket by his plate and asked the waitress to be sure to bring the winning numbers over as soon as they came across on the public bar television.

After more than a few glasses of wine and while his friend was in the toilet, my brother copied his companion's entry numbers and gave them to the waitress with a fiver. He knew his friend had a sound heart and could take a joke, he said.

Just after eight o'clock, the waitress appeared with the pudding and the allegedly winning combination. The victim started to check them, while my brother and the two women sat back to watch his reaction before quickly revealing their little prank.

When he had gone over the figures twice without a word or change of expression, my brother's friend stood up, took the house keys from his pocket, threw them on the table in front of his wife and said: 'I've been sleeping with your sister for three years. Goodbye.'

We shall have to wait till next week for the final *dénouement*, as my brother wasn't able to catch his former friend in the car park, and hasn't heard from him since. As he ruefully observes before ringing off, the joke backfired on him as well, as he was left to pay the bill and it wasn't his turn.

February 12th:

Spring must be on the way. A straggle of jaundiced daffodils has appeared in the farmhouse garden. I call for my wife to share the good news, but she is obviously out on her morning feeding patrol so I look in the fridge to select breakfast. I note that at least half the specially imported catering pack of bacon is missing, together with six eggs and a couple of cold sausages I had earmarked for a fry-up. Obviously, the Cray gang are going to have a better start to the day than me.

While I finish off an unexciting meal of peanut butter on toast, my wife returns in a state of high excitement. Not only has she spotted a red squirrel amongst the giant beech trees lining Hunters Walk, but also something big enough to move in on Reg and Ronnie's territory has taken up residence in the pond. From what I can gather, Donella was feeding Trevor the lone trout when a large, furry creature appeared on the opposite bank, slipped into the water, submerged and swam under the surface leaving a wake like a submarine. I make a mental note to hide the peanut butter and turn to our Illustrated Book of European Mammals. After much discussion and interrogation with regard to the size, shape and colouring of the beast, my wife regretfully rejects the possibility of an aquatic badger. Against all the evidence, however, she will not accept that it is merely a common or water meadow vole or rat.

We are lunching with Jacko and Mauricette Laiznay tomorrow, so will ask them about the mystery creature. That way we can determine whether it is considered edible locally, and therefore should be kept a secret from The Fox.

February 13th:

Setting out early to the supermarket to buy flowers for Mo-mo and a bottle of good wine for Jacko, I check the mail box and see that we have had yet another letter about the roadside mirror from the St Sauveur planning department. The news of our happy arrangement with our neighbour has obviously not reached official quarters yet.

Soon after moving in to the roadside farmhouse, we found that the locals have devised a special game to enliven their travels between St Sauveur and Bricquebec. The frontage to our terrain is just short of 500 metres, and runs downhill from the crossroads to St Jacques and Néhou. This enables drivers to reach at least seventy miles an hour before hitting the hairpin bend after our copse, and it is local sport to see who can clock the highest speed in the measured distance without leaving the road, finding a ditch or killing a stray cow. I have heard them discussing it in the bars. Normally, we don't mind as their speed is such that the one vehicle every five minutes has raced by almost before we hear it. However, as our exit from the courtyard is halfway down the *piste*, it makes it rather risky to leave La Puce without one of us standing in the road with a red flag during the day, and a flashing light after dark. Because of the situation, one of my first installations at La Puce was a large convex mirror located just outside our courtyard wall and pointing in the direction of the oncoming traffic. Apart from attracting a few sniggers from locals at our killjoy and wimpish attitude to their little game, the mirror also attracted an official letter from the *mairie* at St Sauveur. In brief it said we had erected the *gros miroir* without planning consent, and it must go. Appealing against the decision, I threw myself upon the mercy of the court, confessed all and explained in mitigation that I had made the unapproved erection only so that local lives and cows might be saved.

My artifice fell on stony ground, with my anonymous correspondent endorsing the injunction, and pointing out that the mirror was a grave impediment to anyone walking along the public highway (i.e. the bit of verge just outside our yard). Resorting to British irony and very overt sarcasm, I responded by explaining that a full survey of the locals had revealed that no pedestrians had been seen on the relevant stretch of verge since the American infantry in 1944, and that my only neighbour within half a mile was Mr Pigeon, now 85 and not likely to jog past on his way to town three miles away.

But it was all to no avail. Back came a stern letter, warning me that the mirror must go immediately, lest further proceedings be taken. Taking this as a veiled reference to checking out our lack of other planning permission for all sorts of recent additions like the television aerial and the mail box itself, I compromised by taking the mirror off the post between visits. This worked well till we arrived and found the stout piece of oak had been uprooted from the verge and left pointedly by our front door. Taking its presence as a symbolic gauntlet, I then dug a huge hole alongside a suitable power pole on the opposite verge, and set the mirror post in a two foot square block of extra-strength reinforced concrete. Upon our next arrival, we found the mirror, post and block by the door, and the power pole leaning dangerously over the road. Realising that the situation was getting out of hand, I appealed to our mayor for advice and the necessary mediation. After putting on his tie of office and listening attentively, John explained with grim relish that we would never, ever win a battle with the notorious bureaucrats at St Sauveur. Everyone in the region knew that they were almost as unreasoning and unreasonable as the mayor of St Jacques. Far better to consider the possibilities and come to an accommodation which would satisfy all concerned. I should leave it with him.

A week later, he called to say that a solution was in sight. Whereas, he explained carefully, the verge was the property of France and therefore in the sole keeping of the relevant authority at the St Sauveur *mairie*, the ground beneath the hedgerow of the field opposite our courtyard was the property and responsibility of the owner of the orchard beyond. John would approach the proprietor and negotiate on our behalf for permission to erect my mirror in his hedge. Meantime, he suggested that we keep the offending object under lock and key, and take our chances on entering and leaving the road. He knew how dangerous the road could be, and it would surely take someone to be killed before any action would be taken by the authorities to slow the traffic down.

On our next visit, our friend called with good news. He had talked with Mr Margot (the owner of the hedgerow), who would be arriving that evening to begin negotiations.

A small, tidy and most correct personage, Mr Margot tapped at our kitchen door precisely late, and accepted a tumbler of scotch after the mayor had effected the necessary introductions. Following an hour of polite discussion, during which he took us through a recent leg operation and explained that he worked in St Sauveur but tended the orchard to keep his hands dirty with good Norman soil and provide a yearly stock of *calva*, we broached the subject of the mirror. With a flourish, Mr Margot immediately produced a two page document, giving us, our children and our children's children the sole rights and privileges to the twelve square centimetres of land in which our mirror post would rest for all eternity. The paper having been duly stamped, witnessed by the mayor and signed by both parties to the accord, we finished the bottle of scotch, inordinately pleased that the issue had been finally resolved. It was not till much later that we were to discover that Mr Margot not only worked in the planning department of the *mairie* at St Sauveur, but was the informer who had originally laid a complaint against the illegal siting of the mirror.

*　　*　　*　　*　　*

We arrive at the local supermarket and I go in to search for flowers and wine for our luncheon hosts. Donella remains in the car in case there is another *grand tableau* on the meat counter. Last time it was Veal Week, and the display was centred around the skinned yet otherwise complete head of a calf. My wife said she accepted that other cultures must be respected by those who chose to live within them, but it was the way they had left the eyes in place, and how they seemed to follow her accusingly around the store.

Returning with an expensive bouquet and a bottle of wine that, at 20ff seemed neither too pretentious nor too niggardly, I see my wife talking to Mauricette, who is casually wringing the neck of an inoffensive looking old hen. Nearby a struggling throng of eager housewives besiege a lorry which is obviously full of lively if elderly fowls.

Mo-mo explains that the now deceased hen under her arm is the main ingredient of our lunch. Having seen the condition and price of the boiling fowls, I ask her politely if it would not be cheaper and less labour intensive to buy one of the freshly dressed and plucked young chickens lining the shelves of the supermarket outside which we are standing. Patiently, she explains that *poule-au-pot* must be made with an elderly hen, and besides, only by killing it herself can she be sure that it is really fresh.

Three hours later and we are seated around the huge table in the Laiznay kitchen as the flesh of the late hen is boiled into submission.

Mauricette is a local girl, and Jacko a former fireman from Paris who took early retirement some years ago. Our friends live in a tastefully and obviously expensively restored house in a hamlet on the outskirts of St Jacques. I have heard in the bar at Néhou that Jacko left the fire service at the same time as his best friend left the Paris police force. While Jacko bought and restored the house, his friend set up in a bar and restaurant at Bricquebec. When this point in the story is reached, the teller usually winks, rubs finger and thumb together and makes some comment about the unseen benefits of working for the emergency services in the capital. I have no idea what is being alleged, but assume petty jealousy to be the cause. Whatever the case, I shall not ask Jacko. He is a small man, but has a badly broken nose, large facial scar and an air of quiet capability about him. He is also said by the residents of St Jacques to be the finest shot in all the region, if not France.

As Mauricette busies herself at the oven, Jacko shows me his gun room, which would put Woolwich arsenal to shame. The only weapon not in his collection, I jokingly remark, is a heavy machine gun. He looks thoughtful for a moment, then explains that it would not be an efficient way of killing game as the number of bullets used in a single burst would be extremely expensive, apart from making a mess of the carcass.

Back in the kitchen, I hand over the flowers and wine with a flourish. Mauricette is obviously impressed with her bouquet, while Jacko thanks me politely and consigns my careful choice of table wine to the back of a kitchen cabinet. I notice he turns the label to the wall as he selects the replacement.

As she serves the assorted parts of the bird we met so recently, Mo-mo explains the origins of *poule-au-pot*. It was the favourite dish of Henri IV, who issued an edict that it should be on the menu at any time and anywhere on his royal progress around France. Naturally, he was on record as saying that Normandy in general and Cotentin in particular was where they made the finest example of the dish in all France. It is very good, but I would have preferred the vegetables to have been added to the casserole at some time after the three hours the pot has been in the oven. Once again I reflect on the common misconceptions that afflict both our countries. The English believe that the French dislike and mistreat if not actually eat dogs, while we are claimed by them to overcook all vegetables. In our experience, both beliefs are completely untrue. They seem generally as sentimental about dogs as we are, and any vegetable we are given here seems to be cooked within an inch of its life.

The luncheon goes well until I top up my glass of wine with water, as I have seen done in bars all across Normandy.

After almost choking on a piece of chicken and casting a glance in the direction of his gun room, Jacko takes my glass and empties it pointedly down the sink.

I am to learn later from a horrified Freddo that, by defiling the most expensive wine laid on in our honour, I have proffered an almost deadlier insult to our host than claiming he can't shoot straight. Silently, Jacko reaches into the kitchen cupboard, unscrews the top of my gift bottle and pours a generous measure into a large tumbler before pointing pointedly at the tap. It is at this moment that my wife looks across at a nearby worktop, finds herself in eye-to-eye contact with the head of the hen we have just eaten, and thoughtfully relieves the situation by swooning clear away.

February 19th:

It is a momentous occasion. We are to plant the first of the vegetables that must see us through the coming year. My wife says it is far too soon to dig in even the earliest of potatoes, but René has assured us that the finest soil in Cotentin (if not all France) is more than ready to weave its fertile spell. He has also sold me ten kilos of sprouting and withered seed potatoes, which he says will provide more than enough of a crop to keep both our pot and bank balance overflowing if we set up a roadside stall and sell the surplus off to passing trade.

Donella puts a damper on my enthusiasm by pointing out that potatoes are almost cheaper than dirt in the shops, and that it is anyway quite likely that most of the locals will grow their own if not actually steal ours. She also questions the viability of a roadside produce stall, as any passing trade passes so quickly that a suitably placed advertising placard would have to be erected just outside Bricquebec, some five miles distant. Despite her criticism, I spend a most enjoyable day returning to my rural heritage, and am keenly looking forward to the first signs of growth in a month or two's time.

…é appears like a ghost in the early morning mist as I struggle …position unwieldy bags of sand beneath the ancient bridge, …helpfully points out that the rubbish tip is only a mile down …road. I explain that I am constructing, under my wife's direction, …*arrage* to fill the old mill pond and a short stretch of the dry …eam. I don't mention that the real objective is to create a …dator-free frog and goldfish haven.

…My friend looks at the untroubled sky, wags a grimy forefinger …my general direction and announces the arrival of a …understorm *extraordinaire* by midnight. The bags, he says …nfidently, will be no match for the deluge. For once, defending …wife's convictions I disagree publicly with him, and he stomps …to sulk in his caravan. I add another dozen bags of sand before …mbing out of the miniature ravine for a coffee break. …As I walk to the mill it begins to rain.

*   *   *   *   *

…We start our bender at Jackie's bar and grocery store in the …adow of the castle at St Sauveur le Vicomte. Once a thriving …arket town, St Sauveur has suffered more than most as a result …European unity and a common agricultural policy which has …nalised the smallest of French farmers, and money is very tight. …is not a pretty town, and tourism has not been of great benefit. …ostly, the people seem to get by with seasonal farm work and …lp from the government when the winter sets in. As the average …ur visitor spends the evening nursing a single beer and …mplaining bitterly about the hard times, the government and …e invasion of New Zealand lamb via the UK, we are careful not …air our comparative affluence. Most English people we know …em to believe that rural poverty in France is found only in the …ep south, and is somehow picturesque, with the peasants …ntentedly living off the land while wearing striped jerseys and …nusing berets. This is not true, and real life in the Cotentin can …ean getting by in conditions which the average British reader …romanticised twaddle about the joys of living in rural France

58

As I soak satisfyingly in the bath that evening, Donella shouts from the kitchen that Mr Pigeon's pigs are making a fine racket. Probably, she adds, they have been done out of their usual dinner of rotten potatoes.

February 25th:

It is our wedding anniversary.

Given the disappointment of our abortive Christmas Eve run ashore, we decide to celebrate in the evening by going on a pub crawl of all the hot spots in St Sauveur le Vicomte. This will not take long, but will give us the chance to get to know the local socialites better.

Donella declares I must earn my wild night out and presents me with my anniversary present, a pair of thigh length waders. Obviously, it is to be a day of working with the water.

Since she first saw La Puce, Donella has been fascinated by the possibilities of our streams, ponds and waterlogged pastures as additional wildlife sanctuaries. Over the past year, she has spent a great deal of time and money undoing the massive works of past centuries aimed at channelling water past the *moulin de la puce* as quickly and effectively as possible. Now we are here full time, she is daily coming up with schemes to turn the ten acres into one gigantic lake.

What she does not fully appreciate is that running water has a mind of its own, and can turn quite nasty when interfered with.

Built to service the needs of the surrounding estate, the mill was positioned to take advantage of the tiny *Lude*, which sources at the *manoir* of the same name just a mile away. The system used to turn the mill wheel was as effective as it was simple, and common throughout Europe from at least mediaeval times.

When grinding time approached, the miller would simply lower a stone slab across the stream, diverting the *Lude* into the two acre field directly behind the *moulin*. When *le réservoir* field was flooded and the grain hopper full, a slab by the business end of

55

the mill would be cranked up, allowing the reservoir lake to empty over the top of the wheel. The millions of gallons of water would then rush away down an otherwise dry river bed, under the stone bridge which led the carts to the mill, and finally alongside the copse to join up again with the *Lude* on its way off the property and on to the sea.

This simple but ingenious example of 18th-century engineering to create considerable power from a small stream worked happily until around the turn of the century, when a newfangled mill appeared at Néhou and the tiny *moulin de la puce* fell into disrepair and eventual ruin. Over the years, the working end of the mill has been feasted on by local builders and householders like ants on a juicy carcass. The original wheel is said to be a feature at a night club a few miles away and rumour has it that even the local police station benefited from the plunder. One day, we will restore the working end to its former glory and function, but to rebuild our lives and business at La Puce is a far more pressing project.

The plan for the day, Donella explains, is to create a barrier at the stone bridge. By the careful placing of a few sandbags under the arch, rainwater and the constant dribble from the water meadow would be collected in the dry river bed between the bridge and the sadly depleted millpond, creating a natural and comfortable habitat for another hundred or so Hampshire goldfish which she will smuggle in via her collection of Victorian chamber pots still in England. An added advantage of the additional en-suite fish facility will be the protection afforded by the sweet chestnut trees lining the bank at this point. They will deter the heron which has been studying our goldfish pond almost as enthusiastically as René, and the new stretch of stagnant water will attract more frogs to join Triple Salco and his troupe. I forbear to mention that our estate manager has already brought me the good news that our frog colony are of the edible variety, with particularly long and plump legs. He can tell this from a distance by the range and breadth of their diving display from the tops of the flag lilies into the *petit-petit étang*.

Discussing the fine tuning of the damming pr[...] wife how she intends creating a sandbag barrier wit[...] With a snort of impatience at my lack of initiative, [...] that we have an adequate supply of plastic rubbish[...] and a mountain of sand outside the mill which is [...] attract its own cloud formation. I have my dou[...] suitability of the bin liners, but anything which red[...] pile will be to my advantage in the struggle for su[...] René. We have had yet another tractor load from [...] estate manager, who I have now discovered is a c[...] the foreman of a nearby corporation yard. I have [...] the mountain range of sand within seems of a [...] consistency and colour to our own.

In our experience, most Contentinese are as ho[...] summer day when it comes to respect for persona[...] and we have left our garden furniture out and eve[...] during short absences with no loss. However, ce[...] objects like sand, gravel, trees and wild animals on o[...] be regarded as fair game or even a gift from heaven[...] redistributed if left unattended for too long.

On a visit last year, we arrived to find a pile of huge[...] valuable marble slabs dumped by the stream at H[...] After agreeing to a knockdown price when my wife[...] the difficulty of his shifting them again, René explai[...] were almost a gift from yet another friend, and wo[...] unusual and sophisticated *terrasse* outside the carav[...] pond. Apart from one slab which was used as a m[...] stout bridge across the grotto, they still lie beside[...] comfortably hidden in summer by the long gras[...] reluctant to move or use them. There are no names[...] inscribed on the shiny sides that I can see, but their[...] design looks highly suspicious to me, and the fun[...] yard at St Sauveur has a large hole in its fence.

*   *   *   *   *

could not begin or wish to imagine.

Jackie is as usual dividing his time between serving at the Donjon bar and adjoining store and adjusting his wig. Just as the general mood and height of libido of the proprietor of the *Café de Paris* in Bricquebec can be determined from the condition and styling of his moustache, the location of Jackie's wig is a precise indicator of his current consumption rate of *pastis*. Dogs and drink are Jackie's consuming passions, and we find Albert the Alsatian on guard and on the lookout for the occasional tourist with a chocolate bar about their person. His master appears through the bead curtain dividing his two businesses, and we can see by the angle of his hairpiece that he has been almost abstemious this evening. After taking our order and being persuaded to join us in a glass of *Ricard*, he introduces a new member of the household, which is the tiny fox terrier nestling in his cardigan.

Donella immediately falls in love and curses the ridiculous laws that prevent free travel for pets between our two countries. She will not buy and keep a dog at La Puce because of the agony of separation when we must visit the UK together in future, and has strong feelings on the subject of quarantine. In the past ten years, as she will point out to anyone who will listen, hundreds of thousands of dogs and cats have been incarcerated in British pounds, and not one of them has proved to be rabid. Many, though, have died through accident, disease as a result of their imprisonment, or simply from broken hearts. I have to admit that she is right about the situation and the misconception that the whole of France is full of rabid animals decimating the population. The only fatality from rabies in the last decade in France has been that of an unfortunate soul who inhaled bat droppings. Not normally an activist, my wife has been muttering darkly of late about the melodramatic nature of the anti-rabies posters at the ferryports, and is talking about making her own protest with a felt tipped pen if something doesn't happen to change the situation.

A good and sensitive soul, Jackie consoles her and himself with another round of *pastis*, and offers her the unconditional use of the fox terrier between our monthly trips across the Channel. Thus, what we believe may be the first timeshare dog scheme in France is established at *le bar du Donjon.*

*   *   *   *   *

While Jackie slips next door to buy a bar of chocolate from himself for Albert and the as yet unnamed fox terrier to celebrate the arrangement, I visit the toilet facility, which is a minor classic in my list of Cotentin urinals.

Sited most conveniently at the bottom of the yard and alongside a stack of vegetable supplies for the shop, it outdoes even the arrangements at the Bar Ghislaine for simplicity and ingenuity. The system consists mainly of a large, furry and ancient cider funnel clamped to the wall at the optimum height. From this device runs a length of garden hose which disappears down a drain in the middle of the yard. I, and probably Jackie, have no knowledge as to where if anywhere the drain joins the local sewage system, and on a busy night there can be some backfill problems as the route of the hose from the funnel runs slightly uphill. But it works after a fashion, and the open-air toilet offers some of the best views of the sky at night in the area. There is also a keen element of spectator interest for those living in the houses overlooking the yard. One day I will write a definitive guide to the lavatories of Cotentin, which I find much more interesting than many of the more conventional tourist attractions.

Hearing a noise, I look down and see Albert has joined me for a bit of male bonding. He cocks a leg and pees with unerring accuracy over a sack of carrots. I look up at a sea of stars and contemplate the true scale of the universe and the relative unimportance of my petty concerns. As I return to the bar, the rain increases in intensity, and a grumble of approaching thunder rolls across the moonshiny rooftops before echoing round the yard.

As it is a special occasion, the bars of St Sauveur stay open late and all have record takes for a midweek night. It is almost ten o'clock before we arrive at La Puce and Donella puts me to bed.

I awake to find that the ghost of the Allied warplane is re-strafing the cottage roof, but my wife says it is merely a cloudburst. I look at the clock. It is almost midnight, so René may yet be proved wrong. An hour later, the storm is certainly *extraordinaire*, and the rain driving horizontally against the french windows on the balcony is forcing its way between the putty and panes and running down the glass on the inside. I get up to close the storm doors, and hear a roaring noise from the direction of the mill cottage a hundred yards away. Full of foreboding, we dress in wet weather gear and slither down the slope from the farmhouse to the wooden bridge. It is still in place, and we stand above the normally arid river bed and watch in awe as a raging torrent cascades down from the reservoir field into the old mill pond, filling it to overflowing for probably the first time in a hundred years. The flood boils and roars as it is forced along the ravine below us, to be channelled under the stone bridge and away into the night howling in frustrated fury at its containment.

Looking over the parapet, we see that eight hours work and the twenty plastic sand bags have been casually washed away by the deluge. Even now, they are probably heading out towards Jersey. As we battle our way back up the slope and in spite of the deafening roar of the deluge, I am sure I hear a grunt of triumph from René's caravan.

Poule-au-Pot

1. *Take an elderly hen and wring neck till dead*
2. *Dress and joint, reserving the head for garnish*
3. *Place the pieces in a heavy pot with suitable vegetables*
4. *Cook in oven for at least three hours, or until the vegetables surrender*

SPRING

March 15th:

It is not yet dawn, but we are already hard at work over coffee and *calva* in the *Café de Paris*. In the barely aired streets two farmers squabble half-heartedly over the price of a bored ewe as they work themselves up for market day in Bricquebec. The deserted square calmly awaits the arrival of the livestock, hardware, clothing and food stalls, while a pair of rooks take their ease on the church tower, hoarsely discussing the possibilities of rich pickings when the day's trading is done.

It is a very civilised way to start the day.

My wife and I are engrossed in our regular early morning language lesson, with Freddo *le professeur* teaching us to talk like true Cotentinese.

Every region of the country has, quite naturally, its own way of pronouncing the standard words of the language. Each will also have its own special words and expressions. Sociologists will say that this practice is all about creating tribal identity. I believe it's more about putting outsiders in their place, and sometimes even letting them know they are not welcome. Anyone who has walked in to a Welsh pub and heard the conversation switch instantly from the English with which the natives are actually much more comfortable will know exactly what I mean.

As with the other regions of France, Normandy has its own patois. It also has a customised version for the different *départements* and areas. According to some, every commune on the peninsula has its own verbal conventions for mystifying and excluding foreigners from down the road. In extreme cases, individuals in our area may have adapted the local dialect and sub-language, or even invented their own. Quite apart from my own difficulty in communicating with him, there are some Néhou residents I know who find René Ribet mostly unintelligible, even when sober. This is why my wife and I have enlisted Freddo's help to learn to talk if not on equal terms then at least on the same subject with the locals. Interestingly if not surprisingly, as we first started picking up a smattering of Norman French as long ago as 1066, a number of local patois words are pronounced similarly to their English equivalent. *Chair, patate* (potato) and *mug* are good examples. There are also some very interesting insults relating to bodily parts, sizes and functions in which Freddo has painstakingly coached me during my wife's absence. They often come in handy when winding down the window to exchange compliments on driving skills with other motorists.

We have almost reached the end of today's crash course in complimenting a neighbour on the virility and volume of his cockerel when our latest house guests arrive. I introduce Freddo to our friends, Rinaldo and Janet, who have come over to take advantage of the fortnight version of our special 'Real France' package. The standard terms are that we pay for their ferry and food, while our visitors contribute skilled labour to the terrain or restoration work on the mill cottage. We have made mistakes in our selection process and found some former friends arriving under the misapprehension that they are here solely to enjoy themselves, but generally, the system has paid off. Nowadays, we find visiting electricians, carpenters and bricklayers far more fascinating company than marketing consultants and aromatherapists. Rinaldo has been running pubs in Hampshire for the past twenty years, but comes from a remote area of Italy which is almost as rural as Cotentin, so should know the lie of the land and how to best deal with it. He will therefore be in charge of groundworks during their stay. Provided, as I have already warned, he gets on with our estate manager.

As they recover from the effects of an overnight crossing with a restorative *goutte*, the conversation turns to current events at La Puce, and I ask Freddo for his views on the latest inhabitant of the big pond. Listening closely to my wife's description of the mystery beast, our host's moustache begins to quiver like the tail of an overexcited pointer hound. It sounds, he says in sepulchral tones, as if we have a *rat musqé* on our hands. This is very, very bad for the land, and he will come to La Puce tomorrow after school and shoot it.

Seeing my wife's expression, I quickly point out that, in my opinion, the beast is actually nothing more or less than a large water rat, or even an overgrown vole. Freddo shrugs, and says it does not matter what it is, he is still happy to come along and shoot it.

Other locals now enter the debate and make their judgements as to the identity of our new tenant. Whatever they suggest, Freddo declares it to be very bad for the land, and that it will be his pleasure to shoot it for us.

By now, at least a dozen regulars have joined the conversation, and offers to visit La Puce and rid us of our dangerous intruder are coming thick and fast.

With my wife about to forget her normally impeccable manners and explain that she personally is thrilled to discover a wild creature larger than a butterfly still at large in Cotentin, I turn the subject to other matters. Rinaldo, I announce, is a keen fisherman, and I wonder if the assembly can suggest the best sport in the area. Freddo's best friend Pierrot is then universally acknowledged as the finest fisherman in the region if not all France, and kindly agrees to show our Italian friend how to catch trout.

I now see another side of Rinaldo, whose outsize moustache had not appeared as significant when on duty with its master behind the bar of his pub in the Isle of Wight. Speaking in the overly polite tones of a character from *The Godfather* who has had his ability to effortlessly remove a horse's head put in question, he explains that he learned to fish in the limpid mountain pools of the *Abruzzo* before he could walk. Moreover, the teacher was his blessed grandfather, who was recognised nationwide as the finest fisherman in the region, if not all Italy.

Seeing the inevitable outcome of the debate, I ask brightly if anyone has visited the latest Millet exhibition at the Cherbourg *musee*, but it is too late.

Over another round of *calva*, an international challenge is laid down. This weekend Italy, Great Britain and Cotentin will clash at the local fish-it-yourself pond. The one with the smallest catch will pay for the total haul. I remember the sausage game at Christmas, and mutter something about the need to plant a row of onion sets at La Puce, but Rinaldo's Latin blood is obviously up. We will convene in the *Café de Paris* this weekend, and the matter will be resolved.

Now that terms have been made and accepted, the subject and atmosphere changes and the local elders continue the debate as to exactly why our property is called The Flea.

Like all discussions concerning the derivation of local place, property and family names, there are any number of opinions and sometimes wildly improbable theories. In the case of La Puce, we have whittled them down to two front runners. Some locals point out that *puce* or flea is a favoured term of endearment for a female partner, pet or special possession such as a reliable tractor. Supporting this theory is the fact that at least a dozen local dogs are called *puce-puce*, apparently from affection rather than simple statement of fact. Overcome with emotion in a bar before closing time, a man might even refer to his wife as 'my little flea' even when, as is often the case, she is considerably taller and heavier than he. As a vital and life-enhancing resource for the commune over centuries, *le moulin de la puce* might well have earned this affectionate sobriquet early in its long working life. Other elderly residents refer to the ancient water chute outside the mill door, where the village women had the feudal rights to visit every month or so and wash the family's dirty linen in public, in both senses of the term. According to our house deeds, they still have, but we have yet to meet one who prefers the waters and gossip potential of *le Lude* to the services of an automatic *lave-linge*. 'Pushee', however, is patois for washing and *puce* is pronounced in the same way, so the story could well hold water. When the time came to make proper and official maps of the area, it is said, the visiting cartographers confused *puce* with *push*, and established our home

67

forever as The Mill of The Flea. Given the general standards of hygiene at the time, they may well have got it right by default, anyway.

*   *   *   *   *

All appears well when we arrive at La Puce and our estate manager is not in evidence, so I take Rinaldo to see the big pond and our trout colony. After an hour of casting our sliced English bread on the waters, we get a glimpse of Trevor, and I confess my belief that he is the sole fish in residence, though my wife is under the impression that the original four dozen are still there, and merely shy.

On the advice of René and after the big pond had bedded in, we visited the nearest commercial trout lake and bought a dustbinful of healthy yearlings. My idea at the time was to make a start on our own trout rearing business. A spin-off would be the creation of a personal fishing pond, with inhabitants enticed out of the water and in to the pan in moments whenever the fancy took me. Obviously, I did not share the details of this part of the plan with my wife.

In the event, the water in the bin proved a little short of oxygen over the three mile journey, and several of the fish lay gasping limply in the shallows when we released them into our new pond. Without a thought for personal safety, Donella jumped in and administered artificial respiration, after which they happily swam off to join their fellows. Her bonding with them in this dramatic and intimate manner was of course fatal for my ambitions, the pond immediately declared off limits, and my rod briskly parcelled up and taken back to Portsmouth.

It was particularly galling that, while I was banned from fishing in my own pond, the local angling fraternity felt free to enjoy the facilities in our absence. Each visit, it seemed fewer trout came up for their daily feed. It was even alleged by some of our friends that René Ribet had placed advertisements for the new *étang à truites* in bars that he knew we did not visit, and had been selling daily tickets, bait, cold beer and *frites* from his caravan while we were away.

Even if the story is true, now that Trevor is the lone tenant of the pond, the idea of fishing for more than five minutes without a guaranteed catch would have deterred the most earnest Norman fisherman, and he seems safe. Reluctant to restock the pond for the benefit of the locals or tell my wife of our losses, I now spend much of my time throwing feed pellets at the bemused crayfish gang, and claiming to have spotted at least a dozen healthy trout leaping after my solo visits to the pond. Donella says the colony must have developed a special relationship with me, as she has never seen more than one at a time, and they all look remarkably like Trevor.

March 17th:

To Carteret and a special treat for our guests.

Known elsewhere and somewhat ironically as the St Tropez of Cotentin, Carteret is a former fishing village on the west coast which now boasts more restaurants, bistros and bars per head than any other settlement on the peninsula. On the quay is an interesting Italian-style restaurant which is owned by a barking mad patron who seems at permanent odds with his live-in waitress and lover.

On our first visit there, crockery exploded off stage in the kitchen before he fled into the night, leaving customers to rescue their own pizzas from the oven. There followed a series of dramatic phone calls, causing the girlfriend to desert us in mid-serve and follow him into the street before both returned for a tearful reunion at the next table.

Thinking this will all make Rinaldo feel at home, we arrive for the matinee performance and study the menu. Our friend is not amused to find that the only wine on offer is French, which he takes as a comment on the standing of his own country's produce.

After letting off a fruitless burst of Italian at the waitress, he demands to see the owner, and is even more upset to find that he too is French, and that he learned his art and craft when working as a delivery biker for the famous *Pizza Tout d' Suite* in Cherbourg.

The meal goes from bad to worse, as Rinaldo is duly surprised and extremely unhappy to find a French cheese topping on his Neapolitan Surprise Special, and the final straw is the discovery that the English translation of the sweets on offer includes his alleged regional speciality, Banana Shit.

March 19th:

The day of the international fishing competition dawns bright, cold and early, and Rinaldo and I report to the *Café de Paris* respectably late.

Pierrot and Freddo await, and are dressed to kill in commando camouflage, balaclava helmets, freshly waxed moustaches and huge knives dangling from ammunition belts stuffed with heavy duty shotgun cartridges. They are obviously taking the match seriously, and may intend shooting the fish if unable to hook them. As we walk to the car, I notice that each seems to be carrying at least three rods, and ask if others are joining us for the contest. Freddo explains carelessly that it is normal procedure for each competitor to have more than one hook in the water at the same time.

In the car, the rules of the *grand tournoi* are laid down.

The pond and our individual places around it will be decided by the committee, which is to be made up as host nation of Freddo and Pierrot. We will fish for three hours precisely, and the country with the biggest catch will obviously be declared champion. The loser, says Freddo looking directly at me, will pay the fishing fee and for drinks at the *Café de Paris* afterwards. I consider lodging an official objection on the grounds that the French *équipe* will muster twice as many men and six times as many rods as the GB team, but remember my mother's claims about the odds at the Battle of Trafalgar, and keep my own counsel. As we speed through the winding lanes, I fall to musing about the particularly French attitude to freshwater angling. Having exhausted the countryside of most of its natural wildlife, our locals have turned to the new pursuit of trout pond fishing with much enthusiasm. In a parallel with the explosion of golf courses on former farmland all over Britain, every landowner here with a suitably wet piece of land seems to have turned it into a commercial trout lake. Having scooped out a large-ish hole and filled it to the brim with water and fish, he will park a caravan selling cold beer and hot chips alongside, and advertise the new facility by placing enticing hand made posters featuring drawings of trout the size of sharks in every bar and available window in the area. Being Norman, his patrons will naturally demand the very best value for money, which means they must be able to enjoy a day's sport and go away with a satisfying haul of fish at less than they would have paid for the same weight at the fishmongers. Though not averse to sitting still for long periods, Cotentinese are not renowned for their love of the traditional British fishing methods of gentle reflection and patience whilst awaiting the eventual reward of a strike. In England the inmates of pond or river will be given a very sporting chance by fly-fishing-only regulations. Here, as many juicy maggots as may be dangled from any number of hooks are seen as the only sensible way to ensure maximum return on investment.

When the trout fishing fever took hold in our area, one local entrepreneur tried charging by the hour regardless of catch, but soon saw sense when his unhappy patrons started using trawl nets to ensure value for money. Quite apart from the purely financial aspects of the new sport, the opportunity for the head of the household to reinforce his traditional role as provider is a powerful incentive. Having spent as little time as possible in making his haul, the happy and proud hunter will return home and casually lay the glistening, writhing heap on the kitchen table like a cat bringing a captured bird into the home for inspection and approval. Once again, the brave *chasseur* has fed his family in the time-honoured way by confronting nature and outwitting the lesser inhabitants of the countryside. Whenever I go to a local trout *étang*, however, the words 'shooting', 'fish' and 'barrel' spring unbidden to mind.

71

After ten minutes of careering along a bumpy track, we arrive on the shore of a magnificent lake at least half a mile across, and I prepare to eat my thoughts.

Sadly, Freddo ignores the parking facilities and drives on to a small clearing in a heavily wooded and secluded area. Here we find a square pond a little larger than a family size jacuzzi. Unloading the gear and provisions, Pierrot leads us to our positions. I am given the side underneath a huge beech tree, the branches of which brush my head as I stand and survey my pitch. Obviously, our hosts are being considerate by allowing me the only place of shelter should it rain. Rinaldo is invited to take up his position nearby, while Freddo and Pierrot share the rest of the bank. Although they have two sides to our one, I notice that they place their rod holders very close together. We break out our kit, and I see that, as well as two rods each, Freddo and Pierrot have fitted swivel traces, each with two sets of double hooks. The rods supplied for Rinaldo and I are much more modest affairs, and almost of the basic Huckleberry Finn patent.The maggots are doled out, and Freddo kindly sets our floats so that the hooks will hang no more than six inches beneath the water. This, he explains, is to avoid snagging on the roots of 'my' tree, which apparently riddle the bed of the pond. I note that he and his colleague set their hooks at least a yard from the floats.

After consultation, I and Rinaldo steal a march on our rivals and get our lines into the water without delay, while they are held up by the large amount of tackle and the baiting up of at least two dozen maggots each.

The competition proper starts and the French floats disappear almost immediately. In five minutes, Freddo and Pierrot have taken a trio of fat trout between them. Rinaldo has struck once, and I decide it is time to employ my English initiative in bending the rules a little. Although I am forbidden from moving my pitch, I may surely cast anywhere in the pond, and as a former B league Portsmouth darts champion, I should be able to drop my sinker within a whisker of the French happy hunting ground. A quick and dextrous flick of the wrist, and my hook finds a branch of the giant beech. Freddo and Pierrot sympathise and break out the beer while issuing instructions on the best way to disentangle my line. Unfortunately, they add, they have no extra tackle with them.

An hour passes, and the French contingent seem to have more fish in their bin liner than could stand comfortably shoulder to shoulder in the tiny pond. Rinaldo has notched up a handful, and I am halfway up the tree with my Swiss penknife.

A little later and a man appears carrying a dustbin on his shoulder. He shakes hands with Freddo and Pierrot, nods sympathetically to me, and discharges at least a gross of trout into the pond at the feet of his countrymen. The water boils as the fish compete to be the first on Norman hooks. The bin man disappears to fetch another load, while a queue of trout seems to be forming in a very un-French manner at the spot where Freddo and Pierrot are having difficulty in keeping up with demand.

At the end of the allotted time, the tournament is declared over, and the count begins.

The French haul is 72, Rinaldo has managed a round half dozen, and my total tally is two undernourished juveniles and one of Freddo's discarded beer bottles.

*   *   *   *   *

Back at the *Café de Paris*, our host enlists the help of all the customers to carry his haul inside, where the giant glittering, twisting mound is displayed on the bar top as he makes a lengthy address to the assembly. After a blow by blow account of the action, he announces the official figures for the competition, and commiserates with the losers. Obviously he says, it was harder for me as I was in foreign waters. It is also well known that the British have lost the art of fishing, as is demonstrated by their morbid fear of French trawlers appearing in 'their' waters. I respond graciously, toasting the success of the craftiest coarse anglers in the region. I also agree with Freddo about the decline of our fishing fleet, and suggest that this is because we as a nation have been concentrating on efficient farming, which is why our exports of lamb seem to be doing so well in this part of France.

All this badinage is taken in good spirit, especially, I suspect, as the drinks are now on me.

The celebrations commence and Freddo takes up a proprietary position at the door. For the rest of the morning, he distributes largesse, trout and the story of the international fishing tournament in equal measures to passing pensioners. As we leave, he takes me to one side and hands me a bag containing a dozen of his catch with fondest compliments to Donella, and to ensure that we have enough to eat for lunch.

*   *   *   *   *

Late lunchtime, and we have set up our makeshift oildrum barbecue and oven under the balcony at La Puce. Rinaldo has barely got the fire beneath it going when René arrives to take charge. Somehow, he has already heard about our defeat. We should, he says, have enrolled his help, then there really would have been some fish caught. In moments he has gutted, cleaned and lightly oiled the trout before dousing them in *goutte* and wrapping each one tightly in newspaper ready for baking. Rinaldo has been relegated to chopping up the peppers for roasting, which he says is an *Abruzzo* speciality.

It is the first time we have eaten *truit au calva,* and even Rinaldo has to admit that it works.

All agree that it is a meal to remember, and I do not spoil the moment by pointing out that, pound per pound, the trout have cost me more than lobster served at Maxim's of Paris.

March 21st:

Rinaldo and I have started on the treasure hunt. I have let my friend into the secret of the Grey Lady and the miller's gold, and he agrees it sounds very promising. Millers are also known as cheats and misers in Italy, and there is always a pot of gold near

74

the *casa*. René is away on business with The Widow of Negreville, so the coast is clear. We set to with a will at the base of the apple tree, and have hit some obstinate roots when our distant neighbour Mr Bellamy arrives on his ancient khaki *mobylette*.

Renowned in the neighbourhood as the only person who speaks a word of English, he gained his singular skills in 1944 after acquiring a booklet issued to all American GIs to help keep them on friendly terms with the natives. This makes for interesting conversation when he practices on me, and our first exchange began by his asking if we would take a bar of candy for a night's lodging in the barn we didn't have.

His everyday patois is even more colloquial than René's and makes normal conversation impossible, so we have agreed on a happy medium of sign language, wartime Americanese and conventional French.

Apparently believing we wish to move the old apple tree for some good English reason to a point a metre from where it has stood happily since the Americans arrived, he joins us in the hole and shows us how to dig properly.

An hour passes pleasantly, and the pile of earth beside the hole is approaching the size of the sand heap by the mill. It is probably my imagination, but the tree seems to be leaning towards us at more than the normal and accepted angle for orchards in this neck of the woods. So far, we have turned up some interesting old bottles and the remains of a giant horseshoe, but there is no sign of the miller's gold. By now our good friend Marcel Barnard has also joined the party. The first person to arrive to welcome us to the area, Marcel lives in the same nearby hamlet as our mayor, and is the proud owner of an ancient lorry which he allegedly acquired from an enterprising supply sergeant when the American task force moved on in 1946. For as long as anyone can remember, he has hired out himself and the lorry for the odd haulage job and in between contracts, it makes a handy overnight coop for his free range chickens.

Driving past the farmhouse several years ago, Marcel had pulled over and watched in silent bewilderment as we started restoration work by removing at least a ton of vintage straw bales from the loft. As he explained later, they were the local equivalent of fibre glass lagging, and someone had taken a great deal of trouble to put them there in the first place to guarantee a comfortable winter.

Seeing his empty lorry we had asked how much he would charge to dispose of the bales, but he, good man that he is, had refused the commission. Instead, he demonstrated the simple and much more effective countryside way of getting rid of rubbish. Gauging the wind, he made a huge pile of straw, rotted sacking and feed bags and applied a match.

Jealous that Marcel had been the first to show us this trick, René had later attempted to clear our one acre garden of a decade's worth of scrub by the same method. It had worked well until the wind changed, but thankfully the damage was limited to the loss of his trousers and a new set of garden furniture.

Our next guest at the digging party is Coco, returning from his weekly fungi raid on our woods. With its *mélange* of mature beech and oak trees set in leaf mulch which reaches the kneecaps in autumn and has lain undisturbed for a few centuries, the copse at La Puce is renowned for the quality and variety of mushrooms to be found there at all times of the year. This crop and the other natural harvests at La Puce have long been regarded as fair game for anyone who will take the trouble to gather them, and we have long since given up trying to manage or deter the constant flow of locals arriving with stepladders, carrier bags and even the occasional horse and cart. When we first arrived, we had unwisely put up a series of signs at the boundaries of the property warning off all hunters and gatherers, assuming that, as long as we marked the perimeters, they would be respected. On our next visit, the No Entry sign on the track down to the mill had vanished, and the *Chasse Interdite* placards were riddled with buckshot. We responded with bigger, more aggressive signs and rolls of barbed wire, but they too went missing between visits. Finally a truce and compromise was mediated by the mayor, who explained reassuringly that the vandalism was not aimed at us as foreigners, but a manifestation of the locals' objection to our changing the rules of common usage which had existed at La Puce for many years. Normally, trespassers venture on private land at their peril, and nobody would dream of setting foot on a proper farm, but La Puce had been owned by a succession of Parisians and other foreigners who never appeared and obviously didn't give a hoot about who took advantage of the fruits of the land. From now on, John promised, the hunters would respect our peculiar wish to protect the wildlife on our terrain, while all Néhou residents would continue to have access to the nuts, berries, wild flowers and herbs which we did not earmark for our own consumption. We would be welcome to shoot at any trespassers from St Jacques, naturally, and thought even more highly of if we managed to wing a couple. Not a keen nut or berry gatherer, our estate manager had made no objection to the deal as long as the apple harvest was left strictly alone, and we had struck a private treaty with Coco for exclusive foraging rights to the copse. Apart from being the owner of a leading bar and restaurant at St Sauveur and a fervid anglophile, Coco is quite deservedly acknowledged as the finest fungi expert in the region (if not all France), and a true eccentric, even by local standards. In everyday appearance he resembles a gothic engraving of an Old Testament prophet, and drives madly around the peninsula in a very battered Land Rover with *Mission Impossible* crudely daubed on each side. Apart from allowing his wife to run the family business, he keeps busy with his constant quest for ever more exotic fungal growths and by staging musical extravaganzas in the church square next to the restaurant. Some malicious souls in the town allege that his wild eyes and erratic manner can be attributed to the regular consumption of a particular sort of mushroom, but I think it is merely his nature. Our arrangement, struck in his bar late one summer evening, was that he would have the full gathering rights to the copse, while in exchange we would be treated to an annual slap-up meal. Each course, of course, would contain suitable examples of La Puce fungi. Last year, we arrived for our treat to find the town had apparently been invaded by the National Front. As the locals looked on with awe, huge youths with shaven heads, Union Jack tee-shirts and lace-up boots gyrated happily in front of the church while a band advertised as the British Bulldogs performed on a platform beside Coco's Bar. Nervously, we took our free lunch in the restaurant, and before leaving, asked him if he was sure that he had picked the right band for the sleepy town. He smiled dreamily, and assured us that his customers were very fond of traditional English folk music. Surprisingly, the town remained unscathed, and all went so well that the band are booked for a return visit this summer. Coco also tells us that he is negotiating for an exchange visit of the St Sauveur abbey choir to a forthcoming London folk concert featuring the Bulldogs and fellow artistes Die for England and We Hate Fucking Foreigners.

By now, Coco has laid down his overflowing trug basket, and is instructing us on the care and handling of any rare fungi species we may uncover. Marcel Bernard, Mr Bellamy, Rinaldo and I are competing for spade room in the hole, and it is inevitable that René should appear like a pantomime demon king from behind the bike shed.

Surveying the scene for a moment, he pronounces that Donella has gone too far this time. The pond we are digging will be well above water level, and will kill his beloved apple trees stone dead. I have rarely seen him so angry. I make a weak excuse about testing his theory about there being no room for the cherry tree, and we sheepishly fill the hole in under his watchful eye. As usual, he makes withering comments about the small size of my Spear and Jackson edging spade, and a debate begins on the proper way to move earth. Marcel at well over 65 still works at a prodigious rate with his long handled gravediggers shovel, while René prefers a huge bladed spade with a short handle made from an elm branch. Mr Bellamy is loud in his defence of his US government issue entrenching tool. In time and as the debate heats up, the hole disappears, and I give up my plans for finding the miller's gold. I invite the digging party indoors for drinks, and think I hear The Fox making an aside about fool's gold as we enter the farmhouse. The exercise has not been wasted, however, as I have now formed a cunning plan to reduce the sand mountain at a stroke.

*   *   *   *   *

A long and diverting evening is over. Rinaldo and Janet have
retired to the guest room, while our other friends have moved
on to René's caravan for a nightcap to fortify themselves against
the snow they all agree will soon be with us, despite the time of
year and official forecasts of rain as usual until mid July. Our
impromptu *soirée* passed pleasantly with a tasting of the selection
of Italian wines Rinaldo brought with him, and a contribution of
his finest farmhouse cider from Marcel. I weighed in with a pack
of Somerset cider cans, and Marcel, René and Mr Bellamy were
mildly shocked to learn that it can be produced in Britain, and
even more surprised that it is drinkable, even good. They also
expressed surprise that drinkable wine is made in Italy, and Rinaldo
risked a row by pointing out that more bottles of allegedly French
wine are produced each year than the amount of grapes grown
in France could possible provide. It is a well known secret in the
industry, he claims, that many tons of lesser grade Italian grapes
are bought in each year to enable the communes to overproduce
their so-called *appellation contrôlée* wines.

Donella avoided potential unpleasantness by suggesting a game
of ludo, which René as usual won. My wife says that he cheats but
this is hard to prove as he insists on playing by what he claims are
the local rules, though we had thought the game exclusive to
Britain. His version entails throwing the dice under one hand,
then telling us what the number is. Once, Donella tried to get
the better of him by suggesting a game of Scrabble, but that too
was a mistake. He won with a huge score by claiming that all the
nonsense words he laid were *ancien patois*, which must be admissible
as we were playing on his terrain. Nor could my wife possibly
claim them to be false, as it was quite common in Norman French,
which after all had its roots in Old Norse, for consonants to require
no vowels between them.

Now we are alone, and walk out to stand on the balcony

overlooking our land and say goodnight to La Puce. It is a bitter and breathlessly silent night, and yet again I am bewitched by the clarity and number of stars in the big Cotentin sky. In the distant water meadow, the placid surface of the big pond looks no more than a mirrorglass lake on a child's toy farm. An owl hoots on Hunters Walk, and is answered by a tetchy whinny from a horse in a neighbouring field. Beyond the mill, the stream continues its endless cascade into the magical grotto, and the unseen creatures of the dark are surely going contentedly about their business on such a perfect night. In this region they call mills 'listen when it rains' but for once, there is not a cloud in the sky.

Baked Trout à la René Ribet

1. *First catch your fish, or preferably someone else's.*
2. *Gut, then rub skin briskly with olive oil and a generous measure of calva.*
3. *Season lightly.*
4. *Wrap fish individually in outer pages of Normandy West News and place in hot oildrum oven*
5. *Read racing results in remaining sports section (Sunday edition)*
6. *Remove trout from oven, unwrap and serve with deep fried chicory and roasted sweet peppers in a farm cider coulis*

April 1st:

Our guests have regretfully returned to their pub in the Isle of Wight, and we decide to mark the date by playing a joke on René. We present him with a bottle of Rinaldo's Italian wine after pasting the label from a French *vin de table* on it. We meet later that evening and I ask if he enjoyed the wine. He says we were cheated. It was obviously Italian, and probably from the *Abruzzo* region, unless he is mistaken. Lost in admiration, we confess to our little prank, and attempt to explain the April Fool tradition. He is not particularly amused, and bids us goodnight after forecasting heavy snow for the morrow. I smile knowingly and explain that All Fool's Day jokes can technically only be played before noon. He shrugs and begins filling up the cracks in his caravan windows with the newspaper left over from the trout barbecue.

April 2nd:

The joke is again on us, as we awake to find La Puce has become a winter wonderland.

Last year it snowed in late February, but the area has not seen *la neige* at this time of year in living memory, which is a long time. The locals are bound to blame the Common Agricultural Policy. Responding to the drama of the situation, my wife has already begun preparations for a soup run, and the fridge is empty except for René's beer and some *paté* she says is too rich for her animals' delicate digestive systems.

Frankly, I am more concerned about my early potato crop. We wrap up and set out to explore the terrain.

In the baby pond, the goldfish are happily swanning around underneath a thin layer of ice. Donella sets about it lest they drown, in spite of my suggestion that Triple Salco and his aquatic frog troupe might enjoy learning to skate.

We cross the wooden bridge and pause to admire the tableau of ice, snow and water.

Since the flooding subsided, the flow from the meadow has slowed to its usual rusty trickle down the massive stone wall chute to the mill pond. My wife believes the rich red stains are left behind by the clay content of the earth in the reservoir. I think it may be deposits of minerals or even valuable iron ore, and determine to take a sample for analysis. Now that the Grey Lady has let me down, I shall have to find new ways of making La Puce pay its way.

Like every other Briton with a patch of land in France, I have considered countless methods of taking at least a living from the terrain and its resources. Unlike many dreamers, I have seen the obvious disadvantages of taking the local farmers on at the type of inefficient small scale farming and goat growing operations which do not seem to have made their fortunes. I am constantly considering a series of lateral thinking, inventive projects which will flourish with the help of my marketing expertise and flair. Ideas for commercial trout and crayfish breeding, mushroom, sunflower seed, lavender and strawberry growing have all been considered, then abandoned after trial runs or practical analysis of costs and potential income.

One of my first and so far best ideas came when René made an unexpected discovery as he mowed the garden last summer. Hearing a wild curse from where he was shoulder deep in the grass and thistles by the orchard, we thought he had removed a limb along with the weeds, but it was too early in the day and he was still observing his optimum beer bottle rate. Arriving at the scene, we found he had merely blunted his scythe on a flat slab of stone. Underneath was that most desirable status symbol for all British owners of rural French property, an ancient well. Dissuading me from tying a rope to a convenient apple tree and lowering myself into the darkness, René fetched a torch, bucket and length of chain. The surface of the water thirty feet below soon sparkled in the flashlight beam, and looked as clear as crystal.

After taking a sample and rolling it around his mouth knowledgeably, our estate manager declared it pure, and a perfect example of natural Normandy spring water, which everyone accepted as the finest in France. For days afterwards I was in a fever of excitement. Since the Perrier PR disaster some years before, there had been an explosion in the sale of new brands of bottled water from other regions of France. As far as I knew there was not as yet a Normandy version aggressively attacking the market. With a good pump, some piping and a few dozen taps, I could set up a system in the mill cottage, employ local labour and churn out hundreds if not thousands of bottles a day. With some shrewd marketing of Water from the Flea ('Hop off and grab a bottle!'), we would clean up. Perhaps, with a little help from some inventive PR, the well would turn out to have miraculous curative and rejuvenation powers and La Puce would become a shrine for the infirm and elderly. After all, we were right alongside the old *Santiago de Compostela* pilgrim trail to Spain. The potential was surely enormous.

Sadly, it was the mayor who put paid to my dreams when I asked him if he knew about the well. He did, and confirmed that it had been covered over a decade ago after the tenants at the farmhouse had fallen ill and the public analyst had taken a sample of the water and found it very definitely *non-potable*. The problem was not chemical pollution, but the otherwise environmentally sound organic methods for enriching the soil employed by John and other local farmers. Although arriving pure from the heavens, by the time the rainwater had soaked through earth covered with cattle and pig muck, it was totally undrinkable. Discussing the disappointment with my wife and reluctant to abandon the project, I reminded her that our estate manager had originally pronounced our well water as perfectly pure. She responded by pointing out that René of all people was hardly likely to know what water should taste like.

My scheme is far from dead in the water, however. René has told us that there is another natural *source* on our neighbour's land, and he has asked Mr Pigeon if we can have access to it. By his estimates the spring delivers at least four thousand litres an hour, and it will be no problem for him to pipe it to the ditch that runs along the hedge in the water meadow and into the mill pond. Mr Pigeon has long since given up farming his land, so there will be no contamination except for the *merde* from his earth closet, which is of insignificant amounts as our neighbour lives alone and is a frugal eater.

He will start on diverting the spring as soon as he has completed all the other tasks in hand, so we and the rest of the world should only have a decade or so to wait before *l'Eau de la Puce* hits the shelves.

We work our way steadily through the mill garden and grotto, stocking up the dozens of provision points. Although there were at least a million beech nut husks littering the ground after the remarkable summer last year, Donella still insists on providing a regular KP Family Selection Bag for our single squirrel. The nuts are always gone when we return, which, she says, proves they are popular. I think they may be particularly popular with the regular foraging and fishing parties who visit La Puce in our absence, and trout and almonds is a favourite in the area.

Three loaves, two tins of corned beef, a salami, whole round of *brie* and two packets of bacon later and we have reached the caravan overlooking the big pond. Originally, I put it there as a guest annexe for visitors we didn't particularly like and an extra income earner for the summer, but it has become a combination of wild life observation point and feeding substation, crammed with sacks of trout pellets and bird seed. I see that the patio of slabs I painstakingly laid last summer has provided further sport for the local mole colony. I cannot understand what makes them prefer burrowing under and dislodging concrete slabs for fun when it would be much easier to surface at any other point on the ten acres of soft earth. They are surely playing a game with me.

Together with the moles, a variety of other small creatures have taken up residence beneath the caravan, and since a family of water voles has squatted under my upturned dinghy, Donella has forbidden me from launching it except in dire emergencies, such as the rescue of a drowning frog. She has even asked me to bung up the sculling hole in the transom in case it lets in a draught.

Thankfully, the big pond has not frozen over, so I will not be sent out on a dangerous icebreaking mission, and the voles will remain undisturbed. We walk round the pond, and I see that the huge construction of underwater weed in one corner is getting smaller. According to the book, if our mystery lodger is, as Freddo claims, a muskrat, it will have built a lodge of weed to live in and off during the winter, then eaten its way out to go on an orgy of bank tunnelling at about the time Donella spotted it.

Perhaps I will invite the patron of the *Café de Paris* and his shotgun to tea when my wife is not at home.

The Cray gang are not in evidence, but I see they have installed several new front doors below the water line on the west side of the bank. Obviously Ronnie and Reggie's offspring are moving in on other manors, and the odd abandoned claw indicates violent territorial struggle.

After throwing at least a pound of trout feed into the pond, followed by stones while Donella's back is turned so that I can pretend to have seen at least a dozen fish leaping, we catch a fleeting glance of Trevor, so she is content. Now our mercy mission has been completed, tradition demands it is time for cups of coffee and a cigarette at the grotto.

Sitting on the old railway platform bench overlooking the cascade, I open the flask and we look contentedly down at the churning water, each alone with thoughts of how our adventure is progressing. Suddenly, Donella grasps my arm and points. I stare diligently, and finally become aware of a flotilla of small fish, hanging almost motionless beneath the turbulent surface in front of the miniature waterfall. They are baby trout, taking on oxygen from the aerated water before making their journey downstream to be reunited with their mother. The months of backbreaking labour clearing the river have been worthwhile. We look at each other like proud parents, and even I feel the thrill of our achievement. After forty years, the river trout have returned to La Puce.

April 5th:

I am worried that my wife's sense of relative values is catching.

Early this morning, Donella arrived in a state of wild agitation as I was chopping firewood behind the mill and reported a confrontation with a young man on the track to the grotto. When I calmly reminded her of the mayor's compact regarding local foraging rights, she said he was a stranger, and acting extremely suspiciously because he refused to return her greeting. He was also carrying a fully extended fishing rod.

I hastened to the grotto, forgetting in the heat of the moment to lay down my double edged felling axe. The intruder was happily squatting on the other side of the basin, his line in the water at the exact point where we had recently seen the flotilla of troutlings. As I appeared, he looked first at me, then my axe, and hastily reeled in. On his hook was a large fish. Outraged, I forgot all the suitable Norman patois curses so carefully learned from Freddo and fell back on a stream of Anglo-Saxon expletives while charging across the tombstone bridge to discuss the matter further. Obviously unwilling to argue his point, he made off, avoiding Donella's rugby-style tackle as he fled up the track and escaped, with mother fish still writhing on the end of his line. An hour later, we heard the wail of a siren from the road beyond the track, and I began rehearsing my side of the story. Neither the local *gendarmerie* or national riot police appearing, Donella took comfort from the possibility that it was an ambulance, rushing to the scene of a fatal and inexplicable cardiac arrest.

I spend the rest of the day making a number of new No Fishing signs, crudely hewn from the copse with my felling axe, and executed in dripping and blood-red gloss paint.

April 9th:

René brings bad news from the orchard. The old apple tree where we searched for the miller's gold has fallen over. We go to look at the damage, and our estate manager seems strangely pleased to see that his dire warning about digging near the roots has borne fruit. He tells us with grim satisfaction that the ancients believed apple trees to be sacred, and that for whatever reason the catastrophe had taken place, it is a certain harbinger of approaching doom. Someone connected with the land of La Puce is sure to die before long. It is certainly grim tidings for us, as René says he has already ordered not one but three replacement trees from his friend who owns the *pépinière* along the road, and they will be very expensive. He had no choice, he says as according to our agreement, the harvest is his, and the extra trees will barely make up for what he loses in fruit while they grow to maturity. He also claims salvage rights on the old tree for firewood to heat his caravan with the stove I know it doesn't contain. I learn of the cost of the new trees, and realise why we call French apples Golden Delicious. While bidding farewell to the dead tree, Donella points out what looks suspiciously like chain marks round the trunk, but René says that they were obviously made by a passing deer, desperate for food after the late snows.

April 14th:

A choppy crossing on our return from a raiding mission. A pub next to the perimeter fence at Heathrow airport has proved unpopular with potential customers for some reason, so I have been called in to conjure up some positive publicity. As it is directly beneath the main flightpath, I at first suggested painting huge advertisements for the special dish of the day and other attractions on the roof. Rather stuffily, the airport authority objected strongly to my suggestion, as they thought news of a plate of moussaka and chips for under two pounds might distract the pilot's attention. Eventually, my clients settled for the installation of a sealed time vault in the car park, containing a selection of bottled beer, a home made steak pie, a video of the area and a copy of a suitable newspaper so that visitors to the spaceport in the year 2196 will know what life was like in our time. The time vault spoof is always a winner and extremely cost effective. All it takes to set up the photo-shoot is a pile of earth and rubble, a spade or two and the brewery director and publican in hard hats, smiling and holding their wares to camera. That way, they get an extra plug in for company brands, and the story is guaranteed exposure as I change the name of the allegedly entombed newspaper to suit where the press release is going.

Victor the Volvo has sulked all the way. I think it is all getting too much for him and he will have to go. My wife will probably want him put out to grass at La Puce in recognition of his long years of loyal service. I told her at the beginning that it is a mistake to anthropomorphise cars or other possessions by giving them names. Farmers know this, and give their cows numbers so it will not be distressing when it is time for a visit from the abattoir van.

I have to admit, though, that Victor has been a treasure since Don rescued him from a cruel and uncaring owner five years ago. I will have to talk to him and stress what a valuable member of our team he is. During the restoration of La Puce, he has smuggled or openly carried more than twenty tons of materials and fittings either cheaper, better or more readily obtainable in the UK. His previous best was two complete bathroom suites which were on star bargain at our local Texas Homecare centre. It was a bargain we could not afford to miss. Unfortunately, we arrived ten minutes after the advertised end of the star offer, which the assistant said was put on randomly through the month. For weeks after, we haunted the showroom, getting to know his routines and taking shifts to spy on him, and he joined quite avidly in the game.

When he knew we were lurking on the premises, he would flirt with our emotions by picking up the cardboard star and strolling over to the nearest suite before appearing to change his mind at the last minute. It got to the stage when we were considering wearing disguise or attempting bribery, but he finally grew bored and relented. We fell upon him as he put the star in place and immediately paid for two bathrooms, one for the farmhouse, and at those prices, one for luck. Cheap bathroom suites are good bargaining counters in France.

On our next crossing, together with the bathroom fittings, I also carefully packed a bottled gas cooker, a dozen paving slabs and the dinghy destined to become the water voles' winter quarters. Before we left, my wife pleaded with me to lighten the load, but I would not listen. Every ounce taken on each trip makes the cost of the crossing relatively cheaper, I reminded her. Victor would be up to it. Having got to the ferryport early to ensure a long and clear run-up to the linkspan, we were first on and right at the head of the queue for offloading.

When we arrived on the car deck six hours later, we found that Victor had gone lame. A back tyre was completely flat, and we had about two hundred lorries, caravans and assorted vehicles waiting behind. It was particularly embarrassing, because the spare tyre was buried beneath one of the two bathrooms. Eventually, a couple of lorry drivers and a gang of hell's angels on the way to a meeting at Le Mans helped us unload. They started with bad grace, but the truckers were most impressed when they saw just how much could be carried in and on an old 240 estate. Fortunately, it was raining when we finally rolled off the ferry, so French Customs were nowhere to be seen. If I were an international drug smuggler regularly using this gateway to Europe, I'd be sure to keep a weather eye on the forecasts.

*　　*　　*　　*　　*

Having got our undeclared goldfish and bedding plants safely through the deserted customs checkpoint, we arrive at La Puce and visit the mill cottage to see how the restoration is coming along.

Outside, the sand pile is even higher and I make a mental note to launch Operation Desert Storm with all speed.

Inside, we see that René is continuing to make an excellent job. The newly installed but ancient floorboarding and other fixtures look almost as if they belong there. Bearing in mind how the mill was stripped by locals, perhaps the new items do belong exactly where they are, and have been reclaimed in the same way they were originally removed. If so, it has been poetic justice.

As soon as the mill is habitable, we will be able to vacate the farmhouse and let it out to recoup some of the cost of the restoration, which is running at three times the original cost of La Puce. This, we have found, is a reasonable equation for all improvement work on old French properties, even when, as with our efforts, work is theoretically done on the cheap. We have considered holiday letting for the farmhouse, but hearing the horror stories of those who have suffered at the hands of paying guests, have decided to try for a permanent let. That will also give us a good excuse when friends casually ask if they can pop over and use the farmhouse in our absence. When this first happened, we were most enthusiastic and set about compiling maps and detailed instructions on how to turn the water on and milk the goats. We always told guests to treat the place like their own homes, and some of them unfortunately did.

As I open the shutters and set about airing the cottage, I find we have already had uninvited guests. A small rodent is gamely attempting to climb out of the toilet bowl in the bedroom, and another lies dead on the carpet. Resisting the urge to quietly dispose of yet another mouth to feed, I rescue the survivor and flush the corpse away to avoid the expense and emotional cost of the formal funeral my wife would certainly stage. I attempt to smuggle the creature out of the mill, but my wife's animal antenna is working at full strength. Within moments she identifies the beast as a newborn shrew, and it is set up for life in a cardboard box lined with my newest vest as she tenderly feeds it with milk through a tube fashioned from the inside of my favourite fountain pen.

While she is distracted, I return upstairs and open our English-French dictionary at R for rat poison.

*   *   *   *   *

Donella being fully occupied with nursing the rat, I invent an

90

excuse for visiting our local builders' merchant, where they should have copious quantities of poison which I can secrete around the mill and discourage further squatters.

Driving into the yard, I find the usual long gaggle of wagons, family saloons and bicycles competing for access to the sand and gravel heaps. As I watch a smartly dressed lady of middle years shovel loose shingle straight on to the back seat of her Renault Five, I wonder once again at the way local people seem to collect and store sand as if there were a permanent shortage. Perhaps, like the logs, it is a status symbol, and the bigger the pile in your forecourt, the more renovations and improvements you are obviously about to undertake. In a charitable moment, I consider that the real reason René has been creating the sand mountain is not for profit, but to impress us and our visitors with the scale of his ambitions for the mill cottage.

As usual, the single attendant in the yard is under siege from a dozen customers, so I wander off in search of the rat poison. Finding none, I pick up a bag of cement for luck, and start the complicated business of paying for it before the noon curfew.

The computer system at *Boueve et Fils* has been in place for several years, but the staff obviously don't trust it, or prefer to temper the new ways with the old. As ever, the process of making any purchase takes place in a series of carefully orchestrated and sacrosanct steps.

First comes the location, selection and loading of the goods, which must be signed off by the attendant. He will take any customer's word for how many garden patio slabs and bags of sand are on board, but to escape, the client must have an official signing-off docket. This is taken to the counter, where the bearer may then enjoy a stimulating encounter with other docket-waving customers. When the attention and interest of a member of staff has been won, the docket will be inspected scrupulously before being thrown away. Studiously ignoring the expensive new computer screens dotted around the serving area, the attendant will then search for a reference to the item in a huge catalogue before cross-checking in an even bigger price ledger. As the cost of any item may vary depending upon special offers and whether the buyer is a regular or local or both, enquiries as to a suitable charge will now be made of all other members of staff present, in ascending order of seniority. Finally, and if it is not time to cease trading for the lunchtime closure, the transaction will be entered into the computerised system for maximum speed and efficiency. If the customer has an account, the process will take a little longer as the necessary documents have to be prepared and signatures examined, compared and discussed with at least one colleague. I used to have an account, but cancelled it when I found that I had been charged for a lorryload of sand, allegedly delivered in my absence. René was most upset when I brought the matter up, and said that even if he had learned to disguise himself as me and forge my signature, he would not have ordered the inferior grade of sand from Mr Boueve at any price. At the time he lived in a tiny rundown cottage outside the village which grew rapidly during the period he was helping us restore La Puce. A week after he had re-tiled our farmhouse, I called by to take him for a drink and noticed he had fitted a new roof in exactly the same colour and style. It is a pity he has lost his home, as I could have offered him our star bargain bathroom at a special price for France.

*   *   *   *   *

Returning from my fruitless journey, I see a charming display of lily-of-the-valley has appeared in the copse. Although the climate in Cotentin is much the same as in the south of England, we do seem to be well ahead with the seasonal flowers. I recently considered the idea of emulating nearby Jersey and setting up a flower exporting business, but decided that scale would make it uneconomical. My last scheme along those lines was to grow sunflowers for their seeds, and I spent a lot of time laying down an acre in a spare field. It was a poor showing, and became a favourite haunt of our bird population. Later I found a sack of sunflower seeds in one of Donella's feeding sheds, and she eventually admitted she had been training the birds to like them.

After a recent inspection of our bank account, I also thought about poppies and the prospects of setting up an opium smuggling racket, but the risks are too great, and anyway, they don't seem to grow at this end of Normandy.

The rat is sleeping contentedly on my vest in the mill cottage, so I suggest that we visit Bar Ghislaine for some top-up provisions. Rural grocery stores are dying in France just as they did in the UK a generation ago, and the reason is the same. Even the older villagers now make their weekly trip to the local supermarkets for the better prices and variety, and visit the local *épicerie* only for daily necessities.

As we arrive, Ghislaine waves through the window, then scowls at one of the Jolly Boys Club members, who is using the open-air toilet next to the shop entrance. After adjusting his dress he pats his crotch with a proud proprietary air, and Madame Ghislaine responds by grimacing derisively and waggling her little finger in the air. Suitably and particularly chastened as my wife has been a witness to his ritual humiliation, he pretends not to see us and hurries back to more respectful male company.

As a concession to the chilly day, a single oak log smoulders in the cavernous fireplace at the Bar Ghislaine, and the JBC is in full session. Following the usual round of handshaking and polite enquiries as to the state of our livers, we are invited to join the party. This is a particular honour, as women are usually not welcome in rural bars, let alone when the daily debating school is in session and men can be men in public. As in pre-war Britain, the ladies of Cotentin still observe the tradition of letting their men appear to be in charge when out and about, excepting certain obvious arenas such as the shop, church and, when the patron is pushed too far, the Bar Ghislaine.

Today, our panel consists of Mister Maurice, his nephew Alain, Marcel Bernard, René and Old Pierrot. Apart from his age, most things are indeterminate about Pierrot. Few people outside his small circle of intimates seem to know what he used to do for a living, whether he is married or even where he lives, which is most unusual for any village.

The main subject for today's debating circle, we learn, is fuel. I call for a round of *pastis* from Madame Ghislaine as our entry fee, and listen in keenly. The two opposing camps divide into a preference for oak, which is harder to find but burns well and slowly, and beech for its warmth and aroma. There is also some discussion on the comparative merits of open fireplaces and wood burning stoves, and a rumour to be spread that a newcomer from Cherbourg has bought a house outside the village and is having electric heating put in. He is either very rich or very stupid, as everyone knows that wood is free. Especially, I reflect silently, if it comes from someone else's land. We have lost several small trees from the copse this year, but our estate manager has told me that this is a necessary culling exercise to let the others breathe.

As the discussion becomes heated, René ushers me to another table to announce that he has at last located a perfect stove for the mill cottage. It is the property of a friend in a distant hamlet, and they have just concluded a deal at a very good price. The *poêle* is very old and impressive, and is thought to have been looted from a local manor house immediately after the Revolution. Naturally, there is no chimney pipe included, but that, he assures me, will be no problem, as every ironmongery and hardware shop in the region will stock suitable tubing for adaptation.

The price will be a mere 1000 new francs, which is but a fraction of the cost of a new reproduction model, and I will be buying history as well as completely effective and free heating for the rest of our days in Cotentin. To celebrate, I order another round of drinks, and return to the club table to find the conversation has moved on. In a lull after my crushing defeat at the fishing tournament has been sympathetically analysed and explained in detail, René takes the opportunity to mention casually that he has ordered another trailer load of sand. This, he assures me, will all be used in creating the walkway of marble around the big pond.

Grasping the moment while virtually the entire complement of the Jolly Boys Club is present, I decide to launch phase one of

Operation Desert Storm. My friends will have noticed, I begin, that I have a very large hole next to the mill cottage where the machinery used to sit. Over the past year, I have consulted with all the experts on how best to fill it in. Both Henri the Tractor and Mr Janne have ruled out the idea of simply scooping up earth from elsewhere on the property and dumping it in the hole, as the surrounding walls would deter even the finest digger driver in the region. Has any one any other ideas for a solution to my problem? As I appear to wait for a response, I loudly remind René that we now have a huge surplus of sand, even bearing in mind his plans for the marble walkway. At this, Marcel looks up, his face aglow with inspiration. Why not, he suggests, simply put the mountain of sand into the hole? Given a year or so in the rain, it will settle much better than earth, and avoid the expense of a mechanical roller. I look impressed, then smile sadly. It sounds a very good idea, naturally, but because of the walls, every kilo would have to be shifted by hand. My friends all know how incompetent I am with shovel or spade. Furthermore, Donella, though strong for a woman, has little stamina. The proposal is impeccable, but the execution would take forever. To a man, the Jolly Boys Club volunteer. If we will provide luncheon and ongoing refreshments, they will gladly contribute the labour. It will be a community effort and completed in no time. The talk now turns to past achievements with favourite spades and the most effective wrist actions. I order another round to celebrate the arrangement, and as Ghislaine arrives with the bottle, I catch René giving me a look of reluctant admiration. I am obviously learning how to get things done in the local and proper way.

*   *   *   *   *

It is later on the same afternoon and, Ghislaine having evicted us for enjoying ourselves, I have been invited to make my first visit to the house of Mr Maurice.

It is a particular honour to be allowed into any Norman's home, and especially so as a foreigner. As he made his proposal, Mr Maurice also whispered something about allowing me to look inside his wardrobe and try the contents. Even in my current condition, I am still alert enough to realise he is not inviting me to ease his collection of winter tights on, and have heard all about his special collection of *calva*. Mr Maurice's nephew Alain is to be the only other guest as the surviving members of the Jolly Boys Club have rather pointedly not been invited to join us. My wife has returned to La Puce to tend to her flock, and René has buzzed unsteadily off aboard his *mobylette* to make arrangements for the collection of the stove. Although the idea of an afternoon *digestif* in pleasant company seems innocent enough, I can't help feeling that there may be some sort of hidden agenda behind the invitation to share the secrets of the wardrobe.

Like most people in the region, Mr Maurice rents his house, which is located at the bottom of a winding dirt track on the outskirts of the village. It stands in a cluster of ramshackle old buildings, flanked by the usual mountain of firewood and a collection of rusting car bodies recalling a variety of classic Citroën and Renault designs. As we arrive, a handful of consumptive-looking chickens scratch determinedly in the dirt yard, while a three-legged dog investigates the remains of a long dead cat. Inside, the one large room serves as bedroom, bathroom, kitchen and sitting area, and is dressed throughout in an interesting mixture of fixtures and fittings.

A stack of World War 1944 vintage American ammunition boxes provide the main seating arrangements, and the chemical toilet is within comfortable range of the giant fireplace. An oaken table for which any London antiques dealer would kill takes centre stage and bears the remains of a hundred forgotten meals. As if distancing itself from its squalid environment, a magnificent 18th-century solid walnut wardrobe - obviously *the* wardrobe - stands aloofly in the furthest corner, and is undoubtedly worth more than the house and the land it stands on.

As Alain settles at the oak table, I follow Mr Maurice to the corner and respectfully accept his invitation to open the doors of the *grande armoire*. Within, I see that the tales of Mr Maurice's life work have not been exaggerated. On rough shelving made from more ammunition boxes are crammed hundreds of bottles, flasks and sealed jars. They contain, according to the villagers, the fruits of our host's labours for more than half a century. Each holds a different vintage of *calva*, and each has its own distinctive flavouring. A true artist, Mr Maurice has allowed only his imagination to limit the range of fruit, vegetables and flowers marinating peacefully over the decades. Allegedly, certain intimate animal parts also lurk within the serried ranks of dusty containers. Alongside a coffee jar containing cherry *goutte*, I discover raspberry, blackcurrant, chestnut and even sunflower varieties. The deeper I explore the depths of the aromatic *armoire*, the more unusual and exotic the combinations become, and I await our first tasting with interest.

After a brief lecture on the contents, age, history and ingredients of the top shelf, our host selects what looks like a specimen jar, wrapped carefully in a pair of black tights to shield it from either light or prying eyes. I am reminded of the moment when my wife watched in fascination as Mr Maurice hitched his trousers and adjusted his seams during our first encounter. Later, she was quite disappointed to discover that several layers of womens' tights are considered locally to be far superior to thermal underwear, and considerably cheaper.

The jar is reverently unsealed and the tasting begins. After an initial sip, I agree with our host that the flavour is to say the least interesting, and he explains that the hitherto secret ingredient is a very rare type of mushroom. Having dangled the bait, he and Alain continue to ply me with glasses of his special concoctions, each benefiting from the addition after brewing of fruit, flower, herb or even animal parts.

The afternoon wears on, and, as ever, I find that the magical properties of *calva* are on full throttle. My patois has improved to such an extent and density that my host seems to be having no problem in keeping up with me as I let rip with a stream of anecdotes and explanations about English cricket, the history and development of the British Pub (1216 - 1949) and the trouble with our royal family.

Like a scorpion, Mr Maurice chooses exactly the right moment to strike before I become so far gone that I am unable to speak, let alone remember the remains of the day. Casually, he returns to the subject of his mushroom *goutte*.

Nowhere, he purrs as we move on to a particularly piquant sweetcorn vintage, can one find a finer variety of fungi than in a mature copse of mixed oak and beech in a wet soil, with the leaf mulch undisturbed for long years. As I attempt to nod sagely without headbutting the table, my host asks silkily if I am aware that I am the owner of exactly such a copse. Gamely trying to concentrate and avoid the proposition that I just know will arrive with the next glass, I say yes, I do know that the copse at La Puce is such an unique occurrence. Is it not then a shame, he asks, pressing me to try a *soupscon* of the daffodil *calva*, that I am absent so often at exactly the time that the various fungi in the copse are precisely right for gathering, and that they should be wasted on the casual visitors who raid my land without any repayment?

I agree, but ponderously explain that this is precisely why I have come to an arrangement with Coco that he should have full gathering rights in exchange for our annual mushroom omelette orgy.

Topping up my glass, Mr Maurice points out that, as far as all sensible and informed critics are concerned, his nephew Alain is in fact a far superior fungi collector than Coco, accomplished as their good friend undoubtedly is. In fact, he and Alain have been discussing the matter, and have come to an agreement on how best to approach the situation. Would it not be an ideal solution to continue the arrangement with Coco, but allot he and Alain alternate days of exclusive access to the copse? That way, both would be free to indulge their expertise and enthusiasm, I would continue to enjoy my yearly omelette, and would also receive an annual gift of a bottle of the finest mushroom *goutte*...

At this stage, I am beyond argument, and in seconds Mr Maurice has produced an official contract which he just happens to have drawn up in the case that I should be in agreement. I sign away half the harvesting rights to my copse for all eternity, and the deal is celebrated in suitable fashion.

My only problem now is explaining the new arrangement to Coco, and finding my way back to La Puce. I eventually make my excuses and leave, bid an emotional farewell to the dead cat, and begin my unsteady journey home. Over the next hour, I rest frequently on the verge to take my bearings and reflect that, despite my triumph with Operation Desert Storm, I still have a lot to learn about the way business is done in my new home.

*   *   *   *   *

It is not a good time for René to call.

Donella, who I initially mistake for the Grey Lady, has tiptoed in to the darkened room to say our estate manager is here and the stove ready for collection. We must, she says he says, go now lest it be lost to another anxious buyer.

I am helped to dress and stagger into the yard, where René, an unknown accomplice and a very noisy tractor await. I ask him to turn off the flashing light, and climb in the cab.

On board and bucketing on our way through the night, I recover sufficiently to ask sulkily why it is so important we pick up the stove at dead of night. My companion answers only half-sarcastically that his *mobylette* not being quite up to the task, the tractor is the only available and suitable vehicle, and it is booked for a session in a chicory field in the morning. Besides, the roads are clearer at this time. While the first reason holds water, I wonder how the one car a week likely to appear in the lane would pose a problem, but am too ill to start an argument. I can still taste the mushroom *calva*, and concentrate on gulping down the sweet night air and keeping my seat behind the driver's cab.

At last, we turn off the lane and lurch to a stop on an even more potholed track. I fall from the grunting tractor as René takes a torch and disappears into the darkness. A little while later, he returns and silently beckons us to follow. We must, he cautions in a stage whisper, be as quiet as the night, as we do not wish to disturb the pregnant donkey in the ruined barn which looms up beside us. I consider questioning this out-of-character consideration for animals of the field, but tiptoe on and fall over a piece of the stove, which is holding the door to the barn shut. Inside, the torchlight illuminates our goal. It is certainly an impressive sight. Displayed to best advantage on a pedestal of concrete building blocks, the wrought iron *poêle* appears almost as big as Mr Maurice's magic wardrobe, and every bit as decorative with its engravings, relief scrolls and curlicues. Presently, it is being used as a chicken coop, and René quickly evicts the two incumbents by grasping their beaks and holding them firmly beneath one arm. Obviously, he is still concerned about the pregnant donkey's uninterrupted slumber.

It is left to me and my mystery companion to wrestle the giant stove from its pedestal and roll it to the tractor on some convenient lengths of metal piping whilst René attends to his chicken nursing. This done, we collect the doors, grating and other attachments from in and around the barn, heave the stove on to the trailer and depart, with René admonishing the driver sharply to keep the revs low. As we near the end of the track, I ask why I was not required to pay the owner before taking the goods, a usually strictly observed Cotentinese tradition. It would not be fair to disturb him on such a small matter, he explains as if to a child, and I should know by now that all good farmers are soundly asleep at this late hour. I can settle for the stove when we arrive back at the mill, and he will pass the money on in the morning. We rejoin the lane and the tractor roars up the incline as I fancy I hear a dog bark in the distance, followed by an angry shout. René says that I am mistaken. It is nothing but a fox, who as everyone knows, does his best business at night.

*   *   *   *   *

Back at the mill cottage, we unload the stove and stow it safely behind the sand mountain, René considerately covering it with a tarpaulin for protection against the night air.

I hand over the thousand francs, and before leaving, he surprisingly volunteers to start installation work later this very day. He also suggests that I keep the deal to ourselves, as our rivals for the stove will be jealous and bad feeling could be caused by self-indulgent boasting about our bargain.

The driver, who has so far remained totally silent, moves to the back of his tractor to do some unseen business with René, and raised voices temporarily disturb the silence. The obviously disgruntled figure finally reappears, mounts and starts his tractor, and it rumbles truculently up the track and into the gloom. René disappears in the direction of his *mobylette*, and I think I hear a muffled squawk coming from beneath his voluminous poacher's jacket. I retire to the mill, contemplating the pleasures of chestnuts roasting on our magnificent stove by next Christmas.

Donella will be pleased with our latest acquisition, but I will not show it to her tonight, as she is conducting a badger-watching vigil by the caravan, and would not wish to be disturbed. Since hearing the alleged grunting last year, she has spent several fruitless nights awaiting their return and eventual appearance. She is convinced there is a sett in the bramble jungle in the top field, and has shown me the alleged tracks. I suspect they actually reveal a convenient short cut to the big pond by season ticket-holding fishermen *en route* from buying bait at René's caravan, but have said nothing.

I go to bed. It has been a long day.

April 23rd:

St George's Day.

I have spent a frustrating evening trying to explain the origins and significance of our patron saint to a sub-committee meeting of the Jolly Boys Club. They found it difficult to understand why we should choose a dubious Greek saint as our patron. In any case, Old Pierrot said, it is a well known fact that the role model for the dragon-slayer was a minor historical figure who came from

Cotentin, as can be seen from the old wall paintings in the 11th-century cathedral in Coutances, the ancient capital of the peninsula. So the English saint is not only not very important, but actually third rather than second hand, and yet another example of a Cotentinese invention being stolen and claimed by someone else.

The evening was not entirely unrewarding, however, as I believe I may now be on the way to unearthing the long-forgotten reason for the emnity between our village and St Jacques de Néhou. Following me out to the *pissoir* so we would not be overheard, Old Pierrot confided that the proper name of our village is actually St Georges de Néhou, but the full title is never used, though nobody knows why. That set me musing on a recent article in the regional newspaper about the church at nearby Canville-la-Rocque, where some medieval frescoes have been uncovered. They show the *Santiago de Compostela* pilgrim route from England to Spain, and the dotted line goes south-west from Cherbourg along what is now the D900. It passes between the two villages and the front door of La Puce, with the church at Canville as a resting place and devotional point to the apostle who is said to have travelled to preach in Spain after Christ's death. For some reason, the French do not have an equivalent to the name James, so St Iago became St Jacques. The pilgrim route was marked by scallop shells, and the scallop is the main ingredient of *coquille St Jacques*. So, St Jacques de Néhou is obviously named for a saint with his own classic French dish, while St Georges de Néhou only managed a minor player in the religious league, and who was anyway stolen by the English via the Greeks. Perhaps the true reason for centuries of hostility between the two communes is just a matter of simple jealousy, like the new street lamps St Jacques has recently installed, putting our village into the shade in terms of technological advancement and public facilities.

May 6th:

René has been almost as good as his word.

Less than a month after he promised to install it, the giant *poêle* is in place, standing on a stone plinth against the wall at the end of the mill cottage which will be our sitting room area. Inside and with all its doors and fittings attached, it looks even bigger, but René says that we will need all the heat we can get when autumn comes. We have already noticed that it is markedly cooler in the mill than outside and had hoped that the situation would reverse naturally in the winter, but our estate manager says it will decidedly not be so. He has assured us that there are no ghosts on the premises, but takes grim relish in predicting we will need a bigger pile of firewood to see us through the dark days than Mr Janne uses at his rambling *manoir*; and he is the undisputed local champion for yearly *fagot* consumption. The apparent problem with our mill cottage is that the stone block walls are more than a metre thick, and it will take at least a winter of constant habitation and blazing fires to infuse them, like ancient storage heater bricks, with insulating warmth. The mayor has also told us that the building will stand for ever as cows' milk was mixed with the mortar when it was built. This was an early damp-proofing device, and it certainly seems to have worked.

As there was no chimney piping with the stove, I shall have to find some and do the job myself, but René says this will be no problem, as common or garden metal drainage pipe will be ideal, and can be bought at any good builders' merchant. I see that he has also left me to make a hole for the pipe through the gable end against which it stands. It is even thicker than the side walls and I do not think that, excellent for smaller tasks as it has proved to be, my Black and Decker hammer drill will be up to the task. I shall visit *Boueve et Fils* tomorrow and buy a man-sized sledge hammer.

May 7th:

The fridge being empty, I breakfast off the remnants of last night's *pot au feu* and some bread stolen from the bird table in the yard.

As I make my frugal meal, the ship's bell on the gatepost signals the arrival of the mayor, and I usher him in after his usual polite protestations about the condition of his boots and the early hour of the day.

Of all the men I have come to know across the years, John Chevalier is one of the most thoroughly decent, gentle and content. His philosophy is as simple as it is wise, and he is greatly respected throughout the area for the quiet concern with which he fulfils his self-imposed obligations to the community and his small part of France. He has plainly learned the value and spiritual rewards of cherishing what he has rather than looking for more. He has his wife, his faith, his duty and his home, six *charolais* steers and a life of dignity and fulfilment. Devoted to the commune and the continuance of its way of life, he spends more time at the tiny *mairie* at Néhou than at his farmhouse in the hamlet of le Hequet. Amongst a sea of paperwork and petty squabbling, he is an island of calm at the heart of the village. Each weekday afternoon at three, he dons the mayoral suit with flared trousers bought to celebrate the birth of his son, and takes his seat at the desk in front of the crossed flags of Normandy and France. For the next two hours, he will deal with a steady stream of villagers as he dispenses justice and practical advice, and strives to make sense of the latest European directive concerning the banning of dumping rubbish at village rubbish tips. He is transparently in love with his wife, his work and his life. He is a happy man, and far richer in spirit than the most successful Parisian bureaucrat.

His daily visits during our past brief stays at La Puce have evolved into a familiar and pleasant ritual. Following the struggle to persuade him to enter, his cap is doffed and my hand grasped as if we had not met for months. Now that they have been friends for several years, he will respectfully brush his lips against Donella's cheeks, then after apologising yet again for the mud upon his boots, reluctantly allow himself to be seated. Politely refusing all offers of daytime alcohol, he will then accept a small coffee, and our conversation will begin.

On this occasion and as usual, there is much to talk about before we get down to the reason for his visit. First, we must reassure him as to our health, the general well-being of our Queen (who is also the Duke of Normandy) and how my friend Mr Major is getting on with running the country. As he enquires about our premier, he will nod deferentially at where a photograph of my mother and Donella with John and Solange hangs next to a picture of me apparently arm wrestling with the leader of Her Majesty's Government.

Some years before, I had organised the re-opening of an East End pub in London after it had been set on fire by a disgruntled customer, and I had hired the most convincing of the many John Major lookalikes available to pull the first pint. The event was not to be a runaway success, as the pub's locals were rabid socialists to a man, and we had to smuggle the lookalike out through the cellar before he came to harm from those holding him entirely responsible for the state of the economy. Even after I had assured the customers he was actually an accountant from Pinner called Patrick, they still wanted to take a swing at him, but he was quite philosophical about the mêlée he had inspired, as it happened all the time. Before the near-riot, we had posed for a photograph together, and I had framed and hung it on the farmhouse kitchen wall. When a visiting French friend with a business in the UK explained the joke to René, and what the real Mr Major did for a living, the news that I was a personal friend of the *chef* of all England went round the village like wildfire. René had either misunderstood my friend's bad (i.e. non-Norman) French, or deliberately neglected to explain that the man in the picture was not the real PM, a revelation which would naturally diminish his status as my estate manager. Despite the common foreign belief and internal claims that, since the Revolution, France is a truly egalitarian society, we have found the French even more snobbish than the English. To have one of Britain's most (as René had assured them) celebrated and successful writers as an honorary villager was one thing. That he was on arm wrestling terms with the British premier was even more of an honour. I suppose by now I should have enlightened them on both points, but have not got round to it yet.

The main reason for the mayor's visit, he explains after the

105

formalities have been completed, is to ask my permission to put his cows to graze in our mill garden later that day. A thoughtful and efficient farmer, which is not always the case in France, John makes full use of every blade of grass he rents, and it is time to give the top fields a rest. He usually puts his cattle into the mill cottage garden at this time, but knows that we are working there and does not want to disrupt our restoration work, which he has thoughtfully forgotten to check for conformity with planning regulations. When we bought La Puce, we were naturally pleased to learn that there was an existing grazing agreement with the mayor of Néhou. Although he recommended that we maintain the arrangement for all sorts of sensible reasons, Mr Gancel the *notaire* advised us that the property's change of hands meant we were entitled to terminate the long-standing agreement. If we wisely decided to carry on as things were, a suitable yearly fee and conditions would be negotiated and agreed, and a yearly contract drawn up, authorised, notarised, witnessed and signed by what appeared to be half the village. Already having learned that any involvement of a *notaire* is very time-consuming and expensive, I promptly typed up a lengthy and completely meaningless contract full of pseudo British legalese, added a first class stamp, asked my local Portsmouth publican and two of his customers to sign it, and duly presented it to the mayor. The document, I explained, gave him full and exclusive use of the land till his retirement, and there would be no charge.

John was visibly moved by my gesture, and I immediately felt bad about creating the fake contract. However, our verbal accord was known to the *notaire* and village, and therefore just as binding. It was also a lot cheaper.

*　　*　　*　　*　　*

Having told John he was as usual welcome to put his beef into the garden, we shake hands and he departs. I slither down the slope from the farmhouse and undress amongst the paint pots and cement bags on the first floor of the mill ready to indulge in a long awaited treat. I am to test out our new old bath. Taking

René and three other strong men to carry upstairs, it is still a talking point in the village, as it is not only a traditional English bath, but an English lord's traditional English bath. Of 1930's vintage, the cast iron monster is oval, big enough for me to achieve maximum submergence, and is finished off with impressive ball and claw legs. Even allowing for our Texas Homecare star bathrooms deal, it is easily our best buy for France. Like all serial property restorers, we are constantly in search of unusual and useful bargains, and often risk an accident when driving past any interesting junk shop windows. Taking the air in rural Sussex one Sunday afternoon last summer, we had passed the gate to a gypsy settlement and seen the luridly painted and heavily disguised monster, bearing a roughly daubed price tag of £30. Talking to the vendor, we learned that he had recently won the rights to strip and salvage all the outdated plumbing before a refit at nearby Cowdray Park, and the bath was just one of the redundant fittings they were invited to take away. At least, he claimed they were invited to take the redundant fittings away. Tragically, I saw that they had already put the hammer through a treasure trove of old copper shower fittings and brass taps for the scrap value, but the bath had survived as it had seemed saleable for use as a cheap water trough for cattle. I was told it came from a guest wing, but I didn't dissuade René from painting word pictures at the Bar Ghislaine about the great English lord soaking in his bath with the odd chambermaid after a hearty game of polo with the Duke of Windsor and Wallace Simpson.

I am just about to dive into the new bath when Donella calls up the stairs to say that the cattle have arrived in the mill garden, but are unaccompanied by either John or Solange. They are also eating her herb garden, and one of them, to her untrained eyes, looks suspiciously like a bull. It appears to be sharpening its horns on the stone wall behind the mill after having had the five-bar gate off its hinges with a few experimental charges. She is concerned that the herd may now wander unchecked into the water meadow and come to grief in the big pond. I reassure her that there are no bulls in John's herd and that she should have learned by now to recognise an overgrown steer. I agree, however that a fall into the big pond could be dangerous, as the whole herd would doubtless be stripped to the bone in moments by the voracious Cray gang.

Pausing only to don a pair of slippers and my Superman dressing gown, I join my wife in the garden. I still do not know if the proposition that bulls find the colour red irritating is true, but my appearance has an immediate effect on the small herd. The cow that Donella thinks is a bull promptly snorts, paws the ground, lowers its massive head and moves towards me at a considerable rate. This disturbs the others, and as I leap with unaccustomed rapidity into a convenient nettle patch, the whole herd thunders up the cart track to the road. Aware of the consequences of a ton or more of cow meeting suddenly with a car coming down the hill at 90 kilometres an hour, I attempt to keep pace with them, and we burst out on to the road at around the same time. Thankfully, the piste is clear, and I pursue the herd in the general direction of St Sauveur.

By great good fortune, the first vehicle to meet us in our headlong flight is the ancient van of Mr Janne, and even more fortuitously, he is sober.

Within moments he has set up a roadblock and, after taking over from me with an admiring glance at my Superman dressing gown, authoritatively directed the alleged bull into one of his own roadside fields.

A long queue of traffic has now built up, and everyone takes the opportunity to show that, whatever their present situation and professional status, they have not forgotten their basic countryside skills. Smartly dressed men and women desert their BMWs and Mercedes as the peasant just below the skin of all French men and women comes to the surface, and they vie to show off their specialist herding techniques with an array of umbrellas, briefcases and handbags.

Eventually, all the cows have been ushered into the field, and the identity of their owner established. The herd belongs to an elderly lady living near the crossroads, and their rightful home is in a field alongside La Puce. Normally, explains Mr Janne, they would be happy to stay there, but the excitement engendered by the presence of the bull has caused them to follow him on his rampage through a couple of hedges and into our mill garden.

The fuss over, I return somewhat shakily to the mill, where I find the Cowdray bath, without the modern design benefits of an overflow device, has flooded the premises. Thankfully, little permanent damage has been caused, although the cows' milk mortar has proved its value as damp-proofing, and the ground floor is now a shallow swimming pool.

Later, as I steep in the hot water and ruminate on the morning's drama, I consider whether I will be hailed as a local hero for stopping the stampede, or an English fool who can't tell the essential differences between a cow and a bull.

May 10th:

Restoration work on the mill cottage has been called to a sudden halt.

René was trowelling cement into some holes in an outer wall when there was an explosion of colour and sound, causing him to fall off his home-made stepladder. At least five juvenile yellow wagtails had erupted from a cavity, followed by the mother, who shepherded them off the premises after leaving her mark of indignation on René's head. Investigation revealed the nest still contains a tiny egg, and my wife put an immediate preservation order on the whole wall. René has offered to return tonight and finish the job while Donella is on observation duty at the big pond, but even I can't bear the thought of entombing the egg and sealing off the nest.

The wall will have to stay as it is for the present.

May 11th:

Donella is ecstatic now that she has found yet another mouth to feed.

She was watching mother wagtail working her way round the big pond when a large black duck took off from the island and blundered its way through the long grass to Hunters Walk. She could tell just by the way it flew, she said with a misty eye, that the creature was nesting, and was risking its own life to lead possible predators away from its young. Obviously, the island is now totally off limits, even were I allowed to use the boat housing the water voles, and I have been instructed to take my boots off and tiptoe when within a hundred yards of the pond. If this continues, I shall probably be placed under house arrest until the infant population of La Puce has flown.

May 19th:

An eventful overnight crossing from Portsmouth.

We share a cabin with our latest Real France package visitors, and all suffer a sleepless night due to the gymnastics taking place next door.

In the morning, we meet our noisy neighbours queuing for the toilet, and realise that we know the couple. Both are happily married, but not to each other. They explain implausibly that they were unable to book separate cabins and are on an urgent business trip. Over breakfast, my wife suggests that they must be in the bed-testing business.

We exchange stories about how we met our spouses, and I amuse our guests with the tale of my short but stimulating career as a private detective. In between jobs, I had responded to an advertisement for a correspondence course to learn the profession, and managed to persuade a friend to lend me his tiny basement office in a Southsea terrace where a number of solicitors plied their trade. All went fairly well until my first job, which seemed a run-of-the-mill affair involving checking out the fidelity of the client's wife. I studied my course notes and duly set up an observation post in the alleyway behind the house she constantly visited. Immediately after gaining concrete evidence of her adultery as she dallied with a large man over a convenient kitchen table, I fell off the dustbin, was spotted, detained and rather unnecessarily assaulted by her partner before being handed over to the police. Fortunately, I was let off with a caution after my profession and intent was explained and proven. I was also cautioned by the desk sergeant to check up on my facts before taking on any more cases, as it turned out that the woman was happily married to the man who punched me, the scene of the action was their own house, and my client was a known stalker who had developed an obsession for the woman and deluded himself into believing they were married.

I met my future wife early one morning shortly after my first and last case when she arrived for work at the more affluent premises above mine and caught me borrowing their freshly delivered bottle of milk. Rather than turn me in, she tended to my black eye, replaced the bottle, tidied up my office and was doomed. When I decided to cease trading as a private eye and get a more reliable source of income as a gravedigger, she came with me and has been bailing me out of trouble ever since.

*　　*　　*　　*　　*

We arrive in some style at the *Café de Paris* in a fearsome looking Range Rover bristling with bull bars, winches and a row of spare petrol cans lining the roof rack as if we were on safari rather than in Cotentin. We are also towing a battered caravan, which was the main reason for our visit to Hampshire, and our return with Jean-Marie Guedeney and his English wife Kathy. Jean-Marie is Burgundian, and the couple run a chain of sandwich bars in the Portsmouth area. As he has lived and worked in Britain for nearly twenty years, my friend's moustache is much smaller than the rural French norm, but his belief in gallic superiority over us in every sphere save cricket and real ale remains undiminished. This unshakeable credo is perfectly illustrated by his regular shipment across the Channel of great mounds of French dough for the manufacture of his *baguette* loaves. Simple on-site mixing of English flour, yeast and water would simply not, in his considered opinion, rise to the occasion.

As a guest under our special short-stay package plan, Jean-Marie will doubtless prove indispensable for any advanced negotiations with René on the new pond Donella is planning, but his main chore for the visit is to tow the caravan into the water meadow. Originally, it was bought to double our luxury waterside holiday home facilities, but my wife has already claimed it for a secondary feeding station and nature hide at the furthest outpost of our little empire.

With the day hardly awake, the *Café de Paris* is nevertheless a hive of activity, and for a moment it seems we have walked into the regional headquarters of the Palestine Liberation Front. Freddo, Pierrot and a motley collection of customers are going hunting, our host tells us, though the array of high-powered armament has already given us more than a clue to their intent. As Freddo is introduced to our guests and makes a covert assessment of Jean-Marie's moustache rating, he explains that a fox has been sighted on the outskirts of the town, and the posse is getting ready to hunt it down and free the area's livestock, elderly residents and new-born infants from its threat. As a fellow Frenchman, Jean-Marie is invited to inspect the arsenal, and we move to where a selection of rifles, bandoliers, hunting knives, nets and what looks suspiciously like sticks of dynamite is heaped carelessly on a table. Freddo's toddler grandson is at this moment playing with a double barrelled weapon slightly longer than he is, and my wife hastens to take it from him. Giving her the soft verge look, Freddo stiffly assures her that he is not *stupide*. Though the *fusil* is loaded, the safety catch is firmly in place. Obviously, the child is too young to go on the hunt at present, but will be ready for action next year when he receives his first ever rifle as a doting grandfather's birthday present. The patron then offers to shoot anything eatable that comes into his line of fire for Donella's pot, but my wife says not to bother to kill anything especially for her, as she has brought some frozen turkey drumsticks across the water.

Approaching the bar and, I suspect, wishing to impress us, Jean-Marie orders our coffee and *calva* with machine gun rapidity, and is served hot chocolate and *pastis* by Collette's mother. After I coach him in the necessary patois phrasing, he has a brief conversation with *maman*, who congratulates him on his command of the French language, and asks what part of England he hails from.

*   *   *   *   *

At La Puce, we move our luggage into the farmhouse, then drive down the track to the mill, which is now barely visible behind the sand mountain.

Kathy alights from the Range Rover and immediately sinks to the ankles of her expensive high-heeled fashion bootees. She is a town girl by birth and inclination, has only visited Jean-Marie's ancestral home in Burgundy during the searing months of July and August, and has not encountered real country mud before, especially the Cotentinese variety.

Jean-Marie is obviously far more at ease with the terrain and the task ahead. A keen off-roader, he spends his weekends looking for a challenge on the forest tracks of Hampshire, but has never seen anything approaching the promise of our land, even in a comparatively arid May. He becomes even more enthusiastic when he sees that the route to the water meadow runs steeply uphill through the mill garden after passing through a gateway only marginally wider than the caravan. And all before meeting the real challenge of the permanently saturated reservoir field. Taken together with our attendance at the fund-raising *soirée* at the village hall this evening, the visit promises to be a most enjoyable and memorable one, he says, almost licking his lips in anticipation of both the meal and the mud.

Anxious to display his vehicle's capabilities without delay, Jean-Marie loses no time in starting his motor up and skillfully manoeuvring the caravan to line up with the gateway. All goes well for at least ten feet, then the back and front wheels of the all-terrain vehicle disappear in the rich Normandy earth. After a few moments of spraying the caravan and rear wall of the mill and settling even further in the mire, Jean-Marie refuses to concede defeat and announces it is time to bring his brand new power winch into play. He finds a suitable tree on the river bank, hooks up, and begins to pull the sturdy ash out by the roots.

As we stand at approximately eye level with the roof of the sinking vehicle, René arrives to welcome us, collect his bottle of duty-free scotch and savour the moment. I can see that he is particularly pleased that it is a British vehicle which has fallen foul of good Norman soil, and seems even happier when he learns that Jean-Marie is from Burgundy.

After a while and as the stricken vehicle continues to sink, our estate manager tells our guest not to abandon hope, as he will go and fetch his *mobylette*. For a moment I think he proposes using it to pull both the Range Rover and the caravan into the water meadow, but he explains that yet another friend with a tractor is working just up the road. With the pooled resources of René, the tractor and Roland the *spécialiste*, all will be well, and Jean-Marie, his unfortunate vehicle and our caravan will be out of trouble.

*   *   *   *   *

While we wait for rescue, Donella provides our friends with wellington boots and suggests a tour of inspection of the rest of the terrain. I take the opportunity to visit JayPay and seek suggestions for a suitable regional dish to impress our guests at lunch tomorrow.

Jean-Pierre recently moved in to a farmhouse less than a mile away, and has therefore become a close neighbour as well as friend. Up until a month ago, the family of eight had the grandest council house in the region, created specially from the former vicarage next to the church at Néhou. Apart from his status as general manager of the meat and *charcuterie* section of a supermarket outside Bricquebec, JayPay is regarded as the most knowledgeable and formidable chef in the area. He also has a special place in the commune's hearts as for the past decade, he has been battling virtually single-handed to halt the annual fall in the village population. So far, his tally is a mixture of six sons and daughters, all almost identical in their striking dark looks and sunny natures. As befits his past accomplishments, JayPay's moustache is on a par with Big Freddo's, a subject which is the focus of much dispute and the occasional wager between regulars at the *Café de Paris* and the Bar Ghislaine. The claim as to who has the biggest and best moustache in Cotentin (and perhaps all France) has allegedly risked fist-fights between the opposing camps.

JayPay carries his authority, responsibilities and giant moustache with equal ease. Apart from his work, countryside and reproductive activities, he somehow finds time to devise and create the regional dishes for regular fund-raising dinners at our village hall. This month's featured region is the Alsace, and the dish *choucroute,* an awesome collation of pickled cabbage and parts of the pig which most English people would not believe existed, let alone be suitable for consumption.

At their farmhouse, I park the car a safe distance from the attentions of the dozen or so bored dogs looking for a little sport, and call for a safe escort. Eventually, Madame JayPay appears wearing her usual combination of a resigned pout and cigarette. As we walk to the barn in search of her husband, she tells me she is more than happy with their new home, given that there are only four bedrooms. She would have liked more, just for the sheer pleasure of having one permanently spare and empty *chambre.* On the subject of large families and the state's changing attitudes towards rural tradition and culture, she recalls an encounter with an official health visitor shortly before the birth of her youngest offspring. The woman had not even borne a single child, but had presumed to give her advice on preparing for the big day. Worse, the session had included a severe warning about the perils of smoking, and a severe admonition that Madame should at least stop the filthy practice while pregnant. This was a ridiculous proposal, as in earlier years she would hardly have had time to light up between conceptions. Besides, the evidence is there for all to see, as her children are obviously healthier and happier than any mollycoddled town kid. Having often stopped to pick up her beaming offspring during their three-mile walk to and from school, I have to agree with her.

Anyway, concludes Mrs JayPay, she had kept the woman quiet by promising to cut back on the Philip Morris, and is nowadays down to forty a day.

In the barn, JayPay, who obviously likes making things, is working on his new invention, an incubator resourcefully created from an old beer bottle display cabinet and the heating elements of a redundant electric fire.

Correcting my teasing suggestion that it will make a roomy and snug crib for the new member of the family, he explains that it is destined to hold and nurture up to four dozen pheasant eggs at a time. As Freddo and his fellow *chasseurs* seem to be running out of targets on their weekly hunt, he is setting up an intensive breeding programme to re-stock the local shooting range. As he gently cradles and strokes the tiny eggs in a massive hand, I once again reflect on this apparent ambivalence of attitude towards the miracle of creation and the pleasures of the kill.

In the lofty kitchen, we gather at a table marginally smaller than the landing area of an aircraft carrier and Madame JayPay does the honours with home made biscuits and a bottle of *pommeau*. As she busies herself adding cigarette ash to the food cooking on the stove, I toast my friends' happy news and explain my problem. I have a visitor from Burgundy, and wish to surprise him tomorrow lunchtime with my knowledge of and expertise in our regional specialities. I know JayPay has a busy day ahead as he prepares to feed more than a hundred villagers at one sitting, but that, of course, is no challenge to someone of his capabilities, and I am lost for ideas. My friend takes a ruminative sip of his liqueur, wipes his moustache thoughtfully, then calls for pencil and paper. It is almost as important, he says, to choose a suitable dish for the occasion as it is to cook and serve it perfectly. The latter stage is, naturally, to be taken for granted in France, the former sometimes sadly overlooked. Tonight, our friends will be dining on *choucroute*, so my special meal should redress the balance, and be more subtle and lighter in texture and taste. With another sip of *pommeau*, inspiration comes. In the short time at our disposal, he will attempt to school me in the philosophical approach and precise sciences involved in the creation of a truly perfect *salade normande*, followed by scallops in white sauce. The salad will reflect the simple yet inspired approach the Cotentinese take to matters of the stomach, and the scallop dish will mark and honour the ancient pilgrim's trail passing by the kitchen door of La Puce.

For the next hour, I am slowly taken through the mysteries and rites of making a salad consisting of little more than a single lettuce leaf. The secrets of the scallop dish take longer to unveil. Spices are brought from the larder, wrapped in twists of brown paper, labelled, numbered in order of inclusion and placed before me. Apart from the simple recipe and method of cooking the dish, details of the precise vintage and origin of the dry white wine for inclusion are written down, and I am required to practice the correct method of crushing the garlic cloves with a fork a dozen times before my mentor declares himself satisfied. Finally, we come to the inevitable yet vital secret ingredient. Returning from a lengthy visit to the barn, JayPay presents me with an earthenware jug wrapped discreetly in newspaper. He has just drawn a little *calva* from the giant oak barrel where it has been maturing for the past eight years. It is not quite ready for drinking in truly sophisticated company, he says, but is more than adequate for inclusion in the dish. As he escorts me and my precious package past the slavering dogs, he explains that the oak barrel was a most important factor in his decision to buy the house. There were many other cheaper and bigger properties for sale, but none went with a lifetime's supply of vintage *calva*. Had the previous owner not died alone and with no heirs or even distant relations, JayPay would never have pulled the *coup* off. It just shows, he says sagely as I back carefully out of the yard, the good sense of ensuring continuity of life and possessions across the generations by having a reasonably sized family.

*   *   *   *   *

Back at the mill, I find that Norman know-how has triumphed over British technology and Burgundian driving skills.

The caravan is sitting happily at the far end of the water meadow, and the Range Rover and its master are sullenly skulking behind the sand mountain. Roland and his tractor have returned to their labours, and René, as ungracious as ever in victory, has offered to give Jean-Marie some tuition in off-road manoeuvring on his *mobylette*. I calm down a potentially explosive situation by suggesting a glass of good wine and a game of ludo, played to Burgundy rules.

*   *   *   *   *

It is time to encounter the *choucroute* and we make our way on foot to the village hall at Néhou. Jean-Marie initially takes this as a further slight to his driving capabilities, but I explain that it will be a long evening, and we do not want him to join the ditch of the month club after such a demanding and frustrating day.

The mayor is greeting guests at the door, and thankfully appears to have little trouble in understanding Jean-Marie's French. After bestowing a few compliments on the wine, food and agricultural practices of Burgundy, our thoughtful host ushers us in to take an *apéritif* before the festivities commence.

The hall is set with tables laid for more than a hundred, and many of the guests have already arrived. The women of the village have made a special effort to mark the occasion and are dressed in their party finery. Most of the men have changed into clean bib and brace overalls and brown gumboots. Old Pierrot has even put on his Sunday best peaked cap.

118

pond, despite the extra work involved. She has been drinking, so I do not suggest that our estate manager would be most agreeable to any method of ensuring the fish in the new pond will be prolific in their breeding, and consequently justify a further issue of season tickets to the local angling community.

Other business conducted at the bar includes a discussion with the Jolly Boys Club on making a start on Operation Desert Storm soon, and we seal the deal with another round of *pastis* before the mobile disco makes any further conversation impossible.

*   *   *   *   *

By one o'clock, we and our visitors are ready to give the villagers and their children best and retire from the action. Jean-Marie says that all French countrypeople are notorious for staying up till dawn at special celebrations, but I think they are just waiting for us to go first so their reputations may be maintained.

Outside, the early morning air tastes as fresh as the lemon sorbet, and the rain has eased to a fine shower. We make our way home through the silent lanes to La Puce for a brief nightcap and Jean-Marie confesses that his visit has been a revelation. Like the ten million Britons who visit his country each year, he had always honestly believed that real France was to be found only beyond the Loire valley. With England looming less than a hundred miles to the north, he had thought it impossible that such a true Gallic culture could exist and flourish virtually in the shadow of the Isle of Wight. If it were not for the weather, food, drink, local customs, dress and language, he could almost be at home in Burgundy.

We fight our way to the bar, which is in the capable and enormous hands of Mr Janne. He is dispensing the choice of *pastis*, bottled beer and wine at nominal prices and we drink generously to help the night's good cause, which is to buy new books for the school.

Everyone seems to be entering into the spirit of the event and determined to enjoy the evening. Married couples go out together rarely in the Cotentin, but when they do, they tend to get their money's worth. Though there is scant room around the sea of trestle tables lining the hall, the mobile DJ is doing good business, and JayPay's children are filling the floor on their own. Some couples are actually dancing together, though René has not yet decided to do his traditional whirling dervish act. Perhaps he is waiting for the Birdie Song.

Alerted to our presence, JayPay makes an entrance from the kitchens, swathed in acres of white apron and a *Michel Mouse* tee-shirt. Perspiration is rolling down his face and threatening the integrity of his waxed moustache, but he is obviously on good form.

After meeting our friends, JayPay registers our status by showing us personally to our table and we see we have been given a most privileged position, equidistant between the toilets and the bar.

Following tradition, the names of the guests allocated to each table has been written on the paper tablecloth, leaving individuals to sort out for themselves who they choose to sit alongside. I note that our party includes the entire Jolly Boys Club and the mayor and his wife. It is time to choose the wine for the evening, and before anyone suggests a sausage competition, I order a case to be going on with. As usual, the wine committee has obviously worked long and hard in sampling and rejecting candidates to accompany the *choucroute,* and Jean-Marie nods approvingly as he pores over the handwritten list of one.

After another scrimmage and round of drinks at the bar, we take our places and the mayor makes a short address, welcoming all and making special mention of our foreign guests, particularly

Jean-Marie and his wife.

As ever, the service and procedure are simple in the extreme, and the quality of the food unmatchable. Following a rehearsal on a mound of assorted smoked sausages and meats from around Europe which for some highly illogical reason is called Plate of the English, we clear our palates with a shrimp and cream soup, and stand by for the main course. There is an embarrassing moment when the wine is tasted and declared unfit for human consumption by JayPay, who promptly sends it back to himself with a curt demand for a fresh case, but Jean-Marie handles the tide of apologies and explanations like a seasoned diplomat.

With freshly charged glasses, we toast the arrival of what looks like the component parts of a whole pig atop a mountain of pickled cabbage, and the meal commences. For the next half hour, conversation falters as we set to in earnest, and the pile of bare bones beside each plate grows apace. Kathy and Donella do their best to keep up with the rest of the party, but surrender when second helpings arrive. After a cigarette and a lemon *calva* sorbet to aid digestion, we move on to a lightly oiled salad which I suspect is the inspiration for my starter tomorrow lunchtime, then deal with a selection of suitable cheeses, the best part of a loaf of walnut bread apiece, and then do battle with great wedges of apple tart in a layer of cream thick enough to ski on.

By now, the pace of even the most determined eaters has fallen off, and most of our table politely refuse an invitation from JayPay to finish off the remains of the *choucroute*. René brazenly fills a carrier bag with leftovers for his dog, though we all know he hasn't got one.

As we sit and recover, the mayor tells me that work on the Patton orchard is nearing completion. An American tank has been installed in pride of place, the grass trimmed and a car park built, and now he is in search of a suitable boulder to carry a plaque detailing the momentous events that took place there during and after the D-Day landings. I tell him I shall shortly be phoning my friend Robert Simon at Cherbourg to order more gravel for the mill track, and promise to enquire about the possible location

and transport of an impressive *rocher*. Since we have been w on the mill, more than 10 tons of quarry chippings have laid on the ancient track, and all have been swallowed up mud. JayPay claims that we could ask the commune to pay provide the stones as it is a long-established public right but I feel this would only confirm my acceptance that it is of our property. I am not taken with the idea of paying it even easier for the locals to bring their trucks and va the track on scavenging missions, but it can be almost unn in the wettest of weather. I look out of the window and see that it has started to rain quite heavily since we arriv hall. It will certainly spoil our friends' visit if Jean-Marie to move his off-road vehicle from outside the mill cottag the return and assistance of Roland the Tractor.

As we retire to the bar, Donella tells me some unexpe news. René has said he has finally struck a deal wi landscaping specialist, and work on the new pond wil thing in the morning. I say that I will believe it when i as we have only been discussing the project for the months. I also consider asking her why we need y expanse of expensive water, but I already know the a garden pond is even more overstocked with expatri now, and the plan to create a new home for them bridge was a total washout. With the sinister Reggie Crayfish gang holding sway over the big pond, she wil this season's baby *poissons rouges* there. While I was secrets of lettuce salad at JayPay's this afternoon, Jean-Marie and Kathy's help in staking out an area Olympic swimming pool in the water meadow. She in negotiation with René to discuss piping water th the river and out to the mill pond to encourage conditions and optimum breeding. This time, she designer, overseer and clerk of the works, and the be all the better for it. Surprisingly, she has fou agreeable to her demands that he lay in piping t

JayPay's cream of shrimp soup

1. *Make a white sauce**
2. *Sauté carrots, onion, celery and a lot of shrimps in butter*
3. *Add wine, thyme, bay leaf and seasoning and simmer for one glass of wine*
4. *Strain the liquid into the white sauce, saving the shrimps*
5. *Peel some of the shrimps and set aside*
6. *Crush the shells and the unpeeled shrimps, add to soup and simmer for one cigarette*
7. *Strain soup, stir in cream and almost boil*
8. *Take from heat, add lots of butter, a dash of calva and the peeled shrimps*

* White sauce is made from butter, flour and milk with seasoning. (calva optional)

May 20th:

Having spent a surprisingly comfortable night roughing it in the mill while our guests use our bedroom in the farmhouse, we are awoken by the sound of birdsong and a tractor.

Easing myself from the bath, I look down to find René and his lake specialist have arrived to break ground. We dress as they prepare themselves for the work with coffee and *calva* in our makeshift kitchen area, and I wonder exactly why René has actually turned up when he said he would. Following the speed of installation of the stove, his lack of procrastination is becoming somehow worrying. Perhaps in this case and as he told Donella, he wishes to provide a new home for the goldfish as swiftly as possible. Perhaps he wishes to show further evidence of Norman tractor skills before Jean-Marie departs.

After meeting a beaming and reassuringly competent-looking Mr Gilbert and his tractor, I watch the battered machine rumble into the water meadow and reflect on relative values on either side of the Channel. In England, Jean-Marie's Range Rover would be an enviable status symbol. Here a reliable tractor is a far more desirable possession.

We assemble by the stakes marking out the perimeter of the new pond, and are joined by Jean-Marie and Kathy. They report on a blissful night in the farmhouse, and Kathy asks if we had come into the kitchen for some reason during the early hours. Donella and I exchange glances, but decide not to recount the legend of the Grey Lady in case our friends consider visiting again. Since my dream and after a night on her own in the farmhouse, my wife has changed her mind and become convinced that we do have a spectral presence at La Puce. Getting out of the bath and preparing for a peaceful night while I was on a solo visit to England, she was quite surprised to hear a series of bangs and crashes from the kitchen. Locking the bedroom door, she spent the night in some distress, and in the morning found that the kitchen door was firmly locked and bolted from the inside. Even

René in search of beer from the fridge could hardly have got in and out of the house without trace, she concedes.

If there is a *fantôme* on the premises, I feel sure that it is a benign presence, and just wish it would hurry up and lead us to the miller's gold before we run out of credit at *Crédit Agricole*.

Leaving Donella to enlarge on the dimensions, shape and style of the new pond with René and Mr Gilbert, I return to the farmhouse to telephone Robert Simon.

We met Robert and his wife Christiane soon after we bought our first wreck in Cotentin, and they have become valued friends. Apart from owning the largest building supply business in the region, they are both anglophiles, and we have mixed much business and pleasure with them over the years. As well as a shrewd businessman and charming dinner companion, Robert is an academic with a particular interest in the history of Cotentin, and is a fund of information and fascinating stories. Christiane is very *chic* and sophisticated, can knock spots off any Parisian hostess, but has not forgotten her rural roots and delights in telling us earthy stories which would make a British navvy blush. Both have been of immeasurable value in helping us build our new home and life in Cotentin. They have also been invaluable in teaching us the proper way to do polite business in France. We first met when I arrived in their yard and demanded the cheapest possible mass-produced materials for the job in hand, which was to tile the kitchen floor at La Puce. Robert seemed embarrassed at my directness, and suggested politely that I might perhaps consider using a far better quality, more durable, attractive and slightly more expensive tile, which would bring out the character of our ancient farmhouse This, he said, was how a French customer would look at the project. To my shame, I continued with the English approach and pressed for quantity rather than quality. Any old tiles would do, provided they were cheap. He then suggested we went to a nearby bar for a chat about how business was normally conducted on his side of the Channel. After three coffees with *calva*, he gave up trying to convert me, and suddenly remembered he had one pallet of tiles which were seconds and a discontinued line, and could therefore be mine for half the normal price. Later, I found out that the hand-made terra cotta tiles were the best money could buy, and were a regular and popular item at the yard. Since then, I have tried to moderate my aggressive and very British attitude when looking for a bargain buy in France, but Robert and Christiane still continue to provide us with cost-price materials whilst finding excuses for their kindness.

After an exchange of pleasantries with Robert, I order yet another lorry load of stones for the track and mention the mayor's need of a big boulder for the Patton orchard. As ever, Robert comes up trumps. He tells me he just happens to have a special offer on chippings next month, and his lorries pass our door on their way to and from the quarry near Haye-du-Puits. If the driver stops off on his way to Cherbourg and we take pot luck on the size of stones and the time they arrive, we will make a big saving. I tell him I do not believe the bit about the special offer, but will shamelessly take advantage of his indulgence. I send kisses to Christiane and go to investigate progress on the new pond.

In the water meadow, I find an altercation between René and my wife in full flood.

Donella tells me she has carefully described the size, depth and landscaping of the new pond, and stressed that she wants all of the earth piled on one side to make a raised bank where she can build another observation post. René insists that it will be better to heap the earth all around the perimeter of the pond as it is dug. Donella retorts that she is sure that it will be better for him and his specialist friend, as it is easier to dump the earth closest to where it has been excavated, and she does not want to have to use advanced climbing equipment to reach the water's edge at this pond. She is by now an old hand at *étang* building, and not to be trifled with.

Adjudicating, I say that, based on past experience, I have to admit my wife has some cause for concern.

The last specialist employed by our estate manager had created the big pond by the simple principle of starting in the middle of the chosen site and working his way outwards. As soon as the shovel broke ground below the water level in the meadow, the hole in which he and his *tracteur* was sitting began to fill. It was then a race against time and the incoming tide, with the machine becoming more and more bogged down as it churned up great mounds of earth and deposited increasingly wetter bucketfulls to the nearest point it could reach. After the job was finished and the driver had swum back to the bank, another tractor had to be employed to pull his out of the mire. The result that greeted us on our next visit looked like a particularly muddy day on a Somme battlefield in the rainy season. But, I hasten to remind her, when taken to task about the state of our formerly enchanting water meadow, René had merely shrugged and said that nature would take care of it. The grass would soon grow over the mud mountains, and all varieties of reeds and wild flowers would ring the pond, while the ankle-turning clods of earth would eventually be broken down by rain and occasional visits by grazing cattle. He was absolutely right, and a year on the big pond looks as if it has been there since before the mill was built.

Having listened attentively and conceded my main points, Donella is still adamant. This time, being on site, she wants the new pond to be perfect, and exactly to her specifications.

Usually with these matters, we arrive at a compromise, which means René agrees with our aims and then does exactly what he wants. However, on this occasion he is disarmingly amicable and, after smiling grimly, promises to carry out Donella's instructions to the letter. The earth from the excavation will be positioned exactly as my wife desires, down to the last kilo. Surprised and a little disturbed at the ease of our victory, I suggest we leave our workers to get on with it, and return to the mill for the unveiling of my speciality luncheon.

*　　*　　*　　*　　*

The Normandy lettuce salad and scallops in cream and *calva* have proved a great success. René tried a few mouthfuls and grunted reluctant approval, while Gilbert had seconds and Jean-Marie said he was more than surprised with my performance at the oven. He, obviously like me, is not a chef, and there were some areas ripe for considered criticism were he not a guest at our table. But all in all, it was good... especially for an Englishman. His remarks remind me of a run-in I once had on the subject of British food with an associate member of the Jolly Boys Club, who often spoke of his alleged exploits during the Occupation. He had, he said, faced the sort of dangers and peril which would make the beard on my most precious part go white just to hear. But, after a long and adventurous life, the only thing that truly frightened him was English food, cooked by an English chef. I thought at first that he was joking, but the sage nods around the table showed his views found favour with our companions, none of whom have ever actually tasted our traditional dishes, but know what they know about the rest of Europe.

A favourite story here as elsewhere in France concerns how a wealthy widow may find Heaven on Earth. Her cook, naturally, should be French, and her chauffeur German. Her lover should be Italian, and her butler English. Hell on Earth for the widow would be an Italian chauffeur, a German lover, a French butler, and, naturally, an English cook.

*　　*　　*　　*　　*

As our guests are booked on the five pm ferry from Cherbourg, we are in good time to drop in for a farewell drink at the Bar Ghislaine. I take an afternoon's worth of bottled beer to where René and Gilbert seem to be progressing well and following Donella's directions implicitly. As I leave, René asks me if I am really sure that I want all the earth on one side of the pond, and fortified with self-confidence by the reception to my speciality meal, I stand firm.

*　　*　　*　　*　　*

It is approaching four o'clock, and the Bar Ghislaine is heaving.

Following tradition, virtually all the male attendees at the *soirée choucroute* have decided to take the day off and gather for a hair of the dog. JayPay is deservedly the centre of attention, and receiving tribute to his performance in the form of unstinted praise and *pastis* in equal proportion. Our visitors are also enjoying themselves.

Young, vivacious and married to an honorary Frenchman, Kathy is proving popular with the Jolly Boys, and is being schooled in some interesting patois phrases and expressions. When we arrived at the bar, she had refused any strong drinks for herself or her husband, and reminded him constantly of the need to allow good time for the journey to Cherbourg. Since Old Pierrot slipped a large *goutte* in her coffee, she has become much less concerned with the hour, and has already invited the entire Jolly Boys Club to stay at her Southsea home later this year.

*   *   *   *   *

It is twenty minutes to five, and our guests have just left. Both seem confident that they will arrive on time for the ferry. Off season, departure times are elastic, but I think they are optimistic, as even in Jean-Marie's Range Rover it is a good half hour to Cherbourg, unless he is planning to go by a cross-country route. However, they seemed unconcerned, and say they will return to continue the party if they miss the boat. Having waved them off, we decide to return to La Puce and the water meadow to check progress on the new *étang*.

Though yet empty, the pond is perfect.

Obviously of an artistic temperament, Gilbert has brought Donella's vision to life. Naturally shaped and curving gently around the perimeter, the level falls steadily from the bank to a depth of precisely one meter at the centre, and all of the excavated earth is neatly piled at one end. Gilbert has even used his giant bucket to tamp down the mound which will soon provide an elevated picnic and observation area. The pipe which will be taking the

129

overflow water to the mill pond is in place and buried, and the trench from the river is near to completion. An empty bottle count shows that René has been working at optimum rate, and he is about to bury the plastic piping which will draw fresh and constantly running water from *le Lude*. As he explains, the trick is to position the end of the pipe a few centimetres above the level of the river, then slope it steadily down towards its entry point into the pond. Finally, he will use one of the marble slabs to create a barrier downstream. Unlike our plastic sandbags, his *gros barrage* will cause the water level to rise, enter the pipe and feed the pond. A moveable plastic bend fitted on the entry end of the pipe will control the flow, and the cunningly placed overflow pipe will keep the level in our new pond at precisely the desired height. Our only problem will arise from my wife's insistence that we pile all the earth on the far side of his otherwise impeccable creation. Apart from his unspecified prediction of impending disaster, all seems well, but to show off my engineering background I question him closely about the mechanical equations he will use to ensure the correct slope of the entry pipe from river to pond. Would it not be best to borrow a theodolite, hammer in some levelling pegs or at least fetch the spirit level and a ball of string? With a sigh, he pushes me out of the way, then opens and empties a bottle of beer in his usual efficient manner. Re-filling it from the river, he pours water into the pipe. Obeying nature's prime directive, it runs downhill and into the empty pond. The angle of slope is clearly correct.

I humbly open another bottle of beer, hand it to him and slink away.

*　　*　　*　　*　　*

Dusk is falling, and I am sitting beside our new pond. Just as René had predicted, the barrier has caused the river level to rise, and water is gurgling merrily through the pipe. Already, we have a foot of water, and Donella is contentedly splashing around in her waders, positioning tubs of plants and reeds transplanted from the big pond. René and Gilbert have roared off on the tractor to catch up with festivities at the Bar Ghislaine, and peace has descended upon La Puce. Even better, nature is already taking a hand in stocking our new pond. A regatta of water boatmen have taken up residence and are sculling happily about on the surface as tiny mayflies practice touchdowns on the gently swaying tops of the water plants. A distant series of croaks tell us that word is spreading about a new and much more satisfactory display arena for Triple Salco and his troupe, and Donella is considering transferring at least a generation of *poissons rouges* to their new home. As we drink in the quiet contentment of the evening, it seems that news of a new habitat has also reached other sections of our countryside community. While the long Normandy twilight deepens, we hear a series of unfamiliar bird calls, in particular the harsh and, to us, perplexing cry of a herring gull. It is not unknown for seabirds to come inland, especially when a plough or digger has been at work on the land, but we are twenty miles from the nearest coastline on the peninsula, and gulls are rare visitors indeed to our neck of the woods. Donella is at a delicate stage with a flag iris, so I am sent to investigate. On the ridge of the feed store alongside the grotto, I find a single starling is giving a perfect imitation of a gull's jagged screech. In the next ten minutes, this Rory Bremner of the bird world runs through his complete repertoire of impressions until the arrival of our pet feral cat sends it ducking and diving away in search of a safer perch.

At the pond, Donella is extremely sceptical of my claim, and asks if I have been at the goat cheese again. But I know what I saw and heard, even if it must remain yet another unexplained phenomenon of the magical and mysterious Cotentin.

May 21st:

The fish man arrives early to catch us on the hop, and we hide in the bathroom as he prowls around the farmhouse.

In the absence of shopping centres in the depths of the countryside, virtually everything can be bought from the mobile vans which regularly visit each village, hamlet and isolated household. There are weekly vans offering everything from *charcuterie* to the latest video recordings, and a three-piece suite and complete wardrobe of clothes may be had from the back of a removal lorry which fights its way down the narrow tracks of the hinterland each Thursday.

For all these convenience goods, prices are considerably higher than at the supermarkets and stores, but we try to patronise mobile salesmen whenever we can to help keep the system alive. Sometimes, though, they can be over-enthusiastic when it comes to closing a sale, and we were netted by the fish man during our first working visit to La Puce. Having discovered that the place was now owned by an English couple who found it hard to say *'non'* and didn't even know how to order any quantity less than one kilo, he became almost as regular a caller as the mayor. As we seemed always to be at the end of his run, he would take the opportunity of clearing his stocks by pressing vast and expensive amounts of mussels, oysters and fairly lively crabs into our reluctant hands, always with the injunction that they must be prepared, cooked and eaten at once. Finally, too embarrassed to make any more excuses about eating out that night, and unable to claim that we were just dashing off to catch the boat for Portsmouth, we developed a complex hide and seek routine to avoid his high pressure sales pitch. He knows we are there when our car is outside, and we suspect he knows we know he is there and are avoiding him. At first, I would remove the striker from the gatepost ship's bell used to summon us from the fields, but he failed to get the message, and began seeking us out in the copse, water meadow or even the loft of the mill cottage. Nowadays we simply go to earth wherever we are at the time. His persistence has paid little dividend of late, but we believe he is actually enjoying the game as much as us.

*   *   *   *   *

It is just as well that my wife did not stock the pond last evening, as it is completely empty.

Frogs, water boatmen and mayfly have moved back to their

former lodgings, and the pots of reeds and other water plants sit isolated on the dry bottom of the pond like lonely cacti in a desert landscape.

Closer inspection shows that René's tombstone barrier has been toppled by the flow of *le Lude*, and the entry pipe is high and dry. Of more import is that the water already in the pond has drained completely away. Walking around the perimeter, we discover where it has moved to. The low bank where the pipe from the river is buried is now a bog. I raise René at his caravan and demand an explanation. He points out that in some places, the land around the pond is actually lower than its bed. It has been a comparatively dry period, the ground is always thirsty, and water will always find the most convenient gathering point. This is why he wanted to surround the pond with a retaining ramp of sodden earth. We, of course, knew better. But there is no cause for concern, as he will replace the barrier later that day, and once the surrounding earth has soaked up enough water, the pond will fill and all will be well. Perhaps. We can of course hire Gilbert to return and move the banking earth to where they both said it should be in the first place.

We sit and look at our expensive hole in the ground and the morass alongside it. Donella makes the best of it by considering its nurture as a natural marsh area, with a bridge to allow us to reach the caravan and big pond. I make a mental note to phone Gilbert when we return in June after our next raiding trip across the Channel.

Cotentin scallops in white sauce and *calva*

1. *Take a lot of scallops from their shells and remove the nasty bits*
2. *Test the calva*
3. *Slice some mushrooms*
4. *Peel some onions and garlic. Chop the onions, crush the garlic (NB with a fork)*
5. *Melt a lot of butter in a pan and add the scallops*
6. *After again testing, pour some calva into the pan and set it alight*
7. *Add the onion and cook for one glass of wine (my rate of consumption)*
8. *Dust with flour, stir and add some dry white wine*
9. *Add garlic (leaving out the fork), cinnamon, clove, nutmeg and pepper*
10. *Fry the mushrooms in another pan and add to the scallops*
11. *Mix crème fraîche with an egg yolk and pour over*
12. *Stir for another glass of wine (do not boil)*

Normandy lettuce

1. *Test some cider*
2. *Mix some with vinegar and crème fraîche. Season*
3. *Add lettuce*
4. *That's it*

SUMMER

June 2nd:

An uneventful crossing, except for an encounter with the ferry boat's new diversion to defray on-board boredom, a travelling tarot card reader and clairvoyant. We meet as she is taking lunch in the cafeteria, and, as business is slow, Donella is offered a special discount sitting. We discuss the reading afterwards, and my wife says she was very accurate in her comments. Mystic Margaret divined instantly that Donella is an animal lover with a strong and durable personality, who has suffered many years of having to cope with someone with a difficult and demanding nature. I point out that my wife spent the whole lunchtime telling the woman about her menagerie at La Puce, but am quite impressed that she managed to detect the unseen presence of my mother-in-law. I am not impressed, however, with the prediction that my wife will shortly be going on a journey overseas, as the reading took place in mid-Channel.

After leaving the port, we stop off at the giant hypermarket on the outskirts of Cherbourg where more people seem to shop every day than live in the region. We are here to pick up the ingredients for the Desert Storm lunches, and my wife knows that the choice, preparation and presentation of each meal will be vital. The last time I saw her looking so apprehensive was when she confronted the bull in our mill garden.

As usual, Auchan is under siege, but we manage to find a parking spot within a kilometre of the main entrance, and Donella inspects a shopping list the size of a toilet roll while I search for a ten franc piece to release a shopping trolley from the thousands chained together outside the food hall. Some English visitors have discovered that a twopenny piece will fit into the slot on the handle, but as you only get your own money back when you re-chain the trolley, I don't see the point in cheating.

Inside, the aroma of freshly baked bread and newly expressed coffee mingles with the tang of reasonably fresh fish, garlic and gallic perspiration. We pass a sprinkling of British buyers who are feverishly loading their trolleys with cases of wine selected solely by price, and I am reminded of a publican couple who visited us last year. Learning that Auchan regularly puts on ludicrously cheap special offers in the food hall as loss leaders, they stopped off with their van on the return journey to the ferry to see if there were any suitable pub catering bargains. Noting a huge placard advertising the regional equivalent of Bayonne hams at around five pounds in English money, they loaded their trolley with a dozen, reasoning that being smoked, the joints would keep for the year it would take to dispose of that many ham sandwiches for the darts team and proper paying customers.

Having to fight their way through the checkout, hand over their international credit card, load their goods and hurry to the ferry, it was far too late to return the hams when they realised that the price displayed had been for the kilo rather than the whole leg. What made it worse, as they explained later, was that there wasn't much call in their style of pub for the rather acquired taste of raw, smoke-cured meat, and they were constantly getting complaints from the darts team that the stuff in their sandwiches tasted funny, was stale, and definitely going off.

*   *   *   *   *

At La Puce, we discover that summer has been hard at work in our absence.

One of the great pleasures of our fleeting monthly visits in the past was the way the progress of the year would be so colourfully registered on our arrival. We would leave behind a white carpet of snowdrops in January, and return in February to a golden panorama of primroses. The following month, we would be met by daffodils and butterburs, with their bushy pink heads nodding discreet welcome. In April, we would find cuckoo pint and early purple orchids waiting patiently alongside the cart track, then a mass of bluebells and goosegrass would invade the copse to signal the end of spring and the approach of summer.

Today, we stop to explore and enjoy the white clusters of elder flower and the tall foxgloves guarding the entrance to the track, where overhanging branches of beech, hazel, birch and sweet chestnut have been woven together by tendrils of honeysuckle to form a snugly arched progress down to our secret cottage.

It is very good to be home again.

Outside the mill, we unload the three-piece suite, bed and dining table and I apologise yet again to Victor, reassuring him this should be his last really major transport operation. If all goes well with Desert Storm and the finishing touches to the restoration, we shall move in to the mill later this month. Funds in our foreign reserves are at an all-time low, and the farmhouse must be let soon. After a year of sleeping with the cement mixer, then finally putting the last brushload of paint on the walls, it will be a wrench to move to far less grand accommodations, but at least the mortgage will be covered by the extra income.

Since putting the farmhouse up for rent with an English agent, we have had some interesting replies and proposals. One middle-aged couple wanted to move in and take over the fields to keep goats and pay us in hand-woven mohair jackets. Another potential tenant with a ponytail hairstyle and white BMW car dropped in to say it would be profitable for both of us if he set up a cannabis plant production factory so near to the ferry port. If asked, we could tell any visitors that forced and blanched rhubarb was being raised under the black painted glass, and he would take charge of all growing, harvesting and transport arrangements. While in no doubt about spurning the goatherds proposal, I did consider the ethics and risks of becoming an international drug baron, but Donella said that even the French police would know the difference between marijuana and rhubarb.

*　　*　　*　　*　　*

At the far end of the water meadow, the grass has turned bright yellow.

Across the two acres, there must be ten thousand flag irises bobbing in the breeze. It has been a particularly wet winter, and growing conditions have been ideal. The land here is too wet for the mayor to regularly graze his cattle, and the meadow has remained virtually untouched for centuries, so the tall and elegant water-loving plants have taken over. Each year, we are enchanted with the wealth and variety of other wild flowers and herbs which appear around the big pond, along Hunters Walk and about the giant bramble patch by the dry stream. My wife has become something of an expert in identifying and classifying the most obscure, and last year she began experimenting with recipes from an old country cookbook which explains how to cure everything from dropsy to impotence. I put a stop to it when a *ragoût* including marsh pepper leaves made my tongue go numb and I was unable to speak for hours. I later noticed that my wife had turned the corner of the page down as if for future reference.

Robert Simon has told us that flag irises are the model for the national emblem of France, originally adopted by Clovis, a 5th-century king of the Franks, but I am more excited about the commercial prospects as I start a head count. I have seen them in our local garden centre in the UK, and they are priced at more than a fiver for a small pot.

I have reached almost a thousand pounds, allowing for packing, shipping and trade prices when Donella summons me to the small pond. It is still empty, and grass is already growing on the bed. My wife points out that if René does not do something about the tombstone barrier, we will soon have the most expensive dent in the ground in France. I look at the thriving marsh now spreading to the river, and consider reminding her whose idea it was to leave areas of the bank lower than the water level in this part of the field. Instead I come up with a plan to keep her mollified until I can have strong words with René.

Fetching the long hose from the garden shed, I connect up and turn on. Water begins to flow into the pond again, and my wife is content.

While the pond fills, I search the local centres of entertainment for our estate manager, and eventually spot his *mobylette* and distinctive American tank commander's helmet outside a bar in the hamlet of Valdecie. The roads are empty as it is just after noon, and I must be sure to return before three o'clock. A two-bottle lunch is not uncommon in these parts, and it is not a good idea to confront a tractor with lowered digger attachment making full use of both sides of the highway.

As ever, the Bar Pétanque is in the sole charge of Madame Françoise, a young widow whose husband died a few years ago. To help support her struggle to keep the business going, most of the local men visit the bar from time to time, but I see that René is alone in a corner, his glass of wine untouched. It is the first time I have seen him crying.

Madame Françoise quietly explains that it is the anniversary of the death of Papa Ribet, who now sleeps in the churchyard across the road. René comes here every year to explain how it goes for Mr Ribet's only son, and he has been ashamed to tell his father that he has lost his home and his wife, and now lives in a caravan.

I decide that a discussion with René about the barrier is of minor significance, and leave him alone with his grief.

Pulling up at the mill cottage, I see an unfamiliar car parked by the sand mountain. It is a white early model Peugeot with leopard skin seats and at least three CB radio aerials. All these accessories predict a high moustache rating for the driver.

Inside, I am introduced to Hubert, who not only teaches English at a local school, but also speaks the language, which he is demonstrating during what appears to be an intimate *tête à tête* with my wife. I also note that he wears his tightly fitting shirt open almost to the waist, that it is strained across his ample paunch, and that gold glitters amongst the thick matted hairs on his chest. Moreover, his carefully waxed moustache is bigger even than Freddo's. Judging from the bottle beside him, Hubert is on at least his second large malt whisky, and he is sitting in my armchair.

He stands so that we may shake hands and measure each other up. I am pleased to see that though he is younger, I am an inch or two taller, and my belly is considerably bigger, which means a great deal in local terms of prestige. During our somewhat stilted conversation, Hubert explains that he lives in the Val de Néhou, which is an isolated and striking area of marshlands outside the village, and has stopped by as he heard that we are losing fish to local predators. René's name is mentioned frequently, and my wife's expression tells me that I can no longer continue the deception that Trevor is only one member of a thriving trout colony. Hubert goes on to say that he has a friend who is a keen fisherman and likes to catch *gardon* purely for the sport. They are very difficult to catch, and the poorest family will not eat them as they are small and full of bones, so they would make ideal inhabitants of our pond. If we wish, Hubert can also ask his friend to provide a large and voracious *brochet*, which will keep the pond clean and under control. He is obviously not aware that the big pond is the Cray manor. Making a mental note to look up both fish in the dictionary later, I thank him for his kind offer, and ask what the price will be. The quiver rate of his moustache points tells me he is offended, and he says that the fish would be a gift. His friend the fisherman, however, is quite fond of whisky. After looking sadly at the bottom of his empty glass for a long moment, our new friend shakes my hand, appears to think about breaking strict local etiquette and kissing my wife on the first meeting, then roars slithering up the track with car windows open and Johnny Halliday singing *Le Jailhouse Rocher* at full blast.

As the prickles on the back of my neck subside, I remark to my wife how short he was, and that he seemed to have been making himself at home with my whisky and chair. My wife tells me not to be so silly, that he was being extremely helpful, and that she found him quite charming. I go to check on the water level in the new pond, and consider growing a *real* moustache.

*   *   *   *   *

Though the hose has been going for a couple of hours, the bottom of the pond is barely wet. I inspect the tombstone barrier, but decide fixing it firmly and permanently back in place is beyond my skills. As I consider connecting up another hose, I am called away by the sound of a lorry coming down the track. Unless it is yet another load of sand, our latest batch of shingle has arrived.

Looking at the mountain of stone on the back of the bright yellow *Brument-Clot* company lorry, I see that Robert has been his usual generous self. Fortunately, the vehicle has a tipping device, so I ask Denis the driver if it is possible to drive slowly back up the track, raising the tipper and shedding shingle as he goes. That way, we will just have to spread it around a bit rather than having to make countless wheelbarrow trips to and from a pile which would almost match the sand mountain. I realise that this will take a considerable degree of skill, but Robert has told me that Denis is his best driver.

Rising to the bait and challenge, Denis makes a twenty-point turn outside the mill, and sets off back up the track as I walk behind to direct operations. Immediately, I see that the job is much more complex than I had imagined. The slope of the track means that instead of a steady flow, an avalanche of shingle rushes furiously out of the open tailgate every time Denis operates the tilting device. Also, each time the front of the tipper rises above the level of the lorry cab, it comes into conflict with the tunnel of overhanging foliage. Before long, though the bottom half of the track is dotted with heaps of shingle as roughly per plan, the front of the lorry has become firmly wedged under a particularly strong oak branch. Denis explains that if he continues, either the tilting mechanism will shear, or we will lose a tree. I climb onto the cab with a completely unsuitable junior hacksaw, while Donella and Denis begin attacking the shingle piles. As my wife points out, it would have been a good idea to move our car up the track before unloading, as we are now cut off from civilisation until all twelve heaps have been levelled off and the lorry freed.

A couple of hours later, and we have made a reasonable job of spreading the shingle unevenly along the bottom half of the track. It is six inches deep from the turning circle outside the mill up to the lorry's tailgate, but there is not a new stone beyond as we cannot force the wheelbarrow between the banks of the track and the sides of the truck. In spite of his fatigue, Denis enthusiastically suggests that he return to the quarry for another load, which he can discharge on to the top half of the track from the road. That way it will cascade down and make up the level. He graciously accepts a coffee and a small advance on his tip, while we go for another inspection of progress at the small pond.

The bottom now appears to be fairly damp, and I do some quick calculations based on a distant maths exam involving the time taken to fill a bath with the hot and cold taps running at different rates of flow. To the untrained eye, it appears the pond is about the size of two hundred baths, and a timing experiment with a pint glass and the hose followed by some long division and multiplication sums indicates that the water should be at a satisfactory level by the day after tomorrow. The rate of seepage into our new bog is, unfortunately, an indeterminate and therefore incalculable factor.

Denis now appears at my shoulder, whistles loudly, does some brisk ooh-la-lahing after looking at the hose and the work it has to do, then asks if we realise that our water is metered at the road and charged for by the litre. I pretend to know this, and privately decide to cut down on baths over the coming year.

Further bad news from Denis is that his lorry will not move. The obstructing branches of the oak have been removed, but there now seems to be some sort of mechanical fault. We return to the scene and scramble underneath his truck to discover that two of the three nuts and bolts holding the driveshaft coupling together have shaken loose in the struggle with the oak tree. They will now be buried somewhere under twelve tons of pea shingle. Rather than sift through it all or break out my metal detector, Denis and I retire to the tool shed to see if we can find some temporary replacements.

*　　*　　*　　*　　*

Some time later, and we are to be found lying under the lorry in a *mélange* of mud, shingle and tree branches. I am holding a nut fast with a pair of electrical pliers, while Denis is tightening the last bolt with an oversized spanner, the gap made up with a ten franc piece. Eventually, as the blood from our skinned knuckles mixes with engine oil, grease and leaf mulch, the job is completed, and too exhausted to struggle from beneath the truck, we stay where we are and share a cigarette. Denis tells me that his real job is as a helicopter technician, and I tell him all about our former life across the Channel. By now, our mutual adversity has meant we have advanced to pet name terms. He is Den-den, and I explain that, to the villagers I am George-o, though within the membership of the Jolly Boys Club I have the honour of being known as Mr Beerbelly. After our mutual ordeal, I feel we are now close enough for him to call me either. I now attempt to explain the origins and development of the Anglo-Saxon *eckname,* and run through a selection of common modern diminutives in England such as Billy, Chas, Daz and Shaz. To further illustrate the differences and difficulties which can be encountered by the foreign visitor, I tell Den-den about an artist friend called Conrad Barnes who visited us last year for an extended Real France package trip. When I invited him to visit us and paint the restored farmhouse, he took it as a request for a tasteful watercolour impression, but was just as happy when we asked him to apply three coats of traditional powdered whitewash to the outer walls. In the *Café de Paris* to celebrate the end of his commission, I had stopped the conversation by calling his pet name from across the bar. Later, Freddo had taken me aside to say that though the epithet was in fairly common usage in the marketplace, it was not a good idea to call my friend 'Con' in more refined circles, as it was the equivalent of comparing him with a vagina, only more so. As I told him at the time, I already knew that *connerie* meant a cock-up, so should have guessed that *con* would not be too far away in the slang vocabulary.

Prolonging our moment of quiet companionship, Donella passes us coffee as we lie beneath the lorry and exchange anecdotes and ambitions. As we talk, our undernourished squirrel stops by to see what is going on, and I notice what looks like an early ox-eye daisy growing from the bank. A relatively short time ago, I would not have imagined that life would find me stretched out beneath a lorry halfway up a mill track in Normandy exchanging intimacies with a former helicopter mechanic. All things considered, I would much rather be exactly where I am than anywhere on the M25.

Much later, and Denis has delivered his second load and gone, and another twelve tons of shingle have been spread evenly across the top half of the track. To save on the water rates, I have bathed in the new pond, which has already reached ankle height. The water boatmen have taken up residence again, along with some curious ball-shaped creatures which float on the surface for a moment, then drop like a depth charge into the comparative deeps. I have looked in the dictionary and found that the fish Hubert's friend is bringing are roach. I also now know that a *brochet-de-mer* is a barracuda, but reassure my wife that the freshwater version is merely a pike. Nevertheless, she says we will refuse Hubert's kind offer of the predator king of the river, unless I am sure it will really be safe from René's customers, and particularly the Cray terror gang.

Far above, our kestrel is making his teatime rounds. He arrives each day in the morning and afternoon, and follows the same routine. Selecting a suitable part of the terrain, he will hover till spotting a target, then drop like a stone to pick up his instant takeaway. Birds of prey flourish in this area, and seem to be much respected for their hunting skills by those who would shoot a harmless starling without a second thought. René says that our regular visitor is not a kestrel but a *buse* or buzzard, and will often stop work to watch it go about its business. He seems to admire its freedom and dignity, and is obviously pleased when it strikes and finds a victim. He also says there is an eagle which sometimes visits the region, and he has seen it surveying our terrain from a tall beech tree alongside Hunters Walk. I would like it to be true, but he told me at the end of a long and convivial lunchtime, so he was probably only trying to please.

June 3rd:

It is René's birthday.

We discuss a suitable present, and I suggest the two bottles of malt scotch and 400 English cigarettes bought on our recent crossing. My wife says it seems rather unkind to speed him to an even earlier grave with such a gift. Besides, she points out, as René drinks to excess every other day of the year, he might want to have an inverse birthday celebration by staying sober for 24 consecutive hours.

I stand firm and explain that, comparing the strength of the English cigarettes and the purity of the scotch with what our estate manager and the rest of the locals normally drink and smoke, our gifts would probably be classified as health products in Cotentin.

June 5th:

I return from an early morning visit to the big pond to report on two amazing developments.

We have a corn circle, and our frog colony is speaking patois.

Pressed for details, I explain that an almost perfectly round circle of flattened grass has appeared in the water meadow behind the caravan. It is roughly twelve feet across, and the surrounding grass is standing upright at its normal knee height.

Displaying her usual cynicism with regard to all matters supernatural, my wife disputes a visit by a miniature alien spacecraft, but says that foxes are known to create a flattened circle for cover when resting in long grass. When I remind her that, thanks to the local shooting clubs, foxes are slightly rarer than aliens in this region, she becomes even more excited at the prospect of her alleged badger tenants stopping for a picnic in the reservoir field.

When asked about the other phenomenon, I tell her of the extraordinary spectacle I have just witnessed.

Arriving at the big pond, I came upon hundreds of lemon yellow frogs actually playing leapfrog through the rushes at the water's edge. What's more, as they jumped over each other, rather than making their usual croaks, they were all shouting *'wheah'*, which, as every pretentious Briton with a home in France will tell you as he or she uses the word, is national patois for *'oui'*.

Perhaps, I suggest, this eccentric behaviour is the result of abduction and examination by my aliens, who, landing in the depth of night, have mistaken our frogs for the dominant inhabitants of this part of the world.

Perhaps, my wife suggests as if to a particularly unintelligent plank, the frogs are playing leapfrog because its what they do at this time of year, and their excited cries are merely their mating song.

After consulting our wildlife library, I grudgingly concede that she may be right. However, I shall make a point of buying all the local papers tomorrow to see if there are any reports of other mysterious happenings in the neighbourhood.

June 7th:

My alien visitation theory has been destroyed.

Making a closer inspection this morning, I found at least twenty cigarette ends in the centre of the corn circle, and an empty bottle of René's birthday scotch in the long grass at the perimeter. Faced with such forensic evidence, I can only conclude that our estate manager went for a midnight walk with his gifts, returned to the wrong caravan, then spent some time walking round in circles before giving up and settling down for the night exactly where he was.

June 12th:

A red letter day. Our estate manager calls to announce I may from this day forward call him by his pet name, which is Néné. We may also now move on from *vous* to *tu* when addressing each other.

This extremely hard-won and rarely granted privilege does not, I believe, count when employed by Paris taxi drivers, who regularly use our equivalent of 'thou' rather than 'you' as an expression of derisive contempt. It is most popularly employed on passengers who do not tip lavishly, or have the gall to ask if there is more than one Eiffel Tower in the town, as they have just passed an identical structure at least twice during an increasingly expensive journey. It is the first time I have heard René's pet name, as nobody in the village appears to use it. He tells me that this is because they are not allowed to, but his father called him Néné all the time. I tell him I am proud to be in such company , and that he should feel free at all times to call me Mr Beerbelly. Néné says nothing about extending these privileges to Donella, so I think she must still be on trial.

June 13th:

Néné says he has found us a long-term tenant for the farmhouse. He has been approached by a most respectable friend currently living in a nearby village who has urgent need of new accommodation for himself and family of nine. The man is a good worker, and is free to tend the land part-time under our estate manager's careful supervision. He will not require wages, but will expect to occupy the farmhouse within the normal tied cottage arrangements which ensure free lifetime tenure. A further bonus is that our telephone will not be used as the family knows no other customers of *France Telecom*, and the heating and hot water fuel bill should be low as they are a hardy bunch and do not bathe obsessively. I promise to discuss the proposition with my wife, and briefly do. Following her instructions to the letter, I return to his mobile home and politely but firmly reject my friend's proposal. Having heard my decision, I notice he returns to the 'vous' usage when we say our farewells, and believe him to be unhappy with me. I assume it will also be back to René from Néné now.

On arrival at the farmhouse, I find my wife thumbing through the telephone numbers of all the English settlers in the area so that she can determine who has recently split with whom, and will therefore be looking for a reasonably priced roof above their heads.

June 15th:

John and Solange Chevalier appear at the kitchen door to say they have just moved their steers into the clearing in the scrubland alongside the copse. I immediately suspect a more formal reason for the visit, as both are in their Sunday best clothes. When John accepts a small glass of whisky, I am even more suspicious. After a long conversation about the condition of the fields, hedges and gates and his fond memories of La Puce over the past thirty years, my friend announces that he has an important announcement to make. He is to retire this Christmas, after almost sixty five years at his farm in Le Hequet. He and Solange will take a small town cottage next to the fire station in St Sauveur, and have just bought a new car to visit all the places they have never had the time and freedom to see. It will be a wrench to leave the home where their children grew up, but it is compulsory to retire from farming at his age. Their son has a good, clean job in the town and no wish to continue in the family tradition, so the rented farmhouse will go to someone else. He will miss La Puce and will, if I wish, help find a new tenant who will take good care of the land. He will be happy to have more free time, but will miss the feel of the earth through his hands and under his feet. I ask them to wait for a moment and go upstairs to my study. There, I take a piece of my headed notepaper, write upon it and add a first class stamp. Returning to the kitchen, I ask them both to sign it.

The document, I explain, negates our former arrangements and is a contract for life, giving them full, free and exclusive use of the two main fields. John may wish to start a small orchard like Mr Margot over the road, or to grow some fine vegetables. He may prefer just to know that the land is there if and when he wishes to use it. I would be honoured, I say, if he will visit us often, and perhaps teach me how to live with and use the land a one thousandth as well as he has for the past decades. He looks at the paper for a long moment, then gruffly clears his throat and rubs a hand across his eye. For all the difficulties in language we have faced over the past years, we are now both, I think, in total *accord.*

After politely refusing to take another small whisky, John invites me to inspect their new car. We walk out and I admire the small, bright red saloon. It is, says the mayor, the first new car they have owned. With care, it should last the rest of their lives.

I stand and wave as John carefully pulls out of the yard and heads off in the direction of Le Hequet, then go back to pour myself a large scotch and ponder on the news, as I feel somehow uneasy after our meeting. The mayor and his wife have been a constant and important factor in our lives since we bought La Puce, and I find the thought of their leaving unsettling. Perhaps I should be more like the people of the area, and accept life, death and change as an inevitable part of nature.

June 20th:

Our newly-shingled track is put to good use as the Jolly Boys Club arrives in and on a motley collection of vehicles, comprising two *mobylettes,* Marcel Barnard's ancient Renault and a tractor with roof light flashing and klaxon hooting. Bringing up the rear is Mike the Bike, briefcase clasped under one arm and a huge shovel strapped to his crossbar. My friends are obviously in a festive mood and intend to make a day of it. We gather in the mill for a quick coffee and *calva* before beginning our assault on the sand mountain, and Michel takes the opportunity to pass round previously unreleased photographs of himself in various waiting rooms, hospital beds and operating theatres. As we admire a medical magazine picture of our friend sitting with a puzzled looking man in a white coat, Marcel excuses himself and begins to unload a selection of period wheelbarrows, spades and shovels, and the debate begins as to who shall have which. My tiny Spear and Jackson edge cutter is the usual source of ribald remarks due to its small surface area, and René asks yet again if it is only the women who dig the garden in England.

Before we get into another lengthy discussion on comparative techniques and shifting rates, I lead the way to the foot of the mountain we must move and explain my plan and vision for the future. Basically, we have around 30 tonnes of gritty sand outside the mill, and a pit more than eight feet deep between the renovated part of the mill and the original gable wall. If we move one to the other, the unsightly hole will vanish. When the sand has settled, I will lay slabs, repoint the remains of the side walls and the massive gable, and create a patio area. Over the coming months and years we will build a stone archway where part of the side wall has fallen down, and fit a heavy, much-studded oak door with huge hinges contrived to creak satisfyingly each time we enter our peaceful retreat. In the centre of the patio, we will build a perfectly proportioned ornamental fish pond, with water pumped to and from the millstream, and illuminated by an underwater spotlight. Strings of tasteful fairy lights will be draped across the old gable end, and giant earthenware pots will line the restored walls. When all is done, we shall have a secret garden of order and tranquillity, contrasting satisfyingly with the natural wildness all around.

But every journey, I remind them, starts with but a single step. And that step awaits us now. Before we take it, I thank all my friends for their efforts in the long days ahead as they labour so hard to help Madame Donella and I make our dream a reality.

My eloquent description is met with a smattering of applause, a shuffling of feet and a long silence as my friends consider the amount of work and expense involved in building a formal and useless garden in the middle of thousands of hectares of traditional farming land. They are too polite to comment, except for René, who loudly queries the point and purpose of fitting a gate when there is not even a roof to deter the most incompetent burglars. He also questions the sanity of buying and installing a water pump when we will have several thousand litres an hour cascading into the mill pond a few metres away as soon as he has borrowed Mr Pigeon's *source*. He falls silent, however, when Donella brings up the subject of the tombstone barrier he has yet to fix, and turns his attention to organising the workforce into suitable teams and shift patterns.

*　*　*　*　*

In spite of recent experiences, I am still amazed at the way my friends deal with a challenge which would daunt a gang of much younger and fitter Irish groundworkers. Economical with movement and seemingly casual in their steady attack on the sand monster, these men with a combined age of several centuries fill a wheelbarrow to overflowing with no more than a dozen swings of the shovel, and take it in turns to push it along a scaffolding plank and into the pit. They rest often to straighten backs, spit on hands and mock their companions' efforts, but return to the task with renewed vigour in moments. In barely an hour, they have made a noticeable impression on the sand pile, and have established an easy rhythm. At this rate, we may even complete the operation before darkness falls. We have been lucky with the weather as the morning sun is warm upon our backs, and René is actually threatening to take one of his coats off.

I am ferrying armfuls of cold beer from the feed bag larder in the river, and Donella is preparing lunch in the mill as an old Citroën van with a corrugated tin roof rattles down the track. The inhabitants step out, and an orgy of handshaking, cigarette lighting and bantering commences. Hubert has arrived with Jackie the fisherman, and we gather round the back of the van to unload a dozen sloshing dustbins. Hubert explains that his friend has been out early, and the bins are full of *gardon* and other small fish which will be at home in our ponds, with no fear of human predators. He looks deliberately at our estate manager as he says this, and I begin to believe I may have misjudged him and his motives on our first meeting.

Our fleet of wheelbarrows are taken out of service, loaded with the bins and the long trek to the big pond begins. In a touching gesture, Hubert invites Donella to launch her replacement stock into the waters, and I notice how he thoughtfully steadies her with a thick arm around her waist as she leans out from the bank and releases the silvery cascades. Recovering from the shock, the fish gather in a precise formation and dart off to investigate their new home. Donella announces that luncheon is ready, and we retire to dine outside the mill.

*   *   *   *   *

The long lunch has gone even better than my wife had dared hope. Except for René, who is rarely seen to eat in public and is rumoured by his critics in the village to live almost entirely on drink, all our guests have praised the excellence of the *repas d'affaires*. Donella has excelled herself, especially with the main course, which was young pigeons in farm cider. Marcel is particularly pleased that she has used his cider in the ingredients, though René makes a formal complaint about our incessant waste of JayPay's best *calva* on cooking, when Mr Janne's newest bottling would have served adequately well. The case of burgundy left by Jean-Marie has been declared first rate. I have presented Jackie with a bottle of twelve-year-old malt in appreciation of his gift, and he has insisted that it is immediately opened and shared by the company. The extra-strength Somerset cider I have brought to the feast has been declared more than fit to drink, and the river larder is running low on bottled beer. Hubert has contributed a brace of his precious bottles of special reserve *calva*, and Marcel is moved to admit that it almost matches his best vintage for smoothness. As we relax in the early afternoon sun, I sense that we are being watched, and Donella points to where our skinny squirrel is looking enviously from a sycamore tree by the entrance to the copse. The remains of our meal has also attracted the attention of the bird community, who become ever bolder as they dart to pick up morsels of *baguette*, Mrs East's home-made Normandy apple tart and Safeway's extra-fruity Dundee cake. I look at my watch and the sand mountain, and decide that we have done enough for the day; it would be wrong to disturb the moment and break the mood of quiet contentment. Jackie, however, has other ideas. The talk has turned to past feats of labour, and he is stung by the Jolly Boys consensus that the youngsters in the region don't know the meaning of hard work. Having finished off the malt whisky, he claims that he and Hubert can shift as much sand in three hours as the JBC has achieved in the whole morning. René is very happy for him to try, though Hubert seems none too pleased at having been volunteered without consultation. But the wager is struck, and the contest is on. With the senior members of the workforce making themselves comfortable around the pile and Michel as referee, the relative youngsters set to with barrow and spades. Sharp comments on style, stamina and short barrowloads fly as fast as Jackie's spade, and Hubert loses several buttons on his shirt as he strains to keep pace with his partner and push the monstrous loads up the sloping scaffold plank. Rather than slow down, the pace quickens as the moments pass, and as the deadline arrives, the tally of barrow loads is only narrowly in the veteran team's favour. Hubert blames the English wheelbarrow for its poor design, turning circle and overall manoeuvrability, but Jackie concedes defeat more graciously. Of one accord, the entire workforce now joins in a final *blitzkrieg* on the rapidly diminishing pile. We toil solidly for a long hour before I call a halt for coffee and cigarettes all round to get our breath back.

As we relax at the table, another visitor arrives. The Travers family have owned the fields around La Puce since before the Terror, and there is talk locally of noble blood. This is not uncommon in France, especially in the case of an unmarried mother in the family tree after 1780. The theory goes that the hundreds of male *aristos* who escaped *Madame Guillotine* fled to remote parts of the country, changed their names but not their leisure pastime of impregnating local peasant girls. Ergo, any trace of illegitimacy at about the right time enables the descendant to lay claim to noble ancestry. A relative of my wife recently traced the maternal side of her family back more than two centuries, and to the delight of the village found that Donella is distantly French, and that an ancestor in Guigamp had not been married on the birth of her son in 1792. The villagers are naturally disappointed that her aristocratic lineage has been marred by the Brittany connections, but some French blood is better than none.

Mr Travers is said to be a millionaire. His tractor and other important personal possessions are not the trappings of a wealthy man, though this factor, as in any rural area, could be evidence for or against the allegation. After reserved greetings all round and a perplexed frown as he obviously wonders why I and half the village are burying tonnes of perfectly good sand, we get down to business. He has come to tell me of a serious problem. One of my trees has fallen into one of his fields, and represents a great danger to his cattle.

Leaving the workforce to see off the remnants of the sand mountain, we go to investigate.

Climbing the steep slope leading from the ford across the river up to where his elevated fields run alongside Hunters Walk, I see that we have lost one of the giant beech trees lining the western boundary between La Puce and the rest of France. The ownership of these trees has always been a point of contention, as René explained when we first took possession of the property. They line a steep bank rising to Mr Travers' land, and the precise position of their sprawling and exposed roots determines to whom they belong. If they are wholly visible as far as the bottom of the bank, the particular tree under examination is mine. If the roots surface from more than half way up the slope, they belong to my neighbour. If somewhere in between, we each own a vertical half of the tree. As far as I can make out, the law as it is understood and agreed locally is similar to the regulations regarding party walls in England since the Great Fire of London. Broadly, the owner may do what he likes with his side, providing it does not affect the integrity of the other side. Even Norman farmers have not found a way to cut a tree vertically down the middle and leave their neighbour's half flourishing, but there is a cunning device commonly employed by those seeking long-term firewood supplies. Leading me to a nearby field during an early lesson in *bocage* feud tactics, René had shown me where great slabs of wood were missing from the trunk of an otherwise healthy oak. The excuse had been to create a flat surface on which to staple a length of barbed wire marking the division of properties. In fact, said René, it was done to kill the tree. Eventually, the great oak would die from the massive wound and crash to the ground. The neighbour could then claim that it was a natural death and take his share of the wood.

Closely examining our fallen beech, I see that nature rather than malice is the guilty party. The core is rotten, and it has obviously succumbed to a recent south-westerly.

Removing his greasy cap and lowering his head as if paying his last respects to the deceased, Mr Travers declares himself greatly distressed by the problems the fall has caused him. There is now a large gap in the *bocage*, he explains, and his cattle could force their way through and fall to their doom down my bank and into my river. Something must be done. Rather than get into detailed examination and analysis of the precise position of the root holes, I accept responsibility, but have by now learned a little about negotiations of this sort. I look resigned, walk about a bit and make a few heavy sighs. I will, I say, ask René to organise a tractor to tow the tree away in the morning. Then he will repair the gap with barbed wire. This will cost me a great deal of money, but I am willing to pay to avoid any bad feeling between us. The tree will, of course, provide me with firewood for the whole winter, but at quite a price. From his expression, I can see that my ploy is working. Mr Travers puts his cap on and takes it off again for a while, and continues to regard the tree like a detective at the scene of a particularly messy murder. He then examines the corpse intently, kicks it, rips off a piece of bark and crumbles it in his fist. It is obviously, he says, very dead and will burn away in seconds.

156

It will make for very expensive firewood. He has a better idea. If he asks his son to bring the tractor and drag the tree across the gap, it will serve as an adequate barrier. I will not be put to the great expense of employing René nor risk being sued when he doesn't fit the barbed wire for months and a cow falls to its death. Would this, *p'tet*, be a suitable solution to our mutual problem?

I consider the offer for the obligatory ten minutes and agree. We shake hands on the deal and I return to the mill, pleased at how well I handled the encounter. I don't remember ever seeing any cattle going in to that field, and they would have to be driven past the door of the mill to reach it, but nevertheless feel satisfied with the outcome. I have, after all, just taken on a rural Norman negotiator of Mr Travers undisputed class and come away with the shirt still on my back.

At the workplace, the sand pile has gone, and so has the hole in the ground.

The team is celebrating quietly at the table in front of the mill, while Marcel fixes the sticky lock on our new front door, using a broken sickle blade as a screwdriver.

Once again I wonder at the contradictions in the Cotentinese character that the day's activities have so clearly exampled. Notoriously close with their money, they will use all their country wiles and ways to win an argument or preferably an extra few francs. But, when a friend has need of their help, they will labour all day for a meal and a few bottles of beer.

In the countryside, as René often remarks when not pricing a job for us, time is cheap and good friends are valuable.

June 22nd:

I have come up with an idea which may well make our fortune.

Over recent months, Victor the Volvo's interior has become increasingly noxious, yet when I opened the door this morning, the usual odour of stale cigarettes, wet socks and horse manure (for my wife's vegetable patch) had been overcome by a more pungent but not unattractive single aroma. Further investigation revealed a garlic bulb which went missing *en route* from the supermarket some weeks ago, the bouquet of which must have been activated by the fierce heat of recent days. With the cost of one of those revolting tree-shaped deodorisers running at three times that of a whole string of garlic, we could be on to a real winner by marketing an appealingly packaged La Puce Natural Car-O-Fresh Clove to all francophiles and motoring foodies.

Desert Storm Pigeons in Cider

1. *Ask someone who knows how to dress and truss some formerly young pigeons*
2. *Brown them in some hot butter, then season and add thyme and bay*
3. *Pour some calva over, and set it on fire*
4. *Cover and cook for half an hour, then keep warm*
5. *Add farm cider to the meat juices and boil for half a cigarette*
6. *Add some more butter away from heat*
7. *Pour juice over pigeons and garnish with slices of baked cider apples*

Mrs East's Apple *Tarte*

1. *Mix some yeast with warm milk*
2. *Add liquid to flour, melted butter, oil and salt*
3. *Rub together till workable, then leave for two slow glasses of wine*
4. *Butter a tart tin and line with the pastry*
5. *Peel and thickly slice some apples, leaving out the core and seeds*
6. *Mix more flour with ground almonds, caster sugar, cinnamon and butter*
7. *Flavour with calva*
8. *Arrange the apple slices in the tin and cover with the almond mixture*
9. *Bake for another two glasses of wine, and serve with crème fraîche*

July 1st:

Today is a big day, as we officially move into the mill cottage.

It is Sunday, and we are to host a small *soirée* for the friends who have helped us complete the restoration. We have still to find a tenant, but my wife is steadily working her way through the recently separated members of the local British contingent. Sadly, it is a long list.

We start out early for Bricquebec to pick up supplies for this evening's celebration.

The PMU betting shop is busy when we call in to see if we have won the Lottery. It still seems strange to see people drinking cold beer and *pastis* at bacon and eggs time, but we are adapting well to the tradition. In the *patisserie* across the road, Madame is doing a roaring trade in the selections of sweetmeats and chocolates her husband has been making through the night. Boxed and wrapped as only the French can package a small gift, they will be ceremonially handed over by sons, lovers and guilty husbands before a family lunch which will drift lazily into evening.

Our next stop is the *Café de Paris*, where Freddo is enjoying the start to his most profitable and therefore favourite weekly session apart from market day. He interrupts a story about his latest hunting expedition to ask if I would like a few dozen trout for the *soirée*. He has been out with Pierrot, and there is obviously a glut of fish throughout the town. In the square outside, the usual couple of farmers haggle over another tatty ewe as it stares myopically from the back seat of an even more dishevelled saloon. Meanwhile, the town youths are performing their early morning Sunday ritual of screaming by on souped-up *mobylettes* for the entertainment of spectators at the tables surrounding the square.

At the bar, René and Mr Maurice are enjoying a Sunday outing with Bernard, Madame Ghislaine's partner. An otherwise handsome man, he bears the constantly harassed frown of someone knowing he should not be enjoying himself, and also that his partner will ensure he will pay the full price for his pleasure. I call for a round and check that my friends will be arriving in good order for the *soirée*. René grudgingly promises to wear his best *bottes*, and Mr Maurice offers to bring a special jar of raspberry cola *calva*. Bernard looks at his watch and says he is in town to buy a box of chocolates for Ghislaine to make up for an unspecified misdemeanour of last evening. Along the bar, a large *gendarme* is already on his second bottle of Freddo's specially imported muscadet, and looks set in for the day.

I remark to our host that the policeman looks a little unsteady on his feet, but Freddo says it is alright, as he has his official motor cycle outside for the journey home. As usual, the talk around us concentrates on yesterday's sports results, whose car was seen outside whose house in the early hours, and who nearly won the national lottery. It is very like a Sunday lunchtime session in any pub in Britain, only a lot earlier.

An hour later, we make our farewells, shake hands all round and offer to give Bernard a lift back to the village. He refuses, orders another drink and explains he has still to buy his gift for Madame Ghislaine, who will be very upset if he is not back in good time for lunch. We all know that the patisserie will have sold out of chocolates by now, and that Bernard will be late for lunch and will look even more harassed at the evening *soirée*.

July 2nd:

It is a little before three o'clock in the morning. We are sitting beside the new pond, which is full to the brim and holding its level now that the surrounding land is waterlogged. René has still not fixed the tombstone barrier, so we have no running water, but my wife is working on him. As I break out the tomato soup while trying to hold the torch steady with my teeth, she is tempting some newly domiciled *gardon* with the remnants of the buffet from the party, which has only recently concluded. The legendary Cotentin wind has gone to bed, and the surface of the pond is as smooth and shiny as silk.

The *soirée* has been an unqualified success, and even Bernard seemed to enjoy himself. Our guests did their duty and trooped around the mill, admiring the stained beams and whitewashed walls, horse brasses and giant bath. Most were obviously wondering why an apparently sane couple would spend so much time and effort on creating a home from what had been a cattle byre for the last fifty years, but are far too polite to ask. Luckily, nobody expressed familiarity with the stove, and Madame Christian the Goat has invited us to visit her for an intensive training course in its proper maintenance and use.

René has promised to fix the barrier later today, and find us a chimney pipe so that we can have a test run on the stove before the winter.

Madame Ghislaine has presented us with a wall plate which roughly translates as 'Welcome to our home; it's not much, but it's ours'.

Marcel shyly presented a box of light bulbs from a past delivery, and Donella was deeply moved to see that he had painstakingly painted each one with coloured sheep marker to make fairy lights for our secret garden.

The highlight of the evening was the mayoral cutting of a ribbon across the door. John seemed in an unusually reflective mood all evening, and eventually took me to one side to say he will be retiring earlier than originally announced. He will see the summer through, then leave his farm at the beginning of September. There seems no point in staying on till Christmas and the official retirement date, and he has much to do. There are his responsibilities at the Patton orchard, and all the distant friends to visit in their new car. He has talked with Solange, and both feel it will be best to make the break before the deadline.

Taking my hand, he thanked me for my friendship, and said he hoped that our business relationship has been to my satisfaction. With my permission, he would continue to honour his obligations to La Puce, and keep the hedges trimmed and the gates in good order. Perhaps, as we have already discussed, I would be kind enough to allow him to visit every week to continue our friendship.

I reminded him of our contract, and promised there will never be another tenant in the top fields in his lifetime.

*   *   *   *   *

As we sit and watch the mist above the water swirl and dance in the torch beam, we see a flash of silver and hear a satisfied splash. All, apart from constant money worries, is good within our little world. The endless cycle of nature moves on, and our first full summer at La Puce is approaching full bloom.

July 13th:

A stimulating and unusually interesting morning crossing, as we fell in with the company of other serial French property restorers.

Arriving at Portsmouth ferry port for the morning sailing, we joined the queue and passed the time by playing our usual game. The scoring system is variable, but the rules rigid. Taking it in turns, we study the vehicles lined up at the quayside, categorise the types inside, and invent a story explaining why they are here and where they are going. If particularly bored during the crossing, we may track down some of the more atypical travellers, and shamelessly eavesdrop to learn their secrets.

Obvious holidaymakers are of low interest and no point value. International drug smugglers or fleeing murderers earn a big bonus, or would if we could prove their status. A classic example of a low-scoring crossing would be a summer glut of thirtysomething men with red spectacles, new Volvo estates and neurotic wives. They are all called Simon and Cassandra, are ill-at-ease in their new and expensive casual clothing and spend their time wearily nagging two fretful and sullen children called Guy and Amelia. They will either have paid a king's ransom for a *gîte* holiday or are going to freeload with expatriate friends in the south, and despite what they later tell their friends in a Fulham wine bar will only be truly happy when they have boarded the return ferry.

Caravan tourers and booze-cruising van owners are obviously not worth counting in our game. Of much more interest to us are the owners of battered vehicles, laden to the springs with bizarre combinations of furniture and household goods which, to the untrained eye, hardly seem worth the effort of strapping on the roof rack.

Like us, visiting property owners all seem to be taking part in a competition to determine who can carry the most heavy and dangerously placed loads. Normally, Victor is a clear winner, but today he was comparatively lightly burdened with a second-hand greenhouse, two dozen paving slabs and a selection of giant earthenware plant pots from the Philippines. They are shipped over by a taxi-driver friend who owns half a house in Manilla, and spends his holidays in the jungle overseeing the manufacture of exotic pottery turned on old car wheels. The samples are destined for the yard at *Brument-Clot,* and if they sell we shall split the difference with Robert and Christiane Simon. It seems a tortuous way of earning a few pounds, but every centime we can make will help us prolong our time in Cotentin.

On this crossing and in the dangerous load competition, we were hopelessly outclassed by a fellow traveller in a Lada camouflaged with more than two dozen stripped pine doors hung carelessly over the windows as well as balanced recklessly on the rackless roof. Anxious to know whether he has a very large property across the Channel or is a hopeless door fetishist, we struck up a conversation on the car deck, and learned he is actually a former policeman from the home counties who has hit upon a winning scheme to subsidise his pension and the upkeep of his house in Brittany.

Finding out to his cost that a new and bland lightweight interior door at his local *bricolage* cost around £100 and that nearly all French properties described as in some need of restoration don't have them, he now runs a booming export business. Every month, he scours the demolition sites and skips of affluent southern England, salvaging discarded doors and taking them to a dip and strip centre, from where they emerge interestingly distressed and free of their layers of gloss paint.

Our enterprising new friend then ships the doors over and

sells them through his regional freesheet publication to other Britons at half the price of a standard and inferior French door. Business is so good, he confided, that next month he will be bringing over a complete vat and the necessary chemicals to set up operation in his back yard, with British couples coming from far and wide for strip'n'swap parties. Before parting, we added his contact details to our list, and retired to the bar to consider the value of stealing his idea. He has obviously cornered the market in Brittany, but there could be an opening for a similar service for Normandy, sited at La Puce. Better yet, we could reverse the process, as half the solid oak craftsman-built and undervalued dining tables in our region are disguised beneath sheets of starburst plastic veneer and layers of greenhouse paint. Stripped and cleaned up, they would fetch a small fortune in any twee English antique shop.

In the bar, we fall into conversation with a number of owners, marked out by their weatherbeaten faces and characterful working clothes. Like us, they have no need to wear their paint-stained body warmers and tattered denims before even getting off the boat, but they like to show that they are not mere amateur holidaymakers or trippers. We exchange details of useful insults we have picked up in our different regions, and I ask if they know exactly why we are dubbed *rosbifs* by the French. When we first started coming to France, I thought that we were as usual way ahead on the insults front. For centuries, we had been calling our nearest continental neighbours 'froggies' at the very mildest, and the best response they could come up with was to name us for our national dish. It was René who took great satisfaction in explaining that *rosbif* is actually a derisive reference to the appearance of normally pale English faces and bodies after unaccustomed exposure to the southern sun. And the French, he reminded me with spiteful relish, like their beef pink to bleeding.

Normally, we expatriots studiously avoid each other on French soil, but the boat is always a good opportunity to exchange useful information and anecdotes. As usual there is a classic *fosse septique*

165

bore, and, before we can escape he manages to whip out a folder and talk us through his collection of snapshots of each step of the installation of his septic tank in the Charente. Thankfully, before getting into full flow, he is roundly trumped and silenced by a jolly couple who casually mention that, sited in the Auvergne, they had to use dynamite to blast through the volcanic crust and make a suitable hole for their tank.

The operation went precisely to plan, they say, except that the blast blew all the windows out of the house next door, which belongs to their mayor. But there was no comeback, as it had been he who had set the charges. The explosion, they add, finally beating the bore into sullen submission, also disturbed a coven of hibernating whip snakes, who immediately went into a frenzy of precipitous mating.

The anecdotes now evolve naturally into a general discussion on the problems of sewage disposal, as virtually every owner will at some stage have to confront the issue. Experiences and tales told over the years have led me to suspect that a great many owners who fondly imagine that they have an efficient drainage system may have nothing but a very expensive hole in the ground. Our case seems typical, with the installation of the plastic tank taking place in our absence, and the only evidence of its existence being a lot of disturbed earth at the alleged site, plus the assurance of René that he had fitted the largest, most sophisticated and therefore costly tank available. So far, we have had no obvious problems, but each spring a crop of the most exotic and evil-smelling plants appear above the tank's reported resting place. Donella looked them up in her Culpepper, and thinks they may be stinkweeds, but they seem far too large, and are in any case totally the wrong colour.

*   *   *   *   *

Arriving at Cherbourg, we make straight to La Puce and discover that we are landlords, and the sand mountain is back.

René is bearded in his caravan, and tells us that he ordered the new load at a special seasonal discount, and there will be barely enough to construct the reinforced cement terrace outside the mill which we need to put a respectable distance between the building and the moles which tunnel in the front garden like crazed prison camp escapees. He will start work on the *terasse* later that day, immediately after he has finally fixed the barrier. He also informs us somewhat resentfully that Madame Lynn and Charlie the dog have taken up residence in the farmhouse.

Until recently, Lynn Wooster and Graham Braye were our nearest English neighbours, and had spent two years painstakingly restoring a large house just outside St Jacques de Néhou.

Unfortunately, there has been a parting of the ways. The house is now in danger of being repossessed and Lynn has been left homeless. After arriving to employ his skills in treating and preserving ancient timber, Graham's business has failed, the debts have mounted, and he is now living elsewhere.

It is a familiar but always tragic story, and one which haunts us every day.

We often drive past their former house on the way to Bricquebec, and witness how nature is steadily taking its revenge on the property. To see all those days, weeks and years of effort and expense wasted is a truly depressing experience for us. How the thousands who put all their hopes and money into the fabric of an eventually ruined dream must feel is hardly conceivable, and an experience we must not allow ourselves to endure.

The irrepressible Lynn and Charlie combination are now getting by as agents for English owners in the area. For the past few months she had been living a nomadic life, cutting grass, receiving and cleaning up after paying guests and generally giving absent owners peace of mind. As she was weary of living out of her car and we are now settled in the mill, Donella has come to an arrangement where Lynn will take over the farmhouse at a modest rent. All parties involved except René are happy with the arrangement, especially Charlie, who now has a ten-acre back garden. Our estate manager seems to think that Lynn has been moved in to spy on him, and he does not get on with Charlie. I attempt to mend bridges by presenting him with his monthly bottle of whisky, and he unbends enough to offer me a drink and ask if I have heard the rumours about the mayor's retirement. Already, he says, there have been enquiries from local farmers about renting the fields at La Puce, and he is negotiating for the best price and terms. I explain that I have told the mayor that we will not be replacing him, but that I would like René to start thinking about stocking the remaining fields with our own animals. He shows immediate interest, and we sit overlooking the water meadow with a notepad and pencil to begin discussions on how I can be the only farmer in the Cotentin to make a profit.

*   *   *   *   *

This afternoon, we are to visit Haye-du-Puits for our regular browse at the *Bonnes Affaires* depot. With the complete absence of second-hand shops in the region, the depot is an exchange centre for everyone with household items to sell and those in search of a bargain buy.

In the cavernous warehouse, an ever-changing jumble of antiques and junk reaches to the leaking roof, with the price tags including a modest commission for the operators. It is a fascinating place for browsing, and hard to resist snapping up older and more unusual items which would be three times the price in Britain. We are in need of a bedside table for the mill, though will probably return with a carved walking stick or art deco clock with missing pendulum.

Before leaving, we take our traditional walk around the land to see that all is well.

The tombstone barrier is now almost horizontal on the river bed, but a build-up of snagged tree branches, silt and other debris has formed a makeshift dyke, and water is trickling through the pipe into the new pond. I reach the bank in time to secrete a dead *gardon* before my wife stumbles upon it, and looking around, she is pleased with the way nature is reclaiming its own. Already, healthy grass is growing on the earth banking and the weeds and water plants are flourishing. Triple Salco is performing a demanding sequence of exhibition dives from the cairn of stones in the middle of the pond, and wild flowers discovered flourishing in our Slough of Despond include bogbean, spotted orchids and arrow-headed water plantain.

We walk up to the Travers field by the ford, and I see that our fallen beech tree has disappeared. In its place and keeping the non-existent cows from danger is a neat line of barbed wire nailed to gaping wounds on three other beeches. I make a mental note to drive past the Travers home on the way to Haye-du-Puits and see if I recognise any recent additions to the gigantic woodpile there.

Madame Lynn and Charlie are not at the farmhouse when we call, and we decide to move some tools and gardening equipment from the bike shed down to their new home at the mill. A low and totally unrestored stone building opposite the farmhouse, the bike shed has two ancient oak doors, each riddled with what we originally took to be the advanced stages of attack by giant woodworm. Further investigation showed that they had merely been used for shotgun practice over the years, presumably in the absence of any living or moving target. Above each door is a massive stone lintel which has been cunningly set at average forehead height. During our relatively short time at La Puce, the rough stone slabs have claimed at least a dozen victims, and a livid scar above the eyebrows has become a membership badge for our Real France package guests.

Although René has reminded us on many occasions of the good money we could demand for bed and breakfast facilities in the bike shed, we decided from the start that it should remain exactly as it has been for the past two centuries. Everything else at La Puce has been replaced or restored, and we wanted to have just one area left as it was, at least partly to remind us of what we had achieved elsewhere. The beams inside are rotten, there is no power, the floor is baked earth, the tiles leak and the stone walls are mostly held together with ivy, but we find it full of charm and character. It is also home to a family of voles, so Donella would not countenance improvements anyway, regardless of the going rate for B & B in the region.

Remembering to duck, we push our way inside and find that someone has fitted a carpet. Closer inspection reveals that the carpet is actually a healthy growth of blanched grass. A well-gnawed seed sack shows that the vole family has been busy, and the dirt floor and damp atmosphere has provided a perfect environment for an inside lawn that any British gardener would be proud to claim. In one corner and nestling comfortably on top of my plumbers tool bag, we find the tiny nest. Without even putting my case to Donella, I resign myself to the expense of a new set of stilson wrenches, and we tiptoe out, leaving the property in the hands of its contented tenants.

*   *   *   *   *

The depot at Haye-du-Puits is busy, with a score of locals picking through the sometimes bizarre and always wildly contrasting selection of items, which today include a king-size divan in leopard skin finish, with stereo loudspeakers set in the sheepskin-bound headboard, jostling for space with a genuine 19th-century solid mahogany Napoleon bed. The divan is priced at slightly more than the bed, but the depot owners know which will appeal most and sell quickest to local buyers. Apart from the bedside table and against all the odds, I am hoping to find a complete length of stove piping complete with brackets and bends, but settle for an Edwardian parasol in mint condition which seems a snip at 100 francs. Donella likes the look of a chandelier made from an old wagon wheel, but it is full of worm, and I do not want to establish a new colony at the mill. During our tour of inspection, we meet a pleasant English couple who are looking for a front door for their cottage on the coast. I give them the telephone number of the Brittany dip'n'stripper, and they respond by promising to keep an eye out for lengths of stove piping. We visit a nearby café, and Donella drinks half a cup of lemon tea before confiding that it tastes a little weak, even by Cotentinese standards. I look inside and see that the metal teapot contains nothing but hot water and a slice of lemon. Donella does not want to make a fuss and says the surly patron must have forgotten to add the teabag, but I am not so sure. As we leave, he says something to the barmaid, who giggles, but I do not leave a tip so have the last laugh.

*   *   *   *   *

On the way home we stop off at *Boueve et Fils* and have some luck.

In the ironmongery section I find a single elbow bend, and a metal chinese hat which Mr Boueve the elder assures me will protect the open end of my chimney pipe from the worst downpour Cotentin can provide. When I ask about piping for the stove, he looks at me as if I am a madman, and explains that it is high summer. Stove pipes, like mushrooms, will appear in the autumn. I think I will have to visit the *bricolage* in Valognes. It is a twenty-mile round trip, but the nearest thing to a good DIY shop in the region, and I want to have the stove up and running in good time for roasting the first chestnuts from the tree by the wooden bridge.

Rolling down the track, we are amazed to see that René has made a start on the terrace in front of the mill. He has already staked out the area with split logs held in place by sharpened branches, and introduces me to a friend and his wheelbarrow, who are scaling the new sand mountain the hard way. Eric, René tells us, is the star football player for AFC Negreville, but is otherwise temporarily unemployed and homeless, so is moving in with our estate manager till he can be found new lodgings. Though without a home, Eric owns a metal disc grass cutter, which makes him a man of some substance. He will clear the farmhouse garden in a trice, and his rates are most reasonable. Other important events have unfolded, and René has a favour to ask. A relative of Christian The Goat is to be married next week, and the couple need somewhere to spend their wedding night. There is no suitably romantic room for their nuptials in the immediate area, and the hotel at Bricquebec charges a fortune for a night in the bed which Queen Victoria allegedly used. All the village knows about the

171

lace-trimmed marriage bed in the guest bedroom at La Puce, and we would win many friends if we would allow the young couple to spend their first night together there. We also owe Christian a favour in return for allowing his goats to keep our scrubland in check. René will see to all the arrangements, and we will hardly know they have been there. I promise to clear it with Madame Lynne as she is now our official tenant, and after asking René not to cut any more branches from the chestnut tree by the wooden bridge, we leave them to their labours.

July 14th:

Our main task for the day is to clear the waters of the big pond. Although the nearest trees are twenty metres away, the fierce autumnal winds continually blow dead leaves across the water meadow and on to the surface. Over the winter months they sink and form a layer of sludge at the bottom, making the water murky and unattractive. Now we have more than one fish to look at, we intend to tackle the problem with an old country trick told us by René. All we have to do is sink bales of barley straw in the pond, and somehow, they will attract all the suspended detritus. Although I don't understand the physics involved, it's worth trying. If it works we will be able to follow and perhaps frustrate the exploits of the crayfish gang during this hot period, when they are at the height of their murderous activity.

Alongside the caravan, we find the barley straw which René has purchased on our behalf. Disappointingly, it is not woven tightly in rustic string netting, but sealed in modern plastic bags.

With due reverence and respect for our boat squatters, the upturned dinghy is moved for the first time this year and prepared for launching. After the big pond had bedded in, I bought the boat from a fisherman who operates from Portsmouth docks, and has a brisk trade in buying and selling used marine equipment. A shifty little man, not unlike a dead halibut in skin tone and features, he is the only fisherman I know with a sallow complexion, as he seems to work purely at night. When I made contact with him in a dimly-lit waterside Portsmouth pub and said I was seeking a dinghy, he said he had nothing at the moment, but asked for details of the sort of boat I was looking for. Within the week I received a call to say that he had coincidentally just got his hands on the very craft I was after, but I must pick it up that evening, and well after dark. The deal was done and money changed hands before he slid away into the night from Portsmouth Hard, leaving me to heft the little craft on to Victor's roof rack. As I did so, I noticed that the mooring rope at the bow had been cut clean through, and wondered if my supplier might be a distant relative of our estate manager in Cotentin. Having got it safely out of the country, I painted the neat little skiff a suitable puce colour, and Donella inscribed its name on a piece of planking which I nailed firmly to the blunt end. Unfortunately, the nails went right through the hull, but they are well above the water line.

Having shifted *la puce d'eau* from her winter resting place, we are disappointed to see no more evidence of our lodgers than a series of small, perfectly round holes about an inch across. I think my wife was hoping to see the interior of a neatly kept little house, complete with miniature chairs gathered around a cheery fire like an illustration from *Wind In The Willows*, but she is at least content that some wild creature's family has been taking advantage of the shelter.

It is a moment's work to push the craft down the bank and scramble aboard. Donella throws me the first of the barley straw bags, and I paddle out, anchor at a suitable position, and push it over the side. At once, I detect a problem. There is air trapped inside the plastic covering, and the bag bobs happily on the murky surface. Offstage, a frog croaks encouragement as I lean over and stab at the bag with my single oar, but merely send it skimming away to the far bank.

I call for my wife to fetch a screwdriver, then I pursue the runaway bale and continue the attack. Eventually, I manage to puncture the tough plastic surface, and the bag settles fractionally lower in the water. By now, Reggie and Ronnie and a number of their gang have crawled up from the depths to see who has come on to the manor without their permission. A huge, brilliantly blue emperor dragonfly also arrives to settle on the prow of the *water flea* and enjoy the spectacle. On the far bank, I detect a movement in the rushes, and see that the feral cat has joined the crowd. Determined to have my way, I pursue the bag around the pond, spurred on by an excited medley of croaks, grunts and squeaks from my audience. Poking, slashing, stabbing and cursing, I finally make a big enough hole to insert the large stone which I have been using as an anchor. The bag promptly rolls over, and the stone drops out of the hole.

An hour or so later, all six bags have been torn apart, and their contents have spread themselves around the surface of the pond like a strawberry patch protected from the frost. Donella has also found the heap of netting sacks meant to contain the straw where René had left them behind a fresh molehill under the caravan. I paddle wearily back to the jetty, cutting a temporary swathe in the straw surface. At least the leaves will not be able to sink this autumn, and I have made a new friend in Douglas the dragonfly, who has followed my career with fascinated bemusement around the pond all day.

Outside the mill, we find a cow up to its knee joints in freshly laid concrete, and René setting about its hind quarters with a scaffolding plank. The cow's owner is vainly trying to wrest the plank away. Though his farm is two miles distant, Mr Sorrell owns a small field on the other side of our stream, and exercises his right of way to it every summer. There appears to be bad blood between the two men since I commissioned René to enquire about buying the field, and Mr Sorrell broke the unwritten rules by coming directly to me to negotiate. He is, according to the locals, an aspirant candidate for the Euro Green party, which would account for the way he seems to leave his land entirely to nature, and is so obviously concerned about the welfare of his cow.

Mr Sorrell now joins René and his cow in the wet cement, and the tug-of-war for possession of the scaffolding plank heats up. I and Donella enter the fray, and manage to calm the situation down. The cow is persuaded to leave the future terrace and stand in the ford for a hose down, while René and Mr Sorrell are invited into the mill to settle their differences over coffee and a large glass of scotch. The situation becomes much more amenable when Mr Sorrel sees the picture of me posing with the lookalike John Major, and I promise to ask our premier if he can put a good word in for my neighbour before the Euro elections.

July 15th:

It is St Swithin's day, and it is raining. Nobody at the Jolly Boys Club meeting seems surprised or particularly interested when I point out that, in England, we would now be in for another forty days and nights of wet weather. Old Pierrot follows me out to the *pissoir* for our usual private chat at the end of a meeting, and explains tactfully that, given the climate in Cotentin, rainfall statistics are not usually considered an unusual or stimulating subject for debate. As we zip up, he reminds me that it is anyway a well known fact that St Swithin was born in this *département,* and took the weather with him when he settled in England.

July 19th:

The day is not going well.

Donella has spent the morning on the big pond with a garden rake, but has only succeeded in moving the floating barley straw around the surface. She is most concerned that the covering will cut off sunlight and air to the fish, so I have been delegated to oxygenate the water.

Lacking an electric agitator as used by the professional trout pond owners, I park the *water flea* in the middle of the pond, then swirl the oar around as if hand blending an enormous batter mix. René has assured me that this will introduce bubbles of air into the pond, but it is very hard work and I become giddy as the boat reacts to my eccentric paddling and spins round on its axis. Douglas the dragonfly is fascinated and has not left my side, and the frog troupe have reached hysteria pitch. Resting from my labours, I see Christian The Goat striding across the meadow towards me. By the set of his shoulders I can see that he is not a happy man, and he loses no time in passing on the bad news. One of his animals has been found lifeless in the dry stream by the wooden bridge, and Christian has no doubt that the guilty party is Charlie the dog. I offer to buy him a replacement, but Christian is inconsolable. The goat was a favourite with his children, and they are too wise to be fooled by a ringer. We agree that I will visit his home that afternoon to discuss what is to be done, and he leaves without shaking my hand, which is a bad sign.

A little later, Madame Lynn appears in some distress.

She has also received a visit from Christian, and there have been harsh words about the alleged goat-worrying incident. This was immediately followed by the arrival of René, who had called to discuss accommodation arrangements for the wedding on Saturday. As she explains to us, she is quite happy for the couple to take over the master bedroom for the night, but is somewhat perturbed by the six old mattresses René has brought and positioned around the house. The wedding party is going to be much larger than expected, he says, and has claimed my permission for them to find shelter at La Puce. Since he left, several strangers have called at the house with their luggage, and checked that they will be sure to get the full English breakfast they have already paid for. I promise to investigate, and return to the comparative peace of the big pond.

*   *   *   *   *

My reverie in company with Douglas is disturbed by three small boys with large fishing rods. They ask me how the trout are biting, and I ask them why they wish to know. They explain that, as season ticket holders to the pond, they wish to complain to the management - i.e. Mr Ribet - about understocking. It has been a long time since they caught anything except the occasional *gardon*, a species which, of course, is virtually uneatable. I apologise for the poor sport, and promise to speak to my estate manager about upping the fish quota.

July 21st:

The wedding has taken place, and the grand concourse through Néhou has been voted one of the most memorable for years. Following tradition, the wedding party has spent the afternoon driving slowly round and round the village, with horns sounding continuously. Apart from a confrontation with a small herd of cows and a new member for the ditch of the month club, there have been no major incidents. The lead car was, as tradition also demands, driven by the best man chauffeuring the bride and groom. Rather than a string of tin cans trailing from the back bumper, it had an old-fashioned besom broom fixed to the roof. At the reception in the bar at Néhou, I compliment Madame Ghislaine on the magnificence of the wedding feast, and ask if she will give me the recipe for the apple dumplings, which are not at all like my mother used to make. She does not see the joke, and questions how they could be as my mother has only recently become a visitor to the Cotentin. She writes it down anyway. As she composes, I recall the besom on the car and mention reading of old plantation marriages in the French-speaking southern states of America. The wedding ceremony involved the couple stepping over a broomstick to confirm their union, and I wonder if there is any connection with today's display and procession of the old-fashioned broom. Madame Ghislaine snorts at my fanciful notions as she refills my glass, and says that the besom strapped to the car is actually a symbol to show who is really in charge of a French marriage, and also that a broom has been bought and is ready for offensive action if necessary. It might not appear so to the outsider, she adds whilst directing a look which could open a mussel at Bernard, who is dallying with a pretty bridesmaid, but in Cotentin it is the women who wear the real trousers. I know what she means, and it does seem that the more belligerent and swaggering the man, the more he lives in fear of his wife. The

177

boasts in the bar, the aggressive style of driving and the *braggadocio* all seem to be in direct contrast to what probably goes on behind closed doors.

Today, however, all the couples at the wedding feast are on at least outwardly cordial terms, and dressed for the occasion. There is hardly a pair of working boots in sight, and all flat caps have been left at home. And the men look just as smart. Severe haircuts have obviously taken place in kitchens all across the village, and Mr Maurice is sporting his best pair of flared jeans over a new pair of lightweight summer tights. René is obviously avoiding a confrontation over the mattress rental affair, and is said by Christian the Goat to be putting the finishing touches on the marriage bed and settling the happy couple in at La Puce. Christian is at our table, has thawed considerably since our last meeting, and is now prepared to discuss suitable damages and compensation for his recent bereavement.

The mayor has already made two speeches, one involving a very complicated but obviously earthy joke in patois that I could not follow, and Hubert is filming the occasion on his new video camera.

As the shadows from the gravestones in the churchyard opposite lengthen and before we settle down for the evening, I visit the facilities outside the *épicerie*, and am adjusting my dress as the mayor and Solange leave the party. Once again, I compliment them on their new car and John tells me he is looking forward to a trip to see an old army friend who now lives in Paris. Cautioning him to drive carefully, I tot up my intake for the day, and suggest to my wife that we would both be better for a slow stroll back to La Puce.

Night begins to fall in earnest, and bedding Victor down outside the bar, we take the short cut across the open fields behind the village. After four years, we now feel well-known enough to risk the journey across someone else's land, and all the owners are anyway at the wedding feast. In the distance, car horns start up and fade away in the direction of the farmhouse where René and Lynn await the paying guests' arrival, and we are alone in the tranquillity of a perfect summer evening. Beyond a wire fence, a cow lifts its head and regards us incuriously for a moment before returning to its business. A magpie has hitched a ride upon the back of a sheep in an adjacent field, and we both automatically bid it good day for luck. The bats are swooping low, and the full moon makes strange figures beneath the trees as we make the journey last.

The lights are blazing at La Puce as we arrive through Mr Margot's orchard. René is showing an elderly couple how the security lamps work by driving his *mobylette* in and out of the yard, and some local children are happily shying stones at the fairy lights around the patio. Madame Lynn has sensibly retired from the fray and left the revellers to it. Before following her example, we see a flickering light in the bike shed and look inside to discover three mattresses laid out on the grass carpet. The vole *famille* will have company tonight, and René has proven his point about the value of our guest annexe.

Down at the mill, all is tranquil. We take a torch and flask of minestrone soup and set off for the big pond. It is a clear night and a distant chorus of croaks indicate that love is in the air in other parts of our estate. There will be work to be done in the morning, with guests to see off and the farmhouse to be reclaimed, but for now, it is time to say goodnight to the more permanent residents at La Puce.

Madame Ghislaine's Apple Dumplings

1. *Peel and core some apples*
2. *Put some cinnamon and butter in the holes, and cook in a slow oven*
3. *Mix flour, butter, salt and a little water to make a dough*
4. *Make the dough into a ball, then flatten with a rolling pin*
5. *Repeat (4.) several times, then leave dough in cold place for one glass of wine*
6. *Roll out the pastry and cut out circles large enough for wrapping apples*
7. *Place apples on dough circles*
8. *Mix some redcurrant jelly with calva and pour over apples*
9. *Wrap apples in dough circles*
10. *Brush dumplings with egg yolk and criss-cross pastry with fork*
11. *Bake for two glasses of wine, then flambé with calva at the moment of serving*

August 2nd:

7am: It is far too hot to work, so I persuade my wife that we should down tools and go on safari. Instead of working as usual on one small corner of the land, we should spend a whole day exploring every square yard of it. We can take provisions, and draw up a route map which will take us to the furthest corners of our empire, ending up at the big pond for a campfire supper and singalong before sleeping for the first time in our fully-equipped caravan. We will even take drawing pads and pencils, and sketch and log every wild flower and tree on our journey, which will include tracing *le Lude* every inch of its winding way through our territory. Quite simply, I am proposing an adventure and expedition in the footsteps of Darwin, Cook and Livingstone.

My wife agrees after reminding me that at ten acres, La Puce is hardly in the league of the uncharted African interior, and goes off to hard boil some eggs. From the cooker, she vetoes the idea of sleeping in the caravan, and confesses under pressure that it is now the residence of the mouse colony which I had so callously banished from the mill cottage. We shall sleep under the stars, she says. It will be cooler, and we might even encounter the badger family out taking the midnight air.

8am: Suitably equipped, we start our long journey by crossing the wooden bridge, pausing for me to paint a word picture of the mighty torrent which will thunder down from the water meadow and into the mill pond when René has diverted our neighbour's distant *source.* We also see that the sweet chestnut trees shrouding the bridge are ripe with promise for the autumn harvest, and Donella makes a note on her pad to get to them in late September before the main onslaught of human scavengers begins. Arriving at the bottom of the sloping farmhouse garden, we set up camp alongside the goldfish pond for our first rest break. As we take stock, we see that our imported studs have been hard at work, and count over twenty tiny black infants vainly trying to swallow bemused insects at least twice their size. I pour the coffee and discover we have forgotten the sugar. I offer to undertake the hazardous journey back to base for supplies, but my wife says this will be breaking my own rules, and we must improvise. She remembers from her Culpepper that there is a wild flower which can be used as a sweetener, similar in appearance to deadly nightshade. I tell her not to bother to forage in the hedgerow beside us. If we become desperate, I feel it would be safer to fight a bumble bee for its nectar.

Much refreshed, we continue our journey and tramp through the grasslands and up the stepping stones to the vegetable patch, where it is clearly evident that my wife's plot is doing far better than mine. When my early potato crop was threatened by the April snow, Donella became more and more possessive of what was originally agreed to be my sole province, and the situation became so bad that we decided to call a truce and establish our own his'n'her plots. To ensure fair competition, we have both been planting seeds from the same packets at the same time, and there will be a grand vegetable show and weigh-in next month, with the mayor and Solange as judges. Already, it is clear from surface appearances that her crops are doing considerably better than mine. For some reason, the snails and pigeons seem to prefer my runner bean leaves to hers, and comparisons of our rival marrows put me in mind of my yearly sausage game with Big Freddo. From the start of our challenge, she has also spent far more time weeding and watering, and digging in the horse manure that she has sweet-talked Mr Janne into donating each month. I have taken a much more relaxed and organic approach and left nature to do its work, and it seems unfair that it has not paid off. I still expect the potato section to be a walkover in my favour, however. For the past month, I have been making late-night visits to pull up, inspect and carefully replace samples from her neat rows of Maris Pipers, and they do not seem to be doing at all well. I shall take a chance and leave mine permanently buried until the day of judgement.

From the vegetable patch, we return down the slope to the wooden bridge, and lower ourselves down the knotted rope to where the sunken mill pond gently stagnates in the shadow of the ancient gable end wall. Even Charlie the dog has not ventured into its murky depths, but I have already cleared out more than a ton of rubbish, which included the rusting frame of an old bike and, even in this isolated location, the inevitable supermarket shopping trolley. The ten franc piece was missing from its slot, so I suspect that René is the culprit.

We stand for a moment looking at the curved scar and gaping axle hole in the wall towering above us, and try to picture the mighty wheel working at full flood. Down here and sheltered from the ruined elevations at ground level, the centuries fall away and it is not difficult to hear wooden cogs turning, great stones inexorably grinding, and cart wheels rattling on the track as the miller schemed and sweated to skim off another few *sous* to join his secret hoard.

Back in the present, we shoulder our baggage and pick our way across the rocky surface of the dry river bed to the stone bridge. For the first time, we go under instead of over it, admiring the smooth symmetry of the arched roof above us, with not a centimetre showing between the hundreds of perfectly dressed and squared blocks of local stone. Built to take the weight of no more than a cartload of grain, it has withstood the test of our twelve-tonne lorryloads of gravel with ease.

Beyond the bridge, we enter swamp territory.

While we regularly clear the entire length of the *Lude*, we have left this section of the course of the dry river alongside the copse untouched. Over the years, fallen trees and branches have slowed and swelled the trickle from the water meadow, and now it forms an interesting and foul-smelling soup, its surface covered with dense weed and rotting vegetation. It makes an ideal breeding ground for a vast variety of insect life, and we often see quite large lizards basking contentedly beside its stagnant depths.

René has warned us that here there be water snakes and other varieties of deadly poisonous *serpent*, but we think he exaggerates.

We climb out of the dry river so as not to disturb the gently bubbling primeval ooze before us, and rest awhile in the heart of the roadside copse. For the moment, there are few species of fungi on display, mostly bracket growths on dead logs and the odd variety of early *mycenae* emerging from the deep layer of leaf mulch. In a few weeks, the fairy ring will appear close to where we sit, and Coco and Alain will be in serious competition for the choicest and most valuable specimens from the season's crop.

Pressing on, we leave the copse and journey to where *le Lude* leaves our land and passes beneath the D900 on its way to St Sauveur and the open sea. We wade across the clear waters, and take on the acre of wild scrubland that not even Christian's most hardy and rapacious goats dare to confront. Ferocious attacks with our plastic picnic knives having no effect, we bypass the hundreds of vicious bramble shoots waiting to feed upon our unprotected legs and climb back into the *Lude*.

Making steady progress, we soon cover the two hundred waded paces to the stone washing chute and, ignoring the ford to Hunters Walk, splash along the stream under a tunnel of hazel, larch, birch and beech branches to the grotto.

We are weary, and there is no better place for lunch.

1pm: Replete, we sit and watch the cascade tumbling into the wide basin built to avoid flooding when the miller had filled the reservoir field, opened the miniature lock gate and sent the *Lude* surging back *en route*. The artificial and stone-lined basin is not, of course, a real grotto, but roofed with branches and cool and tranquil on the hottest and most frustrating of days, it is a place of magic to us.

2pm: From the grotto, we cross the mill garden to the herb patch, then on to the middle pond. Triple Salco summons his troupe to put on a special display, but we apologise and move on. We have far to go before the day is done.

Carefully edging over the dizzy heights of Tombstone Bridge, we emerge on to Hunters Walk, and see a flash of tortoiseshell and teeth as our feral cat disappears with something furry wriggling helplessly in its mouth. My wife does not know whether to be dismayed at the loss of a resident, or pleased that the cat will dine well this afternoon. I hope that the victim is not our undernourished squirrel, in which case both parties will have had a bad day.

We stroll along the avenue of giant beech trees, stopping for a moment to pay silent tribute at the spot where, several years ago, we saw the last living grouse in all Cotentin. A little further along, we pause to wonder at the Hobbit Tree, a long-dead and skeletal oak that still stands firm against the Manche wind and local woodpile builders despite being almost completely hollow. The track rises steadily, till we come to the end of our terrain and stand to look at the miles of empty fields beyond.

It is a suitable place and time to take high tea, and we settle down upon the corpse of a fallen giant which will see us warmly through the coming winter. Providing, that is, I can find a chimney pipe for my period *poêle*.

4.30pm: We re-cross *le Lude* and squelch our way across the water meadow, my wife pointing out the wealth of wild flowers as I count the flag lilies and multiply each yellow splash by five pounds sterling. A rustic bridge conveniently created by a fallen maple leads to the overgrown and long-redundant cart track where my wife is convinced Badger Hall is located. My suggestion that, with a bit of luck, we may see a visiting Mr Toad arrive in his yellow weskit and motor car does not amuse, and we climb the sloping field to the road and the eastern boundary of La Puce. I try to spot the likely location of Mr Pigeon's *source*, and my wife says I am more likely to see the Toadmobile. She believes that the spring does not exist, and is a ploy by René to keep me sweet.

Deciding not to disturb my friend as it is not long after lunchtime, we leave his mobile home behind and soon reach the field next to the farmhouse, where Charlie the dog is in search of rabbits. I tell him he is wasting his time, and he bounds off in search of other diversions. After pausing to exchange the time of day with two of the mayor's steers, we wave to the balcony and a sunbathing Madame Lynn, and move on to count the wealth of tiny young apples in our orchard.

Anxious now to reach our destination, we briefly inspect the well, walk down the farmhouse garden slope and, ignoring the wooden bridge, climb the ancient retaining wall to return to the water meadow. Now we are nearly at our goal, and it is but a few steps to the big pond and journey's end.

5pm: The heat of the day is still firmly upon us, so we decide to leave bags and bedding packed, take our ease and enjoy the sights and sounds of a high summer afternoon in, on and around our own golden pond.

The entertainment starts with an aerial attack by a squadron of close formation swallows. Flying in from the sun, they wheel off individually to swoop down on the pond, re-fuelling with delicate dips of beak into water as they skim the placid surface. From sheer exuberance and just to show their skills, each pulls out of the low altitude flightpath at the last moment, coming closer to a head-on collision with the caravan roof on each sortie. In the wake of the adult wing comes an inexperienced juvenile, who consistently misjudges his speed and angle of elevation and splashes down heavily before gamely limping away to gain height for another attempt. As if irritated by this display of youthful impetuosity, the black duck crashes free of the long grass on the islet and quacking sourly, lumbers away to the relative peace of Hunters Walk.

While all this is going on, I spot a friendly dragonfly who appears to be helping an injured colleague from one clump of reeds to another. I then see that there are dozens of couples all gamely piggy-backing through the air, and my wife patiently explains that they are mating, and it is quite normal for them to do it at this time of year, in broad daylight and very publicly. I point out that Douglas the emperor dragonfly, who has come to sit with us, is obviously above that sort of thing. She says he is probably of British extraction, or just hasn't found a mate big enough to cope with him yet. If he, of course, is a he.

The *hirondelle* wing continues to make raiding passes on the big pond, and far above them, our kestrel arrives to see what all the fuss is about and study the teatime menu. On the far side of the pond, a single finch has ventured on to the landing platform of the bird table and is sorting through the remnants of our high tea. The Dundee cake seems to be finding favour, and he has sharp words with a grey wagtail come to join the feast. As if to show who is boss of the big pond in pecking order terms, Trevor suddenly rears from the water, snaps up an unseen morsel, and is gone with a twisting flash of pink and silver, and a slap that resounds across the water meadow. Annoyed at the disturbance, Reggie and Ronnie Cray and at least a dozen members of their mob emerge from their front doors and crawl menacingly through the shallows. They are obviously in search of a suitable victim so they can demonstrate who is really in charge of the local manor. After our long trek, I am sitting on the ramshackle jetty with my booted feet dangling in the water, and the cray gang obviously decide to make an example of my Happy Hikers. They swarm up the bank, and Big Ron takes a lump the size of a gobstopper out of my hi-impact water resistant welded seam sole as if it were butter. I withdraw my feet and placate the gang with a large piece of camembert, and become aware of a dead frog drifting into view from behind the island. It looks poignantly human stretched out flat on its back like a lifeless frogman. I try to distract Donella's attention but she has already seen it. Just as I prepare to console her, the creature draws up both knees, then almost casually straightening its legs, goes skimming at least a yard across the still water. It rests there a while, then repeats the process, in the manner of an oarsman in no hurry to make his way through a lazy afternoon on the river. Whatever naturalists might say about the error of relating animal behaviour to human activity, this frog is definitely sunbathing on its back and enjoying, like us, a carefree day away from the everyday worries of its own small world.

Now that Trevor has taken the lead and defied the cray gang, *gardon* begin popping up all around the pond, delicately breaking the surface to feed, then disappearing with hardly a ripple. On the far bank, the action is hotting up as news of the beano spreads, and more and more birds flock to the feeding table. We spot great and blue tits, bullfinch, goldcrests, a reed bunting and a tiny wren unconcernedly rubbing shoulders before a rustle in the long grass sends them careering off to the safety of the hedgerow. The feral cat is hungry again, and looking for a suitable dinner companion.

8pm: The feeding frenzy is over, and calm has returned to the big pond. The sun seems to have enjoyed our company so much that it is reluctant to dip below the *bocage* lining the far end of the water meadow. Donella is deep in *Tales of the Riverbank*, and I am gathering wood to make our camp fire, impatient for flickering flames, long shadows and thick bacon sandwiches.

10pm: At last, the dusk is stealing in to clear the way for night, and the bats appear. Where they spend the day we do not know, nor why they stay so little time with us. Perhaps, like early evening pub crawlers, they are doing the rounds to find the most lively and inviting place to settle for the night.

My fire is going splendidly, and I turn my mind to the mystery which has baffled philosophers, scientists and boy scouts alike for centuries; exactly why does bacon smell and taste so much better when cooked in the open air?

11pm: We are about to turn in when a shadowy figure looms out of the darkness.

It is René, come to see why we are reduced to cooking on an open fire. We persuade him to stay and finish off the cold bacon sandwiches, but he is more interested in the emergency rations of canned cider cooling in the shallows by the jetty.

1am: René has gone, and we are preparing to bed down beneath the stars. I have learned more about my friend in the last two hours than in the three years we have known him. Drawn out by the intimacy of our situation around the fire and at least half a gallon of extra-strength cider, he talked longer and more candidly than during any heavy session in the Bar Ghislaine. He has still not revealed much about his past life, but it has obviously been a hard one, and he has had to survive on his wits alone since a child. Towards the end of our conversation, I sensed that he would have liked to unbend further but, like the wild creatures all around us, he seems ever wary of revealing himself to a potential predator. Perhaps we will get on better after this encounter.

Despite the warmth of our meeting, the camp fire singalong was not a success. It is very difficult to translate the words and meaning of such classics as *Ging Gang Gooley Gooley* and *Green Grow The Rushes-O* to a Norman in a water meadow at midnight, especially after several cans of strong Somerset cider.

2am: Like most of the other residents at La Puce, we are settled down for the night, and have made ourselves as comfortable as possible with the materials to hand.

Moved by the romance of the moment, I bring up the subject of the dragonfly dances this afternoon, but my wife is not responsive. She says that the ground is too hard and the stars too bright, and we are within sight and sound of René's mobile home. Just because she loves animals, she is not going to act like one.

Eventually, I bid her a gruff goodnight, roll over and try to find a comfortable gap between the molehills.

August 3rd:

We have seen a wonderful sight, and one so rare in these parts that even René is impressed.

As if to confirm that he has finally approved of our work, a most important and exotic visitor arrived this morning as we sat at the big pond, recovering from our night in the open.

Scouting for dead wood to start our breakfast fire, I saw a blur of colour amongst the elder trees by the river. Then a small bird with a large beak burst from the foliage and flew straight to perch on the feed table, where he ignored the scraps and crumbs for the common breeds, and focused his attention on the water. After a moment, he darted through the air, swooped, struck and made off back to the trees, a tiny sliver of silver glinting against his rainbow coat.

A kingfisher has come to La Puce.

August 4th:

Our social calendar for the rest of the month is full to overflowing.

It is the week of the St Anne Fair at Bricquebec, closely followed by our village fete, and we have been invited to spend a long weekend in Burgundy. It is the height of the ferry tariff season, so we shall give our monthly raid on England a miss, though our financial situation is at a very low ebb. Bad news has come from Robert Simon, who says that they haven't sold a single Philippino hand-made pot from our vast sample range. He politely suggests that Normandy may not be ready for the eastern ethnic look, and his customers are more interested in plaster board and roofing tiles than strawberry planters thrown on a genuine ex-Manila taxi wheel rim. I report the latest entrepreneurial catastrophe to my wife, who as ever looks on the bright side. We will, she says, at least not have to buy any patio pots for our secret garden when it is finished, and they will make ideal nurseries for preparing the baby goldfish for life in the big pond.

August 7th:

Preparing for our attendance at the *Sainte Anne Fete*, we make the unaccustomed change from our working clothes, and I remark how well her summer print dress suits my wife. This has the opposite effect to that intended, and she caustically enquires if I think she should start clearing out the stream in long gloves and a cocktail dress to set off her gumboots. I make amends for whatever I have said wrong by promising to win her at least a dozen virile goldfish at the fair.

We arrive on the outskirts to find Bricquebec like a busy Friday evening at Junction 12 of the M25. The traffic is at a standstill, so we park by the hole in the fence at the funeral director's yard, and I try not to look at the familiar slabs of marble stacked inside as we set off on the mile walk to the square.

When we first visited the town on a market day, we were surprised at just how many local people would turn out to tour round a handful of stalls and see a variety of farmyard animals go under the hammer. Today, the centre of Bricquebec is busier than Portsmouth's Guildhall Square on a naval payday. Every metre of every pavement has been taken up with stalls doing breakneck trading regardless of what they are selling. Mountains of carpets, furniture and farming tools vie for space and attention with stalls laden down with hundreds of varieties of cheese, and we even see an English couple doing a roaring trade in pirated video cassette copies of recent Hollywood blockbusters. This is particularly remarkable, as they will be in the English language, and I also know that some of the frantic buyers have no video machines on which to play them. Wherever there is a scrap of space, business is being done, especially by the Moroccan street dealers hardly visible beneath armfulls of rugs, scarves, leather jackets, alleged Rolex watches for fifty francs, and, as they proclaim, real gold jewellery for just ten francs. In the heaving thrusting scrimmage of Cotentinese, who are also professional hagglers, they look very much at home.

Whole caravans of boiled sweets of every colour, size and flavour compete with candy floss, ice cream and wet fish stalls, and every corner has at least two *merguez* spicy sausage hot dog stands trying to keep up with demand. Butchers from across the region have abandoned their shops to plunder the rich seam of customers looking for a whole lamb or pig, jointed, cooked or even on the hoof as the customer prefers.

An escaped hen from the poulterer's wagon unwisely seeks refuge under the skirts of the fried chicken and *frites* stand, and even the trestle table selling winter underwear and bobble hats is under siege.

At the heart of the square, it is even busier, as a complete funfair has been shipped in, set up overnight, and is in full swing.

We fight our way through the boisterous hordes eager to pay to be giddily swung, dropped, suspended upside down and whirled round in a cacophony of deafening tinny music and klaxon hooting, and see that there is little chance of popping in to the *Café de Paris* for a quiet drink with Freddo.

Every bar in sight is packed with revellers, and each has thrown up a temporary counter and awning of canvas, scaffolding poles and rough planks which is even busier than inside.

When preparing for the onslaught last week, Freddo had told us that at least fifty thousand people would visit the fair over the three days this year, and we thought he must be exaggerating. Now we see he has underestimated the attendance, and he and his staff of ten will probably serve that many customers in the *Café de Paris* alone. Officially starting on a Saturday morning, the Saint Anne Fair is supposed to close at two each morning and re-open four hours later throughout the three days, but in practice it just keeps going. After a long exposure to his favourite daytime tipple of *kir*, Freddo also told us that he and Collette make enough money from the three mad days each August to take a long recuperative holiday in the Auvergne immediately afterwards, and put more than a little aside for the retirement house they are buying outside Bricquebec.

Giving up our efforts to get within shouting distance of the bar, I reflect that he will probably pay for the roof of their new home in the next couple of hours.

As we try to escape from the maze of fairground rides, tents and stalls, I collide with a large young man who is pointing a pump-action twelve-bore shotgun at me. Reaching for my wallet and preparing to tell him to take what he likes, I see that he is actually a customer at the nearby shooting range, the front of which is knee deep in empty cartridge cases. The man is obviously intoxicated with the frenetic atmosphere, drink or both. I duck beneath the barrels, grab him round the waist and swing him in roughly the right direction. As we stand and watch, we see that the stallholder has cunningly appealed to the Cotentinese love of firing off shotguns at large, preferably immobile and very close-up targets. The object of the challenge to the customers' marksmanship is to hit a dinner plate less than ten feet from the firing position. Given the spread of the cartridge shot and the closeness of the plates, it would be a greater test of skill to miss them. At fifty francs for four goes and the prize for success a cheap baseball cap with *le champion!* stencilled on the peak, the stallholder is actually hiring out the guns at a tidy profit rather than staging a competition. I now also understand why I have already seen at least a hundred men proudly wearing this normally rare type of headgear.

Keeping low, I take my wife's hand, resist the blandishments of at least three Original Astrological Consultants to the President of all France, and finally burst from the fairground maze to collide with a pretty girl in traditional Dutch costume, who happens to be riding a boneshaker bicycle while carrying a tuba. Helping her to her feet, I see that she is not alone.

Behind her stretches a long and wobbling line of young men and women, all in costume, steering ancient bicycles with one hand and playing a trumpet, drum, fife or xylophone with the other. The clogs they are wearing further impede their ability to maintain forward velocity and balance. Thinking quickly and not waiting to make an introduction, I grasp the girl, tuba and bicycle and manage to drag her out of the path of her colleagues, thus avoiding a massive pile-up. I hand over the dented euphonium while the procession wavers past, then all is explained as my wife points out a poster proclaiming that the high point of the fair takes place every day at three pm, when Bricquebec proudly presents a special display by the Only Dutch Cycling Formation Band In The World.

Agreeing that little else could top our recent experiences, we cautiously make our way from the display area and return to the tranquillity of La Puce.

Whatever is on offer at the *Grande Fête et Méchoui* at Néhou this weekend, I feel it is bound to be something of an anti-climax.

August 14th:

Actually, it looks as if the village fete is going to be quite a lively affair.

We arrived at the field beside the church in good time for the open-air mass, followed by fairly orderly and good-natured queuing for the ladies-only portaloo. It was then time for me to make my traditional return to La Puce for our forgotten plates, knives and forks as these are not provided for the *méchoui*, which is the localised version of a North African lamb barbecue.

Now, the fete is in full swing, with every villager having dutifully turned up to support the occasion and provide another boost for the school book fund. There is even a rumour that there are some heavily disguised spies from St Jacques in attendance, but this, of course, is a compliment, as they would only be here to see how things should be done properly at their miserable fete.

In one corner, JayPay and his team of volunteers labour in the fierce heat of the afternoon sun, turning whole lambs on spits above improvised oil-drum barbecues, while Mr Janne and Bernard are coping with the steady flow of customers at the temporary bar set up by Madame Ghislaine.

While not as sophisticated as the amusements on offer at the Bricquebec fair, the stalls lining the hedgerows have their own simplistic appeal and are marginally safer for the spectators. Most consist of rolling, lobbing or throwing *pétanque* balls at pyramids of tin cans, while the main attraction is a lucky dip with a top prize of a full and virtually unused tractor spanner set. Every member of the Jolly Boys Club has been roped in to help; even René has been delegated to sell raffle tickets for the Grand Draw, but I notice that Madame Ghislaine follows him round to take charge of the money. As he tears us off a strip, my friend gives me a stage wink, and loudly declares that he has been working since dawn and his mouth is as dry as a dead cow's udder. My wife having kindly offered to take over the ticket sales, we retire to the bar for an *apéritif* before the *méchoui* is ready.

An hour later, and we are at the head of the jostling queue for a huge slice of lamb, garnished with Normandy green salad and a bucketful of chips. As we steady our plates and stand by to fight off rivals for the delicious outer cuts of seared, crunchy skin infused with JayPay's secret marinade of herbs and spices, he ceremonially unsheathes his weapon. Holding the giant carving knife up to the sun, he squints at the glittering blade, and is obviously not happy with what he sees. As we salivate like dogs waiting anxiously for their dinner to be put in the bowl, he turns to his well-worn whetstone and hones his knife in the manner of a priest preparing his implements for a very special service. Finally, after much examination of the blade and consultation with fellow specialists on the team, he makes the final, crucial test. Rolling his sleeve and exposing a massive and densely hairy forearm, he draws the blade carefully from sweaty elbow to wrist. Holding it once again towards the sun, he runs a sausage-like finger and thumb delicately along the blade, then holds up a thick tuft of damp hair to the crowd, from whom is heard a reverent murmur of admiration and approval. At last satisfied, JayPay wipes the knife casually on the seat of his trousers, confronts the nearest lamb and carves a thick wedge from its saddle. My wife and I exchange glances, then simultaneously step aside to let someone behind us have the honour of bagging the first slice.

Dusk is approaching, and the fairy lights fetchingly draped across the water bowser by the portaloo are twinkling brightly. The mobile DJ is working his way up to the Birdie Song, and René is dancing with my wife. Hubert is filming the day's activities and indiscretions for posterity, and frowns almost possessively as he records our estate manager's attempts to teach Donella a dual version of his whirling dervish routine. René has already disgraced himself by hijacking the tractor train ride and taking the carriageloads of village children on a much more exciting route through the field of cattle maize across the road. As he is firmly but gently led off the floor by my wife, the DJ blows loudly into his microphone and announces the draw for the raffle is about to take place. Shyly mounting the platform, Solange Chevalier reaches into the feed bucket held by Madame Ghislaine and produces a ticket. René nudges me heavily in the back as my wife's name is read out to polite applause. As René was for some reason entrusted with writing the names on the back of all the tickets, I am relieved to see that there are no other prizes but the plump Chinese rabbit with which my wife is presented.

Later, and I spend a pleasant ten minutes at the bar with our mayor, who tells me he has heard from Robert Simon that a suitably large and impressive boulder for the Patton orchard has been located, and will be picked up and delivered free of charge by a *Brument-Clot* lorry in the coming weeks. I say I am more than pleased to have helped with the project, thank him for a wonderful day, and go to collect my wife, who has just presented the large and cuddly rabbit to JayPay's youngest daughter. She is obviously delighted, and runs straight to her father to show off her unexpected gift. As JayPay holds the creature up by the ears and prods its stomach, Donella smiles fondly and says they are probably discussing what best to feed it on. I agree, but would rather wager that he is telling her the best way to cook it.

We prepare to leave, and see René behind the water bowser with a young woman. He is obviously drunk, and concentrating blearily on the unaccustomed practice of taking some notes from his wallet. He gives them to the girl, then sees us watching and hurries her away into the darkness.

About to drive from the field, we bump into Charlie the dog and Madame Lynn, who is looking particularly radiant.

She tells us that she has met someone special. Bathing at Carteret, she struck up a conversation with a man on the towel next to hers, and they got on so well that she agreed to a dinner date. He is not young, but kind, charming and sophisticated, and is the proprietor of two biscuit factories and a grand *manoir* at

Carentan.

We congratulate her on forming a new relationship, and as I encourage Victor over the bumpy terrain, I remark how glad I am that Lynn has met someone new. Fate was indeed kind, I philosophise, to place two lonely and obviously so well-suited people side by side on a crowded beach. My wife is silent for a moment, then observes that Fate was particularly kind in ensuring that Lynn's neighbour was not only lonely, charming, kind and sophisticated, but also the owner of two biscuit factories and a grand *manoir*.

I reflect on the complex workings of the feminine mind as we pull out on to the road, then my heart sinks as we are flagged down by a large *gendarme* swathed in leather, and wearing the standard menacing sunglasses under his visored helmet, even though it has long been dark. We are not two miles from home, and I had thought it safe to go beyond my normal driving ration of two bottles of beer. French policemen persecute all drivers, but seem to take a special delight in harassing the British motorists who contribute millions to the nation's economy each year. Clutching at straws, I take several deep breaths and waggle my tongue frantically around my open mouth as the figure approaches with the familiar cocky strut, leans down to my open window and removes his helmet and sunglasses. I then realise it is the boozy bobby, and that he has been drinking far more than me. He pumps my hand, crisply salutes my wife, and asks if we have had any more temporary guests in the ditch outside our farmhouse.

He also asks if our special emergency supply of *calva* is still in stock, and remarks pointedly on how chilly the night air is after such an agreeable day.

I let out a huge sigh of relief, give him time to find, fall off then re-straddle his *mobylette*, and we create another local legend by becoming the first villagers to receive a motorcycle escort home from the annual Néhou fete.

August 17th:

I am standing on a stepladder and re-staining a suspect beam in the bedroom when a small helicopter enters through the dormer window. The creature hovers menacingly for a moment as it gets its bearings, then joins me at the top of the ladder. I stand very, very still. After prowling along the entire length of the beam and disappearing into various large cavities, it seems disappointed and leaves the same way it arrived. I notice I am sweating even more heavily than usual, and have spilled a considerable amount of *chêne antique* wood preserver on the patchwork quilt my wife spent a month stitching together. I go downstairs for a large *calva* to steady my hand before clearing up and carrying on with the job. Later, I tell Réne of my encounter, and he says it was a hornet looking for a comfortable place to build a nest. I am lucky it didn't decide to settle in the mill, as it would take the combined resources and courage of the St Sauveur fire brigade to get rid of the nest. I repeat my tale to Donella when she returns from a feeding trip, and I believe even she is glad we have not provided accommodation for this particular homeless creature and its family.

August 20th:

The mayor calls to say that the Patton stone will arrive next week and asks if we are free to attend the delivery so as to mark our involvement in the project. Regretfully, I turn his thoughtful invitation down, and explain we are going to spend a few days seeing how life in Burgundy compares with Cotentin.

I wish him well for the ceremony, and remind him that he is judging our vegetable show next month.

August 27th:

We set out for our visit to Jean-Marie Guedeney's ancestral farm in a village not too far from Dijon. Though he was not born there, the property has been in his family for generations, and now that his parents have passed on, he has bought the farm to save it being sold to strangers. He has phoned from England, told us where to find the keys, and said he would be grateful if we could look the place over and give him the benefit of our experience in restoring interesting old French properties.

The trip goes well, except when we become stuck on the Paris ringroute, which is like our M25 round London, only the standards of driving, road surfaces and signs are even worse. The stretch past the capital is supposed to take no more than an hour to complete, but at one stage we begin to think we will be on it forever. The night descends, we stop and change seats at my wife's suggestion, and I do not ease the situation when we see the Eiffel tower three times from different sides of the river and I suggest she should think about a career as a Paris taxi driver.

By midnight, we have thankfully left the lights and sights of the capital behind us, and arrive in the Valley of the Windmills by dawn.

August 30th:

Apart from the extreme heat and the complete absence of mud, we feel almost at home here. In some respects, though, Burgundy is not as French as we are used to. The condition of property and age of the cars suggests that the locals generally enjoy a better standard of living, and Dijon is far, far grander and refined than we are used to with Cherbourg as our main town. There is even an Indian restaurant. We spend the morning visiting museums, exploring the narrow streets with their picture postcard half-timbered buildings, and window shopping at individual greengrocery shops in the marketplace which would make the food hall at Harrods look poorly stocked. There is a sophisticated café bar on every corner, and each has a huge selection of filled rolls displayed in the window, with a hatch to serve the crowds on the pavement. This is obviously how Jean-Marie got his idea for his *baguette* chain in Portsmouth. A couple of drunks who would not even have been noticed in a Cherbourg quayside bar cause a stir by attempting to enter a café where we are taking tea, and the manager promptly phones the police. Minutes later a van arrives and discreetly parks in an alleyway alongside. I move to the window and watch as the two vagrants are efficiently beaten about the head with batons and thrown into the back before the van speeds away, its siren noticeably silent. It is all over in seconds, without any of the weary negotiations, petulant protests or shouting match exchanges between police and yobboes you would expect to see in England after a soccer fixture. Obviously, the authorities don't want anything to lower the tone, distract the shoppers or upset foreign visitors.

In the afternoon, we visit Jean-Marie's birthplace, an imposing four-storey stone building perched next to the church in an elevated village with panoramic views for miles across the rolling countryside. The house is up for sale, and I make a note to tell Jean-Marie in case he wants to buy it as well as the farm. Even within commuter distance of Dijon and as attractively positioned as it is, it will probably fetch no more than a scruffy terraced house in Portsmouth.

We take photographs of the graves of Jean-Marie's parents before we leave. His mother and father are buried alongside each other in the family plot, with a lovely view overlooking the valley. The polished marble and freshly-cut flower displays show that the plot is regularly given loving attention by other members of the Guedeney family. On the way back, I remark on how well the relatives care for grave sites in every cemetery, and we rather morbidly discuss our preferences for a final resting place. Donella says she would like to be buried at La Puce in a bio-degradable cardboard box, so that her body can help enrich the land as quickly as possible. I say she is only thinking of giving her vegetable plot a further advantage over mine, and that I would be happy with a cremation, and for my ashes to be scattered by the *pissoir* outside the Bar Ghislaine. That way, I would never lack company, and would be able to eavesdrop on so many interesting discussions.

As a former gravedigger, I have no romantic illusions about burials, and things happened in my time at Kingston cemetery which would put anyone off the idea of booking space for a traditional interment. Each morning, the foreman would come to our hut and give out dockets detailing the location and dimension of the graves to be dug, together with the time of the ceremony. In those days before mechanical diggers were commonly used, the work was done purely by fork, spade and shovel, and the size of the hole was a crucial factor as to how hard the day would be. A grisly perk and reward for long service was the tradition that the dockets for the biggest corpses were handed out first, and to the newest members of staff. The older hands were given responsibility for the interment of the frail and elderly, who would obviously require less elbow space. The only time I saw a gravedigger unhappy with the prospect of a small hole to dig was the rare occasion when it was an infant or child. Fortunately for my state of mind, I only ever dealt with the largest coffins as I was employed at the cemetery for less than a month. My latest pause on a long and varied career path ended when I stepped back to admire my work on a particularly cavernous grave, fell into the one a colleague was digging next door, and broke his spade handle and my arm.

Exhausting the subject of death and burial, we stop at a bar outside Jean-Marie's village and take an ice cold beer on the terrace. Not for the first time, I notice how easily the Burgundians understand my French. Either they are more used to foreigners, or too polite to give the blank stares and mystified shrugs I still receive on occasion in my home region. As we drive back to the farm, we see a dead hare in the road and I suddenly realise that my friend Douglas the emperor dragonfly will probably not be around when we return to La Puce. I must remember, my wife says comfortingly, that he found a mate before we left, so has served nature's purpose. He will have had, in dragonfly terms, a long and happy life, so should not be mourned.

201

August 31st:

It is my wife's birthday. We are booked in for a special meal this evening at an *auberge* highly recommended by Jean-Marie. I call him to tell him of our adventures so far, and tactfully remind him that he has not sent a birthday card to Donella as I had suggested. Totally out of character for such a normally polite man, he rather testily says that the French do not suffer from the English obsession for sending a greeting card on every occasion from sickness to passing the driving test. Soon, he hazards, we will start posting a card to tell friends we have had a particularly satisfying piss.

As we dress after a lazy day sunbathing in the garden, the phone rings. It is either Jean-Marie to apologise for his tetchiness, or a problem at home. I have left the number with Lynn in case any problems arise, but have asked not to be bothered unless it is something important.

I walk into the cool hallway and pick up the phone.

It is René, and I realise that it is only the second occasion that we have spoken on the phone. The first time was when he called me in Portsmouth to complain about my closing our account with *Boueve et Fils*, and he shouted throughout our conversation as if we did not have the benefits of a telephone link. This time he speaks so quietly I can hardly hear him.

Before I can ask what the problem is, he tells me.

John Chevalier is dead and Solange is in hospital.

Néné thought we would want to know.

AUTUMN

'Life is but a passing shadow'

inscription on a sundial at the manor
house of the Sire de Gouberville et du
Mesnil-au-Val, the author of an
unique journal of 16th-century life in
the Cotentin countryside.

September 1st:

We have driven home through the night, and go straight to René's caravan.

He tells us that our friend had been at the Patton orchard to take delivery of the memorial boulder, and was waiting at the entry to the D900 when a lorry went out of control. The driver suffered a heart attack, and John had no chance to take avoiding action. It is said that the lorry driver may be a relative of the Chevaliers. The impact was on John's side of the car, and he must have died instantly. Miraculously, Solange is hardly injured, except in her mind. René offers us a drink, but we say no and go and sit by the big pond to talk. I cannot help thinking that John was at the junction at that exact moment because of a chain of events I had set in motion. If I had not made enquiries about the stone, he would not even have been there. If I had been there for the delivery, we may have talked for a few vital extra moments or he may have shown me round the orchard, or I may have persuaded him to come to the Bar Ghislaine for a drink, which would have meant us turning out of the orchard in the opposite direction from the main road. Whatever happened, he would not have been sitting patiently at the junction when the lorry appeared around the bend.

My wife does not try to reason with me, and knows it is best to leave me with my thoughts. I spend the night looking at the water and remembering Jean Le Chevalier.

September 5th:

The single bell at the church in Néhou has been tolling slowly all morning. It sounds completely different from its relaxed Sunday tone, or the nagging insistence with which it calls workers in the fields to attend the evening *Angélus*.

We walk towards the village centre and join a gathering stream of people, all wearing their church clothes. I have no black tie, but my wife has made an armband from an old pair of charcoal grey trousers and sown it to my jacket. It is the first time she has worn a hat since her father's funeral.

We pass the field where our mayor opened the village fete so recently, and I see that the water bowser and fairy lights are still there. The field is full of cars, and more are parked along the verges and outside the Bar Ghislaine, which is shut for the day. A gendarme in full dress uniform is directing traffic to an overflow parking field beyond the church, and two policemen on motorcycles sit at either side of the broken gate. They have taken their helmets and sunglasses off, and are almost respectfully ushering the steady flow of vehicles inside. Already, there are at least twice as many people in Néhou as live here.

Although the ceremony is not due to start for more than an hour, the church is full. A large crowd is gathered around the main entrance, where the mobile DJ has set up his loudspeakers to relay the words of the service. There are some familiar faces, but also many strangers, some in military and civil uniforms of very high rank. A row of benches has been placed by the open graveside, and are already filled with older members of the commune, who sit silently looking at the neatly kept rows of marble slabs bearing the names of their friends and relations.

More cars continue to arrive in the narrow lanes than the village has ever seen, or will likely see again, and Néhou has its first traffic jam. The gendarme panics and puts a whistle to his mouth, but a very senior officer in a *képi* festooned with gold braid hurries to stop him and take personal command of the situation as the dignitaries arrive. We had known that John was well respected in the area, and it seems that other mayors, high-ranking Manche officials and important figures from all across the *département* have come to pay their personal tribute. While we wait in the crowded cemetery, men in uniform and wearing extravagant emblems and regalia of office move swiftly amongst the gravestones, nodding here, exchanging a few words there, and shaking hands with everyone within reach. Next to where we stand in the shadow of the church tower, a senior army officer pauses to pump the hand of a surprised and embarrassed chauffeur with a uniform even more splendid than his own.

There is a murmur from the crowd, and we see a procession making its way slowly along the middle of the lane from the distant parking field. At its head, young children carry huge bouquets and arrangements of flowers bigger than themselves, and at its heart is Solange. She is supported on either side by Mr Janne and her only son, and she is totally distraught.

The mass of people silently parts to make way, and she is gently led through the doors and into the dark interior of the church.

Overhead, the bell falls silent, and a single crow flutters back to its roost.

The service begins and the people around the door press forward as if to show that they would join the congregation if there were room.

For two hours we stand stiffly in the hot sun, listening to the words and music coming from inside the church and echoing harshly from the loudspeakers on either side of the porchway. None of those outside join in the hymns or responses made by the unseen congregation, but most make the sign of the cross across their breasts at what must be the appropriate moments.

Eventually, we begin to shuffle forward into the cool porchway, and a few men slip away to relieve full bladders on the low churchyard wall before we enter. They make no attempt to hide themselves, and there is no disrespect in their action.

Inside, we move slowly down the aisle to where the coffin lies in front of the altar. I take the brush from the elderly woman in front of me, and following her actions, dip it into an urn and sprinkle a few drops of water across the casket lid. I have not been to a French funeral before and did not know what to expect. I am disappointed that the coffin is closed, and I will not see my friend's face for the last time. As I hand the brush to my wife, I see Solange leaning heavily on Mr Janne's arm.

Our eyes meet, but she does not see me.

Outside the church, and unsure what to do next, we stand and nod self-consciously to friends and neighbours. There is little conversation and no tears, but their faces show that they know what we have lost.

*   *   *   *   *

The interment is over, and we walk home with Christian, his wife and her mother, who tells us she was christened at the church, and will soon make her last visit there. She is nearly ninety, and it is more than three miles to the family home beyond the crossroads. Perhaps, she says, it would have been easier to stay at the church and wait her time.

September 10th:

It is raining softly as I walk through the gates and stand at the foot of my friend's grave. The flowers are still fresh, and completely cover the marble slab. There is a photograph of John on the headstone, showing him as he was earlier this year and always will be in our memories. I make myself comfortable, and begin to tell him all the news about the village, and how his fields at La Puce are in good form as the summer leaves us.

September 13th:

We return to the church for the christening of a new member of the commune. It is a boy, and he is to be named Jean.

Afterwards there is a celebration at the Bar Ghislaine. I expect it to be a sombre and subdued affair, but all the guests seem in good spirits. I disgrace myself when one of the Jolly Boys Club makes a black joke about our commune population standing still as we have lost one and gained one in the same month and I take strong exception. JayPay calms the situation down, and when I apologise for my manners but question the taste of the *plaisanterie,* he merely shrugs, lays a huge arm around my shoulder and steers me towards the bar to explain something I must understand.

As I would have seen from the funeral, everyone in the commune loved and respected Jean Chevalier for who and what he was. There will never be another like him, and his passing was properly marked with a ceremony which will be talked about all over Manche for years to come. That is the mark of his greatness. We have all lost a dear friend, and grieve for his wife. Unlike elsewhere in what is supposed to be civilised and modern Europe, Solange will not be forgotten and left to face the future alone. But life and death is commonplace in the countryside, and must be accepted as inevitable. Last week we mourned the death of a dear friend and good man. Today we celebrate life. The accident was a terrible tragedy, but it happened and nothing can change that. Now it is time to think about birth, not death.

Life, as even the English would probably say, must go on.

I nod acceptance of what he says and accept the glass he offers me, but still feel angry at the world. No matter how long I live among them, I don't think I will ever really understand these people.

September 14th:

The top fields at La Puce seem strangely shabby and untended when I take my morning stroll. Even though John was due to retire, he would still stop by nearly every day to see that all was in order, and had already started mending a hole in the hedgerow made by a truck careering off the road. I have decided to leave it as it is, and René says it will soon grow over, anyway. Already the grass is getting very long, though I am probably imagining the level of neglect and decay I seem to see around me. René says he has found a farmer willing to put a couple of his horses in to keep the grass down, and it will save the expense of paying someone to cut it. I agree. It won't be the same, but at least there will be some life around the place.

I tell myself to buck up, and go to see how Trevor is getting on with the binful of young trout I secretly bought at Valdecie and tipped into the big pond when my wife was not around. With luck, she will think that Trevor has had an immaculate conception, or that they are a hybrid result of his liaison with a *gardon*.

She needs cheering up, and, as Jean-Pierre said at the christening, life must go on.

September 15th:

The swallows have flown.

I shall miss their joyous aerobatics around the big pond, and their departure is another reminder that the year is dying.

René says that, before France's Age of Reason (which naturally preceded that of any other European country), ignorant peasants believed that swallows hibernated in the mud at the bottom of rivers and ponds.

Now we know that they winter in Africa, but I like the idea of them sleeping contentedly beneath the surface of the big pond, waiting to burst forth and welcome the sun and summer of another year.

September 17th:

I am particularly pleased with myself today. I dropped in to the Photo-Kwik shop in St Sauveur this morning to pick up a roll of film, and the manager told me Helen Patton has engaged his services. He is to fly over the grand house at Néhou and take some aerial shots now that the restoration is complete. As he will be going past La Puce, I asked if he will take some photographs of our terrain while he is up there. We negotiated for a few moments and a satisfactory deal was reached with regard to extra fuel, time in the air, photographic plates and additional artistic output. I handed over 300 francs and left, feeling I had pulled off a major *coup*.

It will be nice to have some panoramic pictures to show the extent of our estate. As we struck the deal, I considered asking the photographer if he has any specialist infra-red equipment which could detect and show buried metal, but don't want the word about the miller's gold to get out; he is a notorious gossip. I still think a friend's wheeze for staging metal detector weekends for enthusiast clubs from England is a sound idea. We could bury little trophies around the terrain, and follow the contestants round to see if they stumble on the treasure. I shall phone Mark Berridge in the morning and ask how he feels about a joint venture, with him having the accommodation rights for his *château B&B*, and me the entry fee and refreshments proceeds.

Sept 19th:

René calls at the mill to say we have a problem. A plane has been circling the water meadow this morning at a very low altitude. He recognises it as the one the photographer at St Sauveur hires for work, and is concerned that he has been paid by the government to take some spy pictures and catch René working while he is supposed to be unemployed. He makes me promise not to tell the Social Security that I am paying him if a snooper arrives. I tell him not to worry, that I have commissioned the shots of La Puce. He is dumbstruck at the thought of my spending money on photographs of grass, and says he could have taken some from the top of the giant cedar tree in the orchard which would have been just as good for half the price.

September 20th:

We have been visiting the *boucherie* at St Sauveur for our weekly joint.

Although an inveterate defender of British produce and cooking, I have to admit that virtually all the meat varieties and cuts seem to taste better here. The pork is particularly good, and I have yet to be given a tough steak in a shop or restaurant. My only criticism is that, in a region that regards butter and cream as health food, the housewives will not have more than a thin layer of fat left on any cut or joint. As most of them have probably never heard of cholesterol, it can only be that they don't see why fat should be included in the weight they are paying for. The other week, we bought a large piece of beef for roasting, and before I could stop him the butcher had whipped off every ounce of fat thickly covering the joint and casually thrown it to one side. As he demonstrated his skill at wrapping and tying our piece of dead animal up like a special anniversary present, I asked him if we could have the *gras* included, as the joint was for roasting. Giving me a puzzled look, he threw what he must have considered to be our unsightly fat into a waste bin and fetched a sheet of specially trimmed, rolled and reconstituted stuff from the cold store. Re-opening the parcel, he spent several minutes artistically arranging it around the meat, then went through the decorative packing process again. The joint cooked well, but would have been even better simply left in its original coating of lard. According to our friend Mauricette Laiznay, meat is rarely roasted here, with the joint put in the oven and basted in stock to achieve the same effect. We shall have to try it that way, but I can't see how it will compare with the traditional British and surely most natural method of roasting the animal in its own fat.

This weekend, we are to feast on a leg of pork, specially ordered days ago and entered in the customer ledger after much discussion on every aspect of the previous owner from age, weight, birthplace and breed to temperament. While this all may seem a little indulgent, the result is always impeccable, and we shall have real crackling today.

Although the most polite of men, our butcher was quite explicit when I asked him recently why crackling in England always had the appearance and taste of indiarubber despite Donella's best efforts with scoring knife, oil and salt. He was sorry to say that it was a well-known fact that all pigs in England are fed very poorly and on a monotonous and unimaginative diet. As French farmers understand, a well-fed and happy pig makes a tasty pig. After all, consider the complexion of the vegetarian. He had seen such a breed of person only once, but the pallor of his skin and his miserable demeanour proved conclusively that not only was his bizarre habit totally against nature, but a practised eye could tell immediately he would have made very poor eating.

Having delivered himself of this judgement, he looked nervously at his wife for approval, and was obviously relieved to see her nodding vigorously in agreement. He is a huge man who can easily heft a whole side of beef from the cold store, but seems a typical gentle giant. His wife is so small she can hardly see over the high counter where she takes and scrupulously examines each coin destined for the battered wooden cash holder. Most Sunday mornings when we call in, the poor man seems to have some sort of facial contusion, and last week he was sporting a huge shiner. When I sympathised and impolitely asked how he got it, he shrugged, put his fist to his nose to indicate extreme intoxication, and said he had walked into an open door the night before. His wife looked grimly satisfied as she counted our change out, so I am beginning to suspect she beats him regularly.

Obviously moved by our interest in his profession and opinions, our butcher slipped me a sample of his special black pudding as we left, together with a hand-written leaflet on at least a dozen ways of serving it. I noticed that he picked his moment when *madame* went out to the back of the shop, so am even more convinced he is a battered husband.

*   *   *   *   *

Strolling for a Sunday morning *apéritif* and chat with Albert the Alsatian at Jackie's Bar, we counted no fewer than two arm slings, one leg in plaster and any number of freshly applied sticking plasters amongst the clientele taking their ease outside Coco's place. Apart from their domestic injuries, the local men seem peculiarly prone to accidents in the fields, especially at harvest time. It is a rare autumn when there is not at least one plaster cast on show in any bar, and broken and badly cut fingers are common currency. It would be interesting to conduct a survey, and discover if most are sustained before or after lunch. The Bar Ghislaine being in such a rural location, we see constant examples of the most bizarre agricultural injuries at this time of year, and have started a private lottery at Jolly Boys Club meetings, where drinks are won for accurately forecasting the arrival of the next walking wounded and what part of his anatomy will be strapped, bandaged or plastered.

September 21st:

I awake in the early hours, certain I am having a heart attack. There is a band of steel round my chest, and the pain is excruciating. I rouse my wife and ask her to phone the emergency services. She claims not to be able to remember the number, and reminds me that we do not have the card which would enable us to claw back medical expenses under the relevant EEC agreement. It would cost a fortune to have me hospitalised, and besides, it is only indigestion. How anyone of my age could eat that amount of pork crackling at lunch followed by black pudding for supper and expect to get away with it escapes her. She fetches a bottle of *cidre bouché*, pops the cork and for once encourages me to drink it all down quickly, and straight from the bottle. The ice-cold fizzy liquid does the trick, and I bring up vast quantities of trapped air for the next hour. I start to feel much better, and the cider has its usual effect of making me feel amorous. My wife sends me to sleep on the sofa bed so she can get a few hours rest, and reminds me we have a heavy day of harvesting ahead of us, as it is the day when the results of our long running vegetable competition will be revealed. I lay awake for a while after remembering that the contest was to have been judged by John and Solange Chevalier.

*   *   *   *   *

We have spent a hard morning in the vegetable patch, and are resting from our labours in the cool of the mill cottage. So far the day has not gone well for my side of the line dividing the his'n'hers plots.

Compared with my wife's mountains of runner and French beans, mine are but foothills. Her beetroots are *pétanque* balls compared with my marbles, and the sprouts do not even invite comparison. Despite my midnight sorties to unearth, inspect and unintentionally retard her main crop potatoes, her overall yield is at least twice that of my miserable pile.

In a sulk, I go to the bar to find sympathy in male company. Jacques Laiznay is there, earnestly treating his liver complaint. Jacko explains that he has been entertaining former fireman colleagues from Paris for the weekend and needed to take a healing infusion of *suze*. This exotic liqueur is based on the gentian flower, and is to my taste absolutely foul. It has a revolting, sickly smell and bitter taste redeemed only by being extremely high in alcoholic content, but the locals swear by its medicinal and restorative properties for internal problems. As most of their internal problems spring from excessive drinking, I think its main benefits are of the hair of the dog variety. All the local men seem to be complete hypochondriacs, with a most peculiar logic dictating their dietary regimes. The attitude seems widespread, and not confined to the masses. I once had lunch with a very senior officer in the Le Havre *Chambre de commerce*, and he suggested we went to his favourite restaurant on the quayside, which specialised in dishes from his Alsace birthplace.

After poring over the menu for a long while with a worried frown, he rejected my suggestion of a crisp white wine in favour of a purifying bottle of mineral water, and explained that he was on a very strict diet. His doctor had just broken the news that his cholesterol level was off the scale, and given him a small booklet detailing the comparative ratings for all meat, poultry and fish, together with items and dishes which must be avoided like the plague. After consulting it in tandem with the menu, he firmly turned down the oysters, and looked aghast when I even suggested a lean steak. Luckily, his favourite *choucroute* was the midday special, and not included as a specific dish in his booklet, so he contentedly ordered then devoured the groaning platter of fatty pork on pickled cabbage with ferocious dedication.

Hearing about my kitchen garden defeat, Jacko commiserates and says it is a known fact that only women can coax any size of vegetable out of the dense soil in the area, and this is said to be because they have had so much practice in the challenge of extracting cash from their husbands' pockets. All the serious and professional growing is done by men in the sandy soil on the coast, where the carrots and leeks come as big as a stallion's business equipment. I take comfort from his remarks and he suggests we order a whole bottle of *suze* and treat our maladies for the rest of the afternoon. I agree, with the proviso that I can have lots of water in mine without risking our friendship.

Black pudding and apples

1. *Peel, core and slice some apples*
2. *Fry them in butter, and season*
3. *Oil the pudding, prick the skin and grill*
4. *Arrange the ingredients in a casserole dish and heat*
5. *Just before serving, flame with a generous dash of calva*

I am convinced my wife's ability to communicate telepathically with the animal kingdom is developing apace.

On the way to Bricquebec this morning, we swerved to avoid an elderly mongrel standing placidly in the middle of the road. I stopped, and Donella ran back to warn other drivers while I approached the dog. Before I could see if it had a collar, it ran off and disappeared through a gap in a hedge. My wife was concerned and wanted to set up an emergency roadside observation post in case it returned, but I assured her it must belong to someone in one of the roadside houses, and had gone home.

Privately, I am amazed at the charmed lives of the pets who reside by the D900. Like their owners, they seem to lack any degree of road safety awareness, and wander about the highway without a care, which should be a very risky business. I have never seen a driver actually aim at an animal unless it is generally considered eatable, but nobody seems to take any drastic avoiding action if a dog or cat chooses to get in the way. Strangely, dead pets in the road are even rarer than squashed hedgehogs or rabbits, and that is saying much. Last year, I was taking our bank manager for a soothing lunch at Carteret, and somehow managed to miss a suicidal pheasant who obviously saw no point in going on now that he was so totally alone in the world. Rather than compliment me on my driving skills and humanity, my passenger seemed quite upset that I had missed such a rare opportunity to bag some free food without even being put to the cost of a shotgun cartridge.

Later in the evening of our encounter with the stray dog, I hear a noise outside and go to investigate. Opening the front door, I see the creature waiting patiently on the edge of the circle of light from our porch lamp. Her animal antenna working at full strength, my wife pushes past me with a bowl of food which she just happens to have prepared earlier, and the dog eats ravenously. It refuses all her invitations to come inside, but is still there in the morning, waiting for the breakfast gong. Donella seems not at all surprised at its appearance, but I am astounded. How it knew where to find us after our brief encounter four miles away is almost worthy of an entry in the *Guinness Book of Records*. My wife decides that she will call him Lucky, and I agree that this is a very apt name. He has no collar and was probably dumped by the roadside now that he is too old to hunt well, but Donella says that she will call the *gendarmerie* at both Bricquebec and St Sauveur tomorrow to ask if anyone has reported a missing dog. I nod my approval of this responsible attitude, but privately place a small wager that she will find lots of things to do well away from the telephone for the foreseeable future.

September 24th:

Donella has started on her latest harvest run to try and outwit the human scavengers who are always with us at this time of year. After the late spring and long, hot summer, the terrain at La Puce is providing an unusually abundant crop of uncultivated nuts, berries and fruit, even for the Cotentin.

Earlier this month, there was a massive haul of blackberries and elderberries, and it is hard to move freely about the mill cottage for jars of jam, jelly and pickle, while plastic bins of gently fermenting and bubbling potions line every available shelf and standing place. My wife has even been looking thoughtfully at our giant bath tub as an ideal vessel for a major brewing of her special hedgerow wine. It will be interesting to see what our cider and *calva* specialist friends make of Donella's inventive blends, as home made wine seems totally unheard of here, and would probably be seen as a gross infringement of France's sacred monopoly on making alcoholic fruit juice. None of our friends will believe that the southern counties of England produce some very drinkable white vintages, and Jacko Laiznay looked at me as if I were a simpleton when I first asked him why Normandy did not have its own wine. He explained slowly and clearly that, though I may not have noticed, we were living above the Loire, and it would be madness to even attempt to emulate the activities of those who create the finest wines in the world from the south of the country. He then went on to remind me that I, even as a settler, should realise that our area docs indeed produce, export and consume vast quantities of its own inimitable beverage, which is called *calvados*, even though it was invented in the Cotentin. I can't wait to see his face when we present him with a rich and fruity rhubarb and apple hock from the stony southern slopes of *le val de la Puce*.

Apart from the abundance of fruits and flowers for her home brewed wines and preserves, my wife is particularly pleased that our animal charges will have such a rich harvest to choose from this year. The hawthorns have been particularly prolific, with their brilliant and firm red berries fighting for a place on the branch, and the sloe berries are hugely full of potential for next month, as long as the locals don't get to them first. They are much prized in the area, and are added in modest quantities to help bring out the flavour in farmhouse *calva*. A huge harvest of hazel nuts is threatening to break the branches of the trees alongside the river and around the grotto, and thousands of crab apples have appeared amongst the oak *bocage* at the end of the water meadow. They are hopelessly tart, but the locals like to use them for an especially piquant sauce. I have also never seen so many truly enormous acorns, and it will be a shame to see them go to waste. I have tried some and, though the texture is firm and crunchy, they are far too bitter for any use I can think of. Perhaps I shall go over René's head and attempt to barter with Mr Pigeon, with our acorns given to his pigs in return for the rights to his *source*.

Across the *Lude*, Hunters Walk is now boasting as many beech nuts as stars in the evening sky. They are quite sweet, but fiddly to open and get at, and the only application for them I have heard of is to flavour chewing gum. Anyway, Donella says the skinny squirrel will need them all to see him safely through the winter.

According to my recollection of country lore, all this fecundity shows we are due for a hard winter, but when I asked René, he just sniffed and said all it shows is that we have had a good summer…

Blackberry and apple *confiture*

1. *First, pick your blackberries and apples before they are stolen**
2. *Simmer the cleaned blackberries until soft, then mash*
3. *Chop the apples and repeat the process, using fresh water*
4. *Mix the fruits, add the same weight in sugar, stir and boil to setting point*
5. *Add a dash of calva before putting the jam in jars*

Green Tomato Fool

1. *Scald 2lbs of green tomatoes briefly, then put them into cold water to make it easy to remove the skins*
2. *Chop and stew until soft with 1 lb of sugar and a little nutmeg*
3. *Sieve and add sugar to taste*
4. *When cool, stir in half a pint of cream and a good whack of calva*
5. *Serve cold*

La Puce Cider Apple Chutney

1. *Simmer some chopped apples and onions in a pan with a small amount of vinegar*
2. *When soft, add pint of still cider, sultanas, pickling spice, ginger and salt, then keep simmering till a pulp results*
3. *Stir in plenty of brown sugar until mixture thickens to satisfying texture, and seal and store in jars until you can no longer resist trying it*

* Make sure you pick your blackberries before the beginning of November, when, as they say in Cotentin, the Devil pisses on them. I'm not sure of the exact date but, as they also say in Cotentin, you'll know when he has by the taste…

September 25th (am):

I shall have to rethink my scheme for the mass production of garlic-based car deodorisers. The plant is apparently very difficult to grow in our soil to any high yield, and besides, the strength factor is diminishing daily as the days grow marginally cooler. I toy with the idea of experimenting with this year's particularly rank Camembert, but decide the aroma is very much an acquired taste, even for the locals.

September 25th (pm):

While my wife is busy with her foraging, I decide it is high time to sort out the stove chimneypipe situation. It is still far too early for roasted chestnuts, but I can't resist the idea of a test run. Although we are in the midst of an Indian summer, it is becoming noticeably chilly in the mill cottage in the evenings, and I want to be sure we shall be snug and warm for the winter.

Valognes is advertised locally as the Versailles of the North, though I have not yet heard a Norman claim it was built before its Paris namesake. Ten miles or so to the south of Cherbourg, the town lost many of its beautiful old buildings and much of its charm when the Americans flattened the town during the D-Day landings. The authorities literally stuck the remnants of the ancient church on the walls of the ugly post-war replacement, but it hardly makes up for the loss. The streets and areas by the river where the 18th-century *bourgeoisie* houses and civic offices survived only serve as a poignant contrast with the ugliness of the new buildings, but show what the town must once have looked like.

Apart from a respected university, interesting cider museum and some good restaurants, Valognes also boasts some reasonable *bricolage* shops for the rare Norman DIY enthusiast. Having exhausted their possibilities, I turn my attentions to a farming hardware store on the outskirts of the town. If all else fails, I know I can buy some proper stack pipes and joints at the specialist stove shop in Cherbourg, but have already discovered that a few yards of heavy metal tubing and some designer brackets would cost more than I paid for the *poêle* itself.

At the store, a terminally disinterested young assistant pretends not to understand my French for a few minutes till I use my best patois to compare his moustache with the hairs round a cat's arse. I realise immediately that I have gone too far, and smile to show that it was just a joke, and he disappears huffily to the warehouse. Returning no more than an hour later, he says yes, they do normally carry that which I seek, but are out of stock until tomorrow morning. I promise to return, and leave him looking thoughtfully at the reflection of his moustache in a sheet of galvanised iron.

While I am in the area, I decide to make a brief pilgrimage to *Le Petit Bijou.*

The Little Jewel was our first second home in France, or anywhere else for that matter, and will always have a special place in our hearts. Turning off the D902 and down the winding lanes leading to the hamlet of Yvetot-Bocage, I see that *Le Petit* looks even more enchanting than when we regretfully sold it to two schoolteachers from Yorkshire. Having seen it before we had properly settled in, they had fallen in love with the tiny one-bedroomed cottage and told us to name our price. We did, and will always wonder how different our lives would have been if we had refused their offer; but it is good to see that the old place is in such caring hands.

After my sentimental journey, I stop off at a restored mill on the Bricquebec road which now trades as a restaurant specialising in finding as many ways to fill a *crêpe* as there are flavours of *calva* in Mr Maurice's wardrobe. As I take my ease by the duck pond, I try to spot any parts of the restored mill which look as if they could have come from La Puce. I could never prove any claim to prior ownership, but Maurice's nephew Alain has a big van, and I hear he is not averse to the odd commission which needs to be undertaken after dark.

September 26th:

At the agricultural store, I am greeted by the same assistant, this time wearing a blank stare and a clean upper lip, which proves he remembers my visit of yesterday only too well. After I ask him how many twenty-stone Englishmen with real whiskers and a smattering of patois he sees during the average year, he sullenly concedes to recall my order, and does his usual disappearing act. On his eventual return he is wearing a smug expression on his newly shaven *visage*, and reports that the piping I seek has not yet arrived, though has been promised for tomorrow. Or, *p'tet*, the next day or the day after that. Fingering his naked lip, he asks me what I would like to do about the situation, and I refrain from telling him my real desires. Instead, I say I will phone each day until the tubing has arrived, and will ask for the man without the moustache on every occasion, which will probably be just before he is due to leave for his lunch. Then, we can have a long chat about progress with the *situation*. He looks more concerned than when I insulted his moustache, and immediately promises to see what he can do to ensure that I am not inconvenienced for too long.

October 3rd:

My persistence with the assistant at Valognes has paid off. The length of shiny metal tube now leans against the gable end wall where it will be fixed to take the smoke from our stove up to the open air above the roof of the mill. Before that can happen and in order to connect the piping to the stove, a large hole must be knocked at knee height through the wall. Although it is more than a yard thick and the stone blocks look extremely hard, I am disappointed in the progress that my wife has made, despite the help of the brand new bolster chisel and lump hammer I bought her at *Boueve et Fils* yesterday.

Taking over to show how it should be done, I spend the next two hours penetrating a further inch, then rest while I consider further options.

Calling on the Jolly Boys Club to rally round and stage a similar joint operation to Desert Storm would, I feel, be asking too much of even their generosity of spirit. I briefly consider emulating the standard method for installing septic tanks in the rocky crust of the Auvergne, but don't like the idea of letting René loose with a bundle of dynamite and fusewire, even if he knew where to find some.

After a few reflective prods at the wall with the bent chisel, I ask my wife to look up the French for pneumatic drill, then in the phone book for the number of the nearest tool hire centre.

October 4th:

We are through. After wearing out two everlasting chisel bits, the voracious *marteau piqueur* has fulfilled its purpose in life. I wait till the dust settles, then peer through the hole to where my wife looks back at me from inside the cottage like a trapped miner seeing rescue finally at hand. She starts clearing-up operations, and has already earmarked the mountain of debris for use in a new rock garden. I commence fitting a piece of the tubing into the collar at the back of the stove, and find that my friend at Valognes has had his revenge. The pipe is far too big.

＊　　＊　　＊　　＊　　＊

Much later, and I have used the lump hammer to persuade the pipe to fit in to the stove. I have also slotted a short piece through the hole in the wall, and used the elbow bend, chinese hat and some ingeniously adapted hanging flower basket brackets to complete the job. We now have a most characterful and rustic chimney pipe, and all we need is some newspaper, kindling wood and logs to bring our period stove alive after its years of humiliation as a chicken coop. I just hope it will provide adequate heat.

＊　　＊　　＊　　＊　　＊

The stove is getting even hotter. In the last ten minutes the wooden beam directly above it has begun to smoulder, and the plastic frame around the picture of me arm wrestling with John Major has melted. Our fireside chairs are now at least ten feet from the source of the heat, and we are stripped to our underwear. The real problem is that everywhere beyond the direct blast range is comparatively cold. In winter, we will either roast in front of the blaze, or freeze away from it. I lob a few more immature chestnuts at the distant furnace and ponder on a solution. It would be nice to site another *poêle* at the other end of the cottage and have stereo stoves to even up the temperature, but the chances of getting our hands on a similar model through René's contacts without being shot at or ending up in court must be slight. I shall seek out Alain and see if he knows where I can come honestly by a similar stove, but one that is much, much smaller.

October 5th:

The Bar Ghislaine is quiet, and Mr Maurice is sitting in his usual spot, as usual alone and looking ruminatively at a large glass of *suze*.

I often speculate as to why, with a far greater stock and range of alcoholic beverages in his wardrobe, he chooses to pay to spend his afternoons in the bar. My wife thinks it is because he is lonely, and, given his continual experimentation with ever more exotic flavours of *calva*, just hasn't got room at home for the amount of medicinal *suze* he needs to get through each day.

Maurice seems more subdued than normal, and when I join him at his table, he says little in response to my polite enquiries as to his health and wardrobe.

When I ask about Alain, he takes a drink, fiddles with his tights, and explains that Alain is dead. He was involved in a crash on the Bricquebec to Valognes route last week. The funeral is tomorrow, and of course I and my wife are welcome to attend. He has not seen René since before the accident, and would be grateful if I could pass on the details of the interment if I see him.

I offer our condolences, but say, if he will excuse us, we will not attend the service. As I leave after a suitable period of keeping him silent company, Mr Maurice says that he is sorry that I did not get to know his nephew better, as he was a good boy. It seems unfair that someone so young should be taken when he is still here at his great age; it is not natural. Our arrangement with regard to the picking rights in the mushroom wood are now, of course, void.

I return home and tell my wife the news. She will write a letter to Mr Maurice, but is relieved that I have not committed us to attending the ceremony. We have both had our fill of funerals at the little church in Néhou.

*   *   *   *   *

Later, I call at the mobile home to tell René about the accident and funeral. He and Eric are both drunk, and seem disinterested. René says he will not be going to the ceremony as he is too busy, and asks abruptly for money to buy materials for breaking into Mr Pigeon's *source*. I respond in an equally blunt manner that I cannot see why he needs money at this stage, as all it will take to start is a couple of spades and some hard work. I will pay when the job is done, as usual. Perhaps if they drank less and ate more, they would be in better condition to take on the work. Eric looks as if he is considering taking offence at my advice, but obviously thinks better of it.

I leave them sitting sullenly amongst the squalor and go back to the mill. I do not like the look of René lately, and he seems resentful of me. I don't know if Eric is a bad influence on him, or the other way round. Either way, they are not good for each other or me.

October 8th:

The situation with René is worsening. He seems to spend most of his time nowadays sitting in the mobile home and drinking cheap wine with his friend. If there are any shopping errands or demands for money from us, Eric is sent to make them.

This evening, things came to a head when our self-appointed gardener appeared at the door, saying that he and René needed money for food, and I must pay something off our bill for his work. I didn't invite him in, but asked that he explain what he had done on our behalf and how much he thought we owed him. Leaning heavily against the door frame, he gave me a crumpled sheet of paper, and said that René said there were many hours of work that he, Eric, had done which had not yet been paid for.

The paper was covered with what I recognised as René's handwriting and calculations, and appeared to show that Eric had spent hundreds of hours keeping the farmhouse garden in trim.

I laughed incredulously, tore the paper up and said that he was paid immediately after last cutting the grass in the garden, which was more than a month ago. Since then we had neither asked him to cut another blade, nor seen any evidence that he has done so. He looked at me without malice as I told him I would be grateful if he would remove his machine from my shed, and take it and himself from the premises. He shrugged and turned to go, but I caught his arm and escorted him to the tool shed behind the mill. I watched as he returned to the mobile home to pack his things and leave, then asked my wife if she would make the journey to *Boueve et Fils* to pick up some new locks for the tool and bike sheds.

October 12th:

To Portbail for a Sunday lunchtime rendezvous with a reader.

Since publication and the modest success of our first book, we, and more particularly La Puce, have become something of a curiosity for a number of travellers on the Portsmouth to Cherbourg ferry run. Sometimes they have bought *Home & Dry in France* on the boat, and leave the southward bound RN13 to do a bit of detective work and find us. Occasionally, they make a dedicated journey to seek us out and see if we and the place live up to their expectations. Often we get letters from the UK asking advice from would-be buyers and settlers, or from existing owners in other parts of France who just want to let us know that they have had exactly the same sort of adventures, problems and encounters. All seem to have a favourite and outrageous rustic character in their area, but none seem to be in the same league as our estate manager.

Now and then, the readers will have property in Cotentin, and phone or write to suggest a meeting to further compare notes. Yesterday, we had a call from a couple who own a converted barn near the coast, and we have been invited for lunch.

Portbail is another village on the west coast which has found it more profitable to net tourists rather than fish. It is an attractive place, with the church, shops and houses huddled around the water's edge, and a long causeway and bridge leading to an area of sand dunes and a rather mundane collection of caravan parks and holiday chalets. The village has one of the most popular tourist restaurants on the coast, with a good menu and striking views out to sea from the first floor eating area. It is particularly popular with visitors because it is one of the few establishments which will accept casual customers after nine pm. Now and then when we were too exhausted to cook on the primus stove after a long day working on the farmhouse, we would turn up starving and filthy, and be welcome to sit amongst the smart decor and diners. We have not, however, returned to the *Rendezvous des Pecheurs* since a visit with my mother a year or more ago.

Not knowing her, the waiter chose to seat us in the midst of a party of German holidaymakers. A little hard of hearing, mother tends to speak rather loudly, and as the evening wore on, she became more and more outraged at the way the waiter was, in her opinion, toadying to the Hun. We left early, just as she was warming to the subject of how the Luftwaffe had targeted our greenhouse in 1941, and she had never received a penny in compensation.

Fortunately, we are served by a different waiter as we wait outside the restaurant for my fan to arrive.

He is a nice man who used to sell mobile homes, and obviously knows more about La Puce and our past lives than we do. We find her rather pretentious, and she airily introduces us to passing acquaintances as a writer friend. It is quite obvious she has not read a page of the book, and seems to think little of the area, weather, local people or our clothing, which is particularly galling as we made a special effort to dress up for the meeting. We make our excuses after an hour, and find another bar on the far side of the village. Feeling lazy, I propose we save the bother of cooking lunch, and buy a ready-cooked lamb joint from the smoky turnspit stall across the road. Going over to where the tourists are busily taking photographs of pieces of meat cooking, I put on my best local accent, point at a suitably large and juicy shoulder and ask the man behind the counter to put our name on it. He nods, snatches the 200 franc note I am holding, stows it away in his pocket and turns to the next customer. I interrupt the transaction and tell him that I am not some stupid *rosbif* camping on the dunes, but as local as him and know the price of a miserable piece of lamb. He looks at me for a moment, then silently produces a 50 franc note, hands it over and continues with his business.

Returning to the table where my wife has been watching my masterful handling of the situation, I tell her I really believe I am learning how to take the less honest Cotentinese traders on at hard bargaining and win. She congratulates me on my success, but points out that, since she has been sitting there, virtually all of the local customers have been handing over the distinctive 100 franc notes for much larger joints than the one I have ordered.

October 14th:

We arrive at Bricquebec for shopping, followed by drinks with Hubert and Madame Audouard at the *Café de Paris*.

My entrance is marred somewhat by Freddo, who calls loudly over that I should avoid drinking milk as the pub cat is loose on the premises. I take this to be a jibe at my moustache, which I have been deliberately growing while keeping the rest of my full set closely trimmed.

As we settle in the corner, I sit opposite Hubert to avoid close comparisons with the huge growth on his upper lip, and take grim satisfaction in noting that Freddo sends Madame Collette for our order rather than putting himself within the judging zone.

We enjoy a leisurely conversation, during which I have a mild disagreement with our teacher friend about the comparative merits of our two languages. He says that while English is useful for ordering hot dog relish or landing aircraft at an international airport, French is a pure and original language which has not been overly diluted or defiled with foreign words and expressions. I counter that, unlike some cultures, we have always had the self-confidence to absorb and adapt suitable words from foreign countries, especially those we have conquered, colonised and civilised. This gives a variety and subtlety of communication which is, in all modesty, unique. As a former magazine editor, I can assure him that any article I have written in French needed to have at least one third more words and therefore room on the page. Any language, I conclude, which has to call a simple typewriter 'the machine which writes mechanically' must be constructed by and for a race which prefers to hear its own voice rather than getting to the point. This, in my humble opinion, is the situation and position. Hubert now politely refers me to the fact that every one of the words in my native tongue ending in *ion* has been lifted directly from the French, and I have just used three of them in one sentence. There are hundreds of other examples where we have had the good sense to use their language rather than our own. I should also remember where I am sitting, which is in the country and region that virtually taught the English to speak after 1066.

As Donella sees that I am about to move on to a detailed tally and description of English away wins after that long distant home defeat, she suggests we change the subject. Hubert immediately complies, and asks me how I am getting on with René. I explain that our relationship has not been too sound lately, and he tells me that he must be honest, and that many people in the village think that I am too gullible as far as he is concerned. I may think I am doing the Fox a favour by opening the gate to the chicken run, but we will both be the losers if I continue to invite him in.

As I ponder over this oblique parable, we make our farewells on cordial terms, and are invited to dine *chez* Audouard the following evening.

October 15th:

A dramatic and distressing confrontation has taken place at the Bar Ghislaine.

We had met with our dinner host so that he could show us the way to his isolated home in the *val de Néhou*, and René staggered in to join us at our table without an invitation, which I could see annoyed Hubert.

Seemingly pleased with himself, our estate manager called loudly for a round, and ostentatiously pulled out a thick wad of notes to pay, both of which actions are most unusual.

We tried to make polite conversation for a while, but René was obviously in a cocky mood, and several times looked blearily at my wife, laughed at some private joke and grunted something in rapid patois which was obviously coarse and caused Hubert discomfort.

As we stood to leave for the dinner party, Hubert asked if we are happy with the horses in the top field, and I said that they are doing a good job in keeping the grass down, and that we are pleased that René managed to find them. Hubert appeared puzzled, and said that it was he that had arranged with a friend for them to be put there. Looking at René, he loudly asked if we are satisfied with the rental agreement of 1000 francs for the year, which is a fair price. Especially when paid in advance.

There was a long silence, and Madame Ghislaine and the other customers began to pay keen attention as René tried to brazen the situation out before lurching to his feet, pulling a handful of notes from his wallet and throwing them on the table. I asked him why he had not passed the money on to us before, and he at first protested his innocence, saying that he had not seen us for more than a week, but Hubert quietly said he knew the money was paid over even before the horses arrived more than a month ago. Normally, I would have covered the situation by taking the money and making some excuse about René already having mentioned he had it. But I was very angry. I reminded him loudly that it was my specific instruction not to let the fields out as this was my small way of showing a lasting sign of respect for our mayor. I had allowed him to take advantage of me for a long time, but now he had insulted the memory of John Chevalier with his petty greed. His father would be ashamed of him.

Nobody spoke for what seemed a long time, and René looked at me as if I had struck him.

He left his drink and the money on the table, and pushed his way through the door.

We listened to the furious buzz of his *mobylette* fading away in the distance before settling the bill and leaving.

*   *   *   *   *

The meal at the Audouards was a sober and awkward affair after the incident at the Bar Ghislaine. We left early, and returned straight home. There was a light burning in René's mobile home and I thought about going to see him, but decided against it. I said to Donella that I must have hurt him deeply, and had broken our special relationship by speaking to him like that in front of other people. My wife said I am too soft, and he deserved to be shown up for what he is. It will also show the villagers that we are not totally gullible, and besides she had already counted the money he threw down, and it only came to six hundred francs, and not the one thousand he charged Hubert's friend.

*   *   *   *   *

Midnight, and I am woken from my slumber by a series of blood-curdling screeches from the direction of the water meadow. I wake Donella and remind her of the ancient Norse legend of Helquin the Huntsman. I have heard the old locals talk of how he still leads the battalions of Hell across the night skies, all carrying coffins upon which ride the ghosts of the dammed, filling the air with their pitiful cries of terror and remorse. She turns over and goes back to sleep after reminding me that we now live in the countryside, where owls are quite common. Or perhaps, she adds, it is merely René mourning the loss of his six hundred ill-gotten francs.

October 16th:

René has gone.

All that remains to remind us of his tenancy in the top field is a cardboard box overflowing with empty bottles, two long gouges to show where the tow tractor arrived and left early this morning, and a broken gatepost. Obviously, the driver was not Roland the *spécialiste*. I am saddened more than I would have thought. In their different ways, René and the mayor have played a huge part in our lives for the past three years. We shall just have to make our own way in the future now that both have left us.

October 17th:

Another unexpected departure.

Lynn calls at the mill to tell us she and Charlie are also leaving La Puce. Her friend Yves has made an arrangement with his wife and rented a house for Lynn on the hill overlooking Carteret. It has all happened so quickly. The couple will be married when Yves' divorce comes through, and Lynn will move in to the *manoir* as soon as is decently possible.

We congratulate her on her good news, and promise to keep in touch. We are very pleased that she has found happiness and won this chance of a new life. But Lynn's good news means we must start looking for a new tenant very quickly, as the rent for the farmhouse is a vital part of our survival plan.

I shall also miss Charlie the dog, but I suspect Lucky will be pleased to take over as sole proprietor of the woods, fields and streams at La Puce.

October 19th:

To cheer ourselves up, we decide to go on a mushroom gathering expedition.

It is a good time to choose, as the copse is full of fungi, and Coco is away organising next year's festival of traditional English skinhead folk music at St Sauveur.

We spend the first hour wandering around and trying to decide which of the bewildering variety to pick, and which we should leave. We have got the Big Book of British Fungi with us, but the differences between those said to make delicious eating and the deadly poisonous types seem slight.

Donella scoffs at my caution, and says we should pick them all, and take it in turns to try a little of the ones we think are safe over the coming weeks. That way, if we make a mistake, only one of us will suffer, and we will know in future which types to avoid. Besides, by taking the poisonous ones as well as the edible varieties, we will save any of the animals in the copse from making a mistake.

I put my foot down and suggest a better idea. We will pick them all, but wait until the morning, then take them for analysis by the chemist at Haye-du-Puits. Even the most knowledgeable locals take advantage of the service, I point out, even if only because it is free.

In the evening, we dine on a thick and delicious stew, made with our own vegetables, which is very satisfying. I believe my wife was joking when she suggested that we use ourselves as guinea-pigs for testing the mushrooms from the copse, but remembering my experiences with the marsh pepper *ragoût,* I sift carefully through the ingredients on my plate while she is not watching.

October 20th:

We arrive at the *pharmacie* in Haye-du-Puits, and are surprised to find a long orderly queue shuffling patiently towards the counter. We are even more surprised when two people ahead of us offer their places. I wonder at this unaccustomed courtesy, then realise why none of the customers is eager to be served. It is a homeopathic chemist's shop, and all the people here seem to have unusual, often dramatic and therefore particularly interesting things wrong with them. The customers are hanging about as long as possible to see what the others have got, so as to have something stimulating to discuss over dinner tonight and in the market tomorrow. Also in complete contrast with the usual situation when money changes hands, those who have been forced to the counter make no protest about the charges for their nostrums and potions. They hand over large notes without question, and take the small amounts of change as gratefully and respectfully as if receiving Holy Communion.

We make speedy progress to the front of the queue, and soon stand in front of the chemist, a severe man in a pristine white coat, the pockets of which are bristling with pens, thermometers and slivers of wood for depressing customers' tongues regardless of the malady of which they complain. The *apothicaire* seems disappointed when he finds we have no exotic rashes to show him, and that our only fungal growths are confined to the two Safeway carrier bags we carry. With an impatient flick of his head, he summons an assistant, and he and the customers immediately lose interest in us as the next client is pushed to the counter for diagnosis of something hopefully more demanding than a kilo of mushrooms. The young assistant takes the bags to a curtained cubicle next to the shop door and disappears to examine our crop. We wait long minutes to hear the verdict, then I grow impatient, sidle over and take a peep through a chink in the curtains to see how he is getting on. I return to my wife's side and explain in a whisper that he seems to be looking each of the varieties up in an illustrated publication very similar to the Big

Book of British Fungi. This does not fill me with confidence, and I am quite relieved when he returns to say that he cannot, alas, recommend that we eat any of them. Some may be safe, but it is best not to take a chance, as all are rather unusual and even rare. My wife reaches out to take the bags from him, but he pulls them smartly away and says he will dispose of them for us.

Outside, I remark on how thoughtful for our safety the young man was. Obviously fearing that we might ignore his advice, he had kept the bags so we would not be tempted to dice with death. She is not convinced, and prefers to suspect that he is under permanent instructions from his boss. If everyone who comes for advice is told that their fungi are inedible and has them all confiscated, no member of the staff need ever pick or buy a single mushroom again.

October 21st:

Our main activity this evening is an official visit to the Bar de la Place in St Sauveur to inspect the new owners. We have avoided going there in the past, and dubbed it the Fun Factory because the previous owner was so miserable. Even the townspeople found the place depressing and the service and decor appalling, which is saying something in rural Normandy.

Now that Mr Heureux has departed and new owners taken over, the bar is packed with customers who, like us, want to have a look at how things have changed. It is said in the village that the middle-aged couple now behind the bar are foreigners from Mayenne, but they must already have heard of our consumption rate as the husband immediately rushes over and shows us to the only vacant table.

I order a beer and a *pastis* and reach for my cigarettes, and our host promptly whips the *non-fumeur* card from our table and places it on top of the juke box. He returns with our drinks in moments, and tells us they are on the house, which indicates strongly that he is indeed from another part of the country.

A little later, we are joined by Jackie from the Dungeon and

Madame Nellie, who have come to wish the newcomers well. They do not seem unhappy to see the size of the crowd, which includes many of their regulars, and I know they know the honeymoon is unlikely to last. The locals are treating the event as a special occasion and an opportunity to take a look at the new hosts. The free beer would also have overcome any sense of loyalty to their regular haunts, but they will not all be back in the Bar de la Place tomorrow. When the takings dip to its normal share of the business that the five bars in town can sustain, the new owners will begin to know if they have made a wise move.

The evening wears on, and as I start to explain to Jackie that it is the anniversary of the Battle of Trafalgar, Madame Nellie tactfully changes the subject by asking if we had heard that Guy the slaughterman is dead. He was only in his early forties, she says as my wife and I exchange glances, and though he was such a big and powerful man, his heart was not strong. I say I have not seen him since our encounter in her toilet last Christmas, but it is always sad to hear of a sudden passing.

We return with Nellie to take a simple supper of *croque monsieur* and chips, and Donella and I talk in low tones about the latest demise in the area.

Scaling up the figures to allow for the difference in population, I work out that this would represent nearly one hundred Portsmouth people we know dying in a couple of months. We may have opted for what seems a healthy and relatively stress-free life, I observe, but it seems a rather short one for men. Is this the real reason Donella was so keen for us to spend a whole year in Cotentin?

My wife smiles affectionately, wipes a tendril of melted cheese from my burgeoning moustaches and says that now I am learning to take such a philosophical attitude to life and death, I am obviously beginning to adapt to our new environment.

October 25th:

It seems there are some advantages to René's departure. Though I am missing his company, this will be the first year we shall be able to get our hands on our own apples. We spend the whole day harvesting, then most of the night wrapping and storing those we cannot use before the end of the year. I am as fond of apples as the next man, but my wife is eyeing the giant bathtub again, so I think I will call Hubert in the morning and offer him a hundredweight or so for professional DIY *calva* production.

October 27th:

I narrowly avoided an encounter with a drunken hornet this morning. I don't know if it was the same one which buzzed me in the mill cottage this summer, but he seemed to cast a bleary and knowing eye in my direction while lurching out of the orchard. René told me last year that they like to feast on rotting apples at this time, and can become totally intoxicated after a long session. He sounded quite envious. As I took shelter behind the bike shed, the beast zigzagged unsteadily off in the direction of the water meadow. If he disturbs the Cray gang as they settle down for winter, there could be big trouble on the waterfront tonight.

Boiled leg of lamb from Yvetot

1. *Simmer some carrots, leeks, turnips, onions and a bouquet garni for at least three glasses of wine, then add salt and a generous helping of calva*
2. *Rub the leg of lamb all over with garlic*
3. *Put the lamb in the stock and cook in oven for another three glasses of wine, basting occasionally*
4. *Make a roux with flour and butter, and thin it down with some of the stock, and continue to cook it for a leisurely cigarette. Away from the heat, add crème fraîche and capers*
5. *Serve your lamb on a long platter, garnished with the stock vegetables and the cream sauce*

November 4th:

The Indian summer is over and the land is closing down for the winter.

The days are short, the legendary Cotentin wind is working itself up to a suitable fury for the long dark months ahead, and someone has turned the heavenly shower mixer from warm to cold.

Most of our bird and animal lodgers have packed up and bedded down or gone to more hospitable quarters for the winter, though I can't imagine where they will find them.

Nobody in the village has heard of or from René, but, for us at least, his memory lingers on.

This morning, I found the larger of the top fields being turned into a quagmire by a tractor in the control of a complete stranger.

Quite politely in the circumstances, I asked him what he thought he was doing, and he retorted that he knew exactly what he was doing, and if I didn't, he suggested I get a good pair of spectacles or a book about farming. My nose should also have given me a clue as to the enterprise, which involved digging a great deal of *merde* into the ground to give it back some of the life which had obviously been drained from it for so long by an uncaring farmer.

From then, the tone of our conversation went downhill, and we almost came to blows before he explained that he had a verbal contract to work not only this field but all the others, and if I had a problem, I should consult the owner, Mr Ribet. After taking the golden opportunity to tell him that a verbal contract is not worth the paper it isn't written on, I explained the true situation *vis à vis* ownership, and gave him his money back, plus healthy compensation for his wasted pig manure.

In spite of the situation, I have to admit to a sneaking admiration for the Fox's negotiating skills. I had to repay the farmer much more than I would have thought a fair rent for the fields would have fetched.

November 5th:

More fireworks when my wife discovers some strange horses in the big field.

I reach for my wallet and go to negotiate a settlement with their owner.

November 11th:

No temporary tenants have appeared in the top fields this week, so it looks as if we are free to walk through them without upsetting anyone.

November 13th:

We have heard from Hubert Audouard that René's friend Eric is happily working at the cider factory in Brix. As my wife says, it is not surprising that he is happy in his new location and situation, which seems along the lines of holding regular meetings of Alcoholics Anonymous in a pub.

We often pass through Brix on our way to and from Cherbourg, and sometimes stop to enjoy the scenery from the bar in the square. The village is at one of the highest points on the peninsula, with striking views almost to each coastline when the legendary Cotentin mist is having a rare day off. With its huddle of neat grey stone buildings, narrow streets and tiny church, it somehow reminds me more of the Highlands of Scotland than Northern France, and according to our historian friend Robert Simon, there may be a good reason for this impression. He has told us that, in ancient patois, Brix is pronounced *Broow*. This was the name of the 11th-century *seigneur* of the village and a large chunk of the top end of the peninsula, who was so helpful in 1066 that William the Conqueror gave him most of Scotland as a small thank-you present. From there came the title of his direct descendant, Robert the Bruce, or *de Broow*, king of the Scots in the 14th century. I hope it is true, and if it is, the story may go a little way towards explaining the similar reputations for parsimony of Normans and Scots. Another indicator towards some enduring affinity is that Scots visitors seem particularly welcome in Cotentin, and the locals seem to be more at ease with their guttural attempts at French than many Britons are with the Scottish version of the English language.

Historical note:

Some years after Robert Simon told me about the legend, the heart of The Bruce was unearthed during an archaeological dig in Edinburgh, and an excited article in a French newspaper confirmed the Brix-Broow story. I thought about passing on the news to the remaining members of the Jolly Boys Club, but decided against it as they would inevitably point out that, as they had always claimed, Scotland as well as the rest of Great Britain is actually the rightful property of Cotentin...

November 15th:

To Carteret to say another farewell to Lynn and Charlie the dog. They are packing when we arrive, and will soon be off to their new home at Yve's *manoir* in Carentan.

Helping Lynn with the removals is a friend who has had a traumatic and unusually busy emotional life since her arrival on the peninsula. She tells us over drinks of an embarrassing encounter shortly after she moved in with her latest French boyfriend. Having split with her husband six months after settling in the area, she had discovered that the legal complexities of dividing mutual domestic possessions are even more convoluted than in England. During the process of separation, she had found the assistance of the local bailiff or *huissier* invaluable in helping her relocate some of her possessions to the home of her new lover, and from there to her next male friend and *ménage*.

After parting with him and starting a more serious and hopefully longer-lasting relationship with a separated but married man, she found that the law of France required graphic proof of his adultery before divorce proceedings could begin in earnest. Accordingly, appointments were made, and two policemen arrived apologetically on the doorstep at a suitably early hour, accompanied by an official witness. He made careful note of the dressing gown and tousled hair of the householder, then went upstairs to cough discreetly and enter the bedroom. He came through the door just as Lynn's friend sat up in bed, arranged her flimsy nightdress and steeled herself to be officially recognised as the Other Woman. Their eyes met, and she saw that the official witness was none other than the bailiff who had been so helpful in her three past romantic disentanglements. After a polite conversation as he, the police officers and the current lover took coffee at the bedside, the *huissier* declared himself completely satisfied as to the circumstances. Before leaving, he gave her an admiring glance and handed her his card, with a reminder that he was only a telephone call away, and his rates were very reasonable if she decided to continue her magnificent progress through the bedchambers of the peninsula.

November 16th:

The election of a new mayor of Néhou has taken place, and we meet at the unofficial reception in the Bar Ghislaine shortly after the announcement. He seems a decent enough chap, but it is the general opinion that he will never replace Jean Chevalier. I think we should give him a chance, but my wife is not an admirer, as he won on a hunting and shooting ticket. For the past months, graphic posters reminding the commune of the need to be ever vigilant against any threat to their rights to kill have been plastered all around the village. There was quite a fuss when someone went round scrawling 'murderer' all over the candidate's features, but the culprit was never found. At least, the word was written in French, so the finger of suspicion was not pointed at anyone living at La Puce, but I know my wife's handwriting when I see it.

November 19th:

We have received an early Christmas card from Colin and Ann Scott. Inside, they write to tell us that all has not gone well at their café in Catus. They have lost their home and are living above the business till the lease runs out, but have had to close the restaurant, so there will be no more English specials at Scott's to threaten marital accord in the area.

All their news is not bad, and they report that they are making a reasonable living using their experience gained at Anne's trading post corner to sell carefully selected British foodstuffs in markets around their area. They are also talking to an English owner about living at and looking after his holiday complex, and will let us know when they have a settled address. They visit England to stock up at a Hampshire cash and carry every month, and will stop off at La Puce next time they are passing our way.

We are glad to hear that they are fighting on, but it is always depressing to hear yet another dream of an idyllic lifestyle in France ending unhappily. One day during a book signing session at a French property exhibition in England, I will probably use their story with the names changed to warn a would-be restaurateur of the dangers of his plans to set up in a rustic *auberge* and beat the French at their own game. He will doubtless give me the standard dreamer's lecture on how it is better to have tried and failed than never to have done it at all, and I will want to punch him squarely on the nose. I will not, of course, as he will need to learn the lesson for himself if he ever dares to make his dream reality, and I will need the slim profits on the book sale to help us continue our pursuit of survival in the real world of making a living and life in France.

November 20th:

Even colder today. It looks as if the country tale about the abundance of berries in autumn signalling a long, hard winter may not be such an old chestnut. I am now spending at least an hour every day trying to maintain the level of the wood pile behind the mill. It is a perfect example of the law of diminishing returns, as the more effort I put in to ensure a comforting and respectable size, the more it seems to shrink as Donella makes raids to feed the endless demands of the giant stove. I cannot believe we are using this much wood, and am beginning to suspect we may be keeping half the houses in the village warm. After scouring Hunters Walk for the last scraps of dead wood, I suggest we go to town and look at the price of electric fires.

It is market day at St Sauveur, and a miserable affair. The small band of hopelessly optimistic traders have deserted their stalls and are huddled together around the brazier at the *merguez* stand, which is the only place likely to do any business today. The wind rushes furiously through the streets in search of victims, and we take refuge in our butcher's shop. Behind the counter, a young man is carefully making Catherine wheels from long tubes of white pudding, and seems mildly amused when we ask if our gentle giant is on holiday. He has been dead for almost a week now, and Madame has gone to live with her sister on the coast. The new butcher has taken the business over and hopes we will continue to patronise the premises. When I ask how our friend died, he merely shrugs and holds his fist to his nose before returning his attention to the *boudin blanc*. We go for a calming *calva* at Madame Nellie's, and are relieved to see that she and all the regulars seem in reasonable health.

November 25th:

We visit Cherbourg for our regular brush with civilisation, and to buy modest Christmas presents for our friends and neighbours.

Instead of eagerly looking forward to the monthly trip, we are finding it more and more difficult to make the effort. When we first moved over, I would often come up with excuses to visit the town and savour the bustle, noise and traffic, but since then have become increasingly acclimatised to life in the countryside. As the winter sets in, we are less and less inclined to venture even as far as Bricquebec. We will, however, force ourselves to make the journey, if for no other reason than the joy of showing the town a clean pair of heels as we hasten back to La Puce.

We lunch at a bar near to the ferryport which specialises in real English chips and offers British television to homesick day-trippers. As we eat, a pretty blonde weather girl in a pink suit hands over to a stern blonde woman studio presenter in a pink suit who hands over to a severe blonde woman reporter in a German stormtrooper's mackintosh to talk to an even grimmer female MP about how awful it is to be a woman in a man's world. A couple at the bar are having difficulties asking the patron for a bottle of HP sauce, and I offer to help translate their request. I then tactfully explain that they may be better advised to ask for things in English, as most of the bar staff speak it quite well, and can have difficulty understanding their own language when used by a foreigner. It is often best, I advise, to simply mime and point, relying on body language and making spoken communication unimportant. I example my brother, who has developed an infallible technique in this respect. On a recent visit with us to a bar, he acknowledged the barmaid with a crisp '*bonjour*', then ordered a hot chocolate, lemon tea and two beers by simply pointing at the bar pumps, using fluent sign language and repeating '*bonjour*' continually. After getting exactly what he wanted, he said that he had developed the skill over a number of years, and now believes he can convey any message or meaning anywhere on earth simply by using a subtle range of inflexions and stresses on a single word of the host language.

November 27th:

It has been raining liquid ice for two days, and we have been competing to see who can get closest to the stove without becoming part of it. Having counted the wormholes in the main beam for the hundredth time, I take to reading the old newspapers in the kindling box. There is an absorbing article by a British writer about one Gilles Picot de Gouberville, who was the *seigneur* of Mesnil-au-Val in the 16th century. With plenty of time on his hands, Gouberville kept a diary between 1549 and 1562, writing between ten and thirty lines every day. According to the modern-day editor of his work, Gouberville used the phrase 'I did not leave the house' 3,310 times in the thirteen years. While I understand exactly how he must have felt, I hope that my work will offer some rather more interesting observations on daily life in the Cotentin to readers in the 24th century.

November 29th:

I tire of my daily battle with the wood pile, and persuade my wife that we should spend the afternoon in the Bar Ghislaine and take advantage of the free heating.

It must be remarkably cold, as there are two smouldering logs in the giant fireplace. I notice immediately that Mr Maurice is not in his usual position, and Ghislaine breaks the news we are already expecting, but hoping not to hear.

She tells us that he was at Marcel Bernard's house two nights ago for supper. They walked out into the yard to say goodnight, and as they shook hands, he looked up at the night sky, commented on how clear, bright and *calme* it all was, and fell gently at his friend's feet. The doctor says his heart just gave out, and he would have felt no pain. The same man has been telling Maurice for years that drinking would be the death of him, she says, so at least our friend has had the last laugh.

We ask if René has been told, and Ghislaine says that he has not shown his face since leaving La Puce. He is probably too embarrassed after his last visit to the bar. There is talk that he has gone to work for the farmer at the grand *manoir* at St Jacques, and has a cottage there as part of their agreement. If that is true, he is a traitor and has yet another reason for not appearing in Néhou. But it seems a shame that he may not know his oldest friend in the village is dead.

We return to La Puce, wrap a bottle of my precious malt whisky in Christmas gift paper, and set out to track the Fox of Cotentin down to his new earth.

*   *   *   *   *

246

Under cover of darkness, we cross the unmarked but scrupulously observed frontier between Néhou and St Jacques de Néhou. My wife rides shotgun and keeps watch for hostile natives, but the streets are deserted. The bar in the square is closed and unlit, as is the restaurant next door. Our villagers are apparently exaggerating when they say the residents of St Jacques only go out at night to indulge their unspeakable feeding habits, and spend their days sleeping on beds of local soil in dark cellars.

At last, we see a lone figure, furtively darting between the pools of light cast by the new street lamps of which the Néhou commune is so jealous.

I take a chance and pull up, crank the window down and call him. The man looks wildly about for a bolthole like a rabbit caught above ground in a field of hunters, then shuffles over when he sees we are driving an English car. Deliberately speaking in my worst French so that he will not suspect I am actually a member of the community across the crossroads, I ask him if he knows René Ribet and he says everyone knows René Ribet, and many people to their cost.

I ask him if he knows where Mr Ribet is staying as I have a business matter to discuss, and he tells us that I should look for a small cottage at the end of the track leading to the grand *manoir*. I will know it from the new roof tiles and window frames, and the mobile home by the broken gatepost.

As we drive away, he shouts after us to be on our guard, and makes off in the direction of the church. Either, my wife says, he realised we are from Néhou and is planning to ring the bells and raise the village, or to pray for our souls because we are going to talk business with René Ribet.

*   *   *   *   *

We find the cottage, mobile home and familiar roof tiles as promised, and park beside the recently broken gate post. A light is flickering beyond the sacking curtain across the new window frames, and I take the bottle of scotch and leave my wife and Victor on guard. As I walk down the path, my wife reminds me to count my fingers after shaking hands if we do effect a reconciliation.

For some reason, I hesitate and adjust an imaginary tie before knocking, and quickly consider how I will approach our first encounter for more than two months. I decide to take the bluff no-nonsense English approach, and rap smartly on the door. From inside, I hear movement, and eventually the door is opened and René peers out into the night. He has put on weight and looks well, and is obviously sober. For a moment, his face is expressionless, then he sees who his visitor is, and steps back from the doorway. I nod and he nods, and we remain motionless till I hold out the bottle. He reaches out, hesitates for a long moment then takes it. He looks at it, then back at me, then steps further away from the door and nods at the table.

I nod stiffly back, walk in and sit down as he starts to unwrap the bottle.

* * * * *

Two hours later, the bottle is nearly empty and René has spent more time talking than the night by the big pond in August.

He has told me further stories of his childhood and happy years in the countryside, and how he met his wife and had a daughter, then lost them both. His wife is with someone else, and his daughter lives in Cherbourg with her child. We may have seen her with him at the *méchoui*. He tries to give her money when he can, and wants to impress her and to make her see that he is not just a tramp who has been living in a caravan on someone else's land. He explained how he lost his home when the Parisian owner of the cottage at Néhou threw him out when he heard about all the English who would pay crazy prices for worthless country properties. And this after René had worked so hard to restore the place with materials left over from other jobs. He said how he had resented the clever English writer and his wife for being rich enough to buy La Puce and pour money into making it so grand. He said how, in spite of all this, he grew to like me and respect my wife, and thought we were true friends until the bad night in the Bar

Ghislaine. As to the arrangements between us, he did not really intend to cheat us, but we seemed to have so much and I seemed so stupid with my money and my ignorance of the land, and my mad spending on putting fairy lights on a farm.

He had always wanted to have the life and status of a farmer, but it is just a dream that he knows can never come true. Now, he is truly sorry for what has happened between us, but I must bear some of the responsibility. I have been a chicken to his fox, and even opened the gate of the coop myself.

Then it was my turn, and I told him that, far from being a wealthy writer, I am in debt to the bank in England, and we may have to sell and leave La Puce soon. That I may have been stupid with my money and ideas for making a home and a future in this part of the Cotentin, but he must know that we are not like others who come to take over, change the local ways and be absent and uncaring owners. I am here to stay and to learn, and have learned a great deal. Especially from him, who I would still like to be my friend, whatever has happened in the past. As I paused to drain my glass, he said that, whatever happens between us in the future, we have no choice but to be friends; as they say in the countryside, he is my *pote* for life, and there is not much we can do about it.

*   *   *   *   *

Another hour passes, then I rise to leave. Before I walk unsteadily back to where my wife sleeps in the car, he asks me to wait, then returns with something wrapped in an old newspaper. It is his present to us for Christmas, and perhaps I will put it in the mill cottage, next to the pictures of Jean Chevalier and Mr John Major.

As he stands and watches from the doorway, I unwrap the parcel on my lap and see that it is a photograph of a young René with a middle-aged man who must be his father. I wave and start the car, and as we bump along the potholed track back towards St Jacques, my wife stirs, makes herself comfortable and sleepily asks if I still have all my fingers.

EPILOGUE

December 21st:

We are gathered in the Bar Ghislaine to prepare for the Christmas warm-up party.

JayPay is at the counter, having managed to slip away from preparing the spicy *couscous* which will set the North African theme for our *soirée* in the village hall. He has one giant arm resting affectionately on his wife's shoulders, while Madame JayPay is smoking more furiously than ever as she considers the odds on a child-free year.

All around me, the Jolly Boys Club is in full convention, but the seat from where Mr Maurice would have been looking thoughtfully into his *suze* has been left vacant.

As chairman of the wine committee Freddo is consulting with himself and Madame Ghislaine about final amendments to the list of one. He sees that I am watching, smiles knowingly, nods and holds up his two index fingers as if demonstrating the size of one of the hundreds of hapless trout he has caught this morning. I smile back as he nods towards the *pissoir* outside the grocery shop window and tap my watch to indicate that we will meet later to play the sausage game. What he does not know is that I have already visited the village hall and adjusted the names written on the relevant paper tablecloths. I shall now be sitting elsewhere with the older and more diminutive members of the Jolly Boys Club, while I have ensured that he will be sharing a table with Hubert Audouard. I went swimming in the big pond with Hubert this summer, and know that it is not only his moustache that is bigger than Freddo's.

At my side, Néné Ribet is making plans on the back of a beer mat for our farm at La Puce.
He has been almost rehabilitated into the commune, and next year, we have decided, we are going into partnership to beat the

bloody English at their own game. We shall produce the finest lambs in all Normandy, and perhaps France.

While he happily scribbles details of stock numbers and costs, overheads and potential resale prices, he stresses how important it is that we must be totally honest with each other and share all expenses and whatever profits may be made in our first year as real farmers.

As he gets to the part about his specialist knowledge of negotiating for the best prices for buying and selling, and how it is vital that the control of all financial matters be left entirely to him, I merely look knowingly at him, and he falters, smiles wryly and goes back to his plans.

A little later, the Jolly Boys Club prepares to move on to the village hall and I excuse myself, leave the bar and cross the road to spend a few moments alone with Jean Chevalier.

*　　*　　*　　*　　*

In the churchyard, the flowers around John's grave are as fresh as ever. I sit down and begin to tell him about the latest news from La Puce and his commune. He will be pleased to know that Néné is back with us, and I am sure that John will not mind if we use his fields by the road for our sheep farm. I know the grass is good and the land well drained, but I shall need his help and guidance to make a success of the venture. There is also what may be good news from England. I have sent some pages of a book I am writing about our past year at La Puce and Néhou to a big publishing company, and so far they have not sent it back, which is very encouraging.

As he will know, it looks like being a long and hard winter, but the new year and seasons will arrive as always, and we will do our best to make the most of what time we have left to enjoy the good days and put up with the bad.

I hear the sounds of laughter as the villagers make their way to the hall, and stand to say goodnight. Before I leave, I tell John that Donella has still not met her badgers, and I have finally given up my plans for finding the miller's gold.

Now, though, I am beginning to see that the real treasure at La Puce has been all around us, all the time.

FRENCH LETTERS

As promised at the start of this work, there follows a glossary of those French words and expressions I feel may benefit from translation and further explanation. They are roughly in order of appearance, and my thanks are due to Jean-Marie Guedeney and Robert Simon for attempting to curb my worst mistakes and excesses. I would only add that the reader should remember that my interpretation of most or all the following may still be totally inaccurate, as they, like the book itself, represent a very unscholarly and individual approach to the subjects covered.

bocage	Distinctive Norman countryside feature resulting from the tradition of hedging small fields with sturdy trees to ward off the legendary *vent* (wind). And, of course, to make it *very* clear where one property stops and the next begins...
pissoir	Self-explanatory. The original and official men-only very public urinals in big towns were as ornate and striking as they were unique. Nowadays, virtually all have gone, to be replaced by much cruder but nevertheless fascinating examples of male French inventiveness under pressure.
épicerie	Grocery shop. In a village setting, often to be found doubling as the local and only bar, and therefore more than likely to be situated within close proximity of the *pissoir* (see above).
Académie Française	Very exclusive club for a collection of venerable old buffers whose avowed and statutory role is to preserve the language, culture and Establishment values of France. A bit like our House of Lords without the hypocrisy.
saucisse paysanne	In this context, 'countryman's sausage'. Not to be confused with the subject of the traditional Christmas party game on page 9.
calva	If you need an explanation of this word, you have been reading the book backwards. Please skip to page 20. On second thoughts, if you have been reading the book backwards, it is quite probable that you are already familiar with *calva*, so don't bother.

mobylette	The French equivalent of our moped, only much noisier and able to tow and carry quite incredible loads. Often seen in the countryside posing as a builder's van or, in extreme cases, heavy earth moving equipment. The reason for this vehicle's popularity and adaptation to all sorts of functions is that it requires no driving licence or tax disc, only minimum insurance and can cover more than 150 kilometres for every gallon of petrol - providing it is not towing a broken tractor.
poissons rouges	Goldfish. Very popular in some regions, especially cooked *à la* whitebait in flour.
boeuf bourguignon	Burgundian Irish stew.
fantôme	Ghost, as in 'Of The Opera'.
chambre d'hôte	Bed and breakfast establishment, usually rural and often offering a fascinating glimpse of how real French people really live.
apéritif	Technically, any drink taken to stimulate the appetite. In our part of the Cotentin, the usual understanding of the word is any drink taken to stimulate the appetite for the next one.
quarante quatre	Literally 'forty four'. In this context, a fiery home-made orange liqueur, but also used in Cotentin to refer to the D-Day landings. The identical usage is coincidental, though both have had significant long-term effects on the Norman psyche and landscape.

Louis d'or	Gold coin, which every *paysan* (see 'sausage') believes to be buried in vast quantities on his land, if only he can discover where.
Huit à Huit	Eight (am) to Eight (pm). A grocery store franchise that doesn't live up to its name in our neck of the woods.
charcuterie	Cooked cold meats, or the shop that sells them. Usually, every village or town has the undisputed Finest Charcuterie Store in Northern France (at least).
Disque Bleu	Foul smelling cigarette, even by French standards.
non-fumeur	Non-smoker/smoking. Still as rare a breed as vegetarians in rural France. NB. A *fumerie* is an opium den, while a *fumier* is a dunghill. This can make for some interesting reactions if you make a slight slip while asking someone if you are allowed to smoke on the premises, or if they are a smoker.
le Lude	Our river, which is really a stream but gets big billing because it is named on regional maps.
tout d'(de) suite	'At once' or 'very quickly', but meaning exactly the opposite when used by most Cotentinese tradesmen.
étang	Any confined piece of water of a size between a goldfish pond and a proper lake.

mairie	Mayor's official place of administration, which can be anything from a grand town hall to a room in the local school. Unlike the UK, even the smallest communities have their own elected mayor. A man of enormous fixing power locally, and sometimes in effect a marginally milder version of a mafia godfather.
manoir	Overblown farm house (see *Home & Dry In France* by same author for detailed explanation).
pastis	The favourite drink for French workers, which is a more sophisticated and less deadly version of the original aniseed-based liqueur, *absinthe,* traditional choice of all mad French artists, poets and authors.
Ricard	Cotentin's favourite brand of the above beverage.
lave-linge	Washing machine.
frites	Like English chips, only different.
grand tournoi	Big match.
équipe	Team, as in the above.
chasseur	Hunter, an expression used to describe anyone in possession of cartridges, a gun, blood-lust and generally very bad eyesight and aim.
Chasse Interdite	Optimistic legend on the 'No Hunting' signs which are the second most popular targets for the above.

appellation contrôlée	Cunning French system of labelling certain wines to persuade the buyer to pay more for a perfectly ordinary bottle of wine just because the makers say they know where it all comes from.
cidre	Cider. Not to be confused with SIDA, which means AIDS, but is pronounced very similarly, as the author has found to his cost (also see *Home & Dry in France*).
non-potable	Not drinkable, which may apply to any beverage not containing alcohol as far as many Cotentinese are concerned.
pépinière	Horticultural nursery.
douanerie	Customs checkpoint, usually manned by bored and anglophobic officials who would (allegedly) happily let tons of smack cocaine go through in favour of catching a bloody *rosbif* trying to smuggle a new three-piece suite in to the country.
digestif	Supposed to be the opposite of *apéritif* (see above) and taken only after eating, but actually having exactly the same application and usage.
poêle	A stove for burning wood (preferably someone else's).
fagot	Technically a conveniently sized log for the above, but in practice anything up to a fair sized dead tree if you are a dealer trying to buy one, or kindling twig if you are a dealer trying to sell one.
chef	Actually 'boss', but inevitably applied in the UK to any cook with pretensions.

notaire	In rural France, a combination of solicitor, estate agent and local mafia boss (as in 'mayor').
fusil	Shotgun. Not to be confused with *fusée*, which is a guided missile capable of great destruction and loss of life if used indiscriminately. Bearing in mind the way many French hunters use their shotguns, the similarity of names is probably more than coincidental.
chambre	Room, though usually referring to one with a bed in it. Not to be confused with *chambrer* or *chambrière*, which mean, respectively, bringing wine to room temperature and a chambermaid. In France, of course, there is a natural affinity between the pursuit of the last two subjects in the confines of the first.
choucroute	Alsatian (the region, not the dog) dish of boiled pork on a bed of pickled cabbage. Actually, much nicer than it sounds, and popularised in Normandy by refugees from war-time Alsace.
rocher	Boulder, large stone or rock, as in Gibraltar.
tracteur	Tractor, unless in the case of a moped in disguise (see '*mobylette*').
ragoût	Stew when made by pretentious cook (see '*chef*').
tête à tête	Literally 'head-to-head' and used to describe an intimate conversation or position, which may actually involve a little more than talking.

mélange	Mixture or mess, as in 'you look a right *mélange* this evening, *cherie*'. Also used for mixed oil and petrol fuel for a *mobylette*.
pot au feu	Another type of stew.
repas d'affaires	Business lunch.
bottes	Boots. In the Cotentin climate, invariably of the Wellington variety, though it is not wise to use his name in a dockside bar on a Friday evening.
sou	Ancient French coin of insignificant value (five old centimes), alleged to be secreted in vast hoards by Normans who know they are worthless nowadays, but can't bear to let any form of money out of their custody.
méchoui	Barbecue of lamb (the event), popularised during France's North African adventuring.
kir	A sickly sweet and highly intoxicating *mélange* of white wine and cassis, allegedly invented by a bishop of that name. The pretentious version is made with champagne and called *Kir Royal*. Our local version is *Kir Normand*, with sparkling cider making a much, much cheaper and therefore much, much more enjoyable substitute for the champagne.
chêne antique	Old oak.
auberge	Country inn.
képi	Peaked uniform cap, as in French Foreign Legion.

boucherie	Butcher's shop or department.
cidre bouché	Norman equivalent of champagne, without the ridiculous overpricing.
pétanque	Oversized steel marbles and game, of which the author is supreme local champion (Valdecie *Ricard* league).
Chambre de commerce	Professional version of our Chambers of Commerce, excepting that their executive officers are voted in and actually do a great deal more for local business than holding cheese and wine parties and going on goodwill trips.
croque monsieur	'Mr Bite'. A Welsh Rarebit sandwich, with ham inside and cheese outside.
ménage	Household, as in *ménage à trois*.
merde	A multi-purpose slang word or curse, as in 'oh, shit' or 'you little shit'.
boudin blanc	White pudding, as in Cornwall, but different.
pote	'Mate', as in special male friend.
couscous	A North African speciality dish of semolina flakes and hot stew. Like our Indian curry, popularised as a result of colonial conquests.
Home & Dry in France	Fascinating book and recommended reading for francophiles and francophobes alike.